RESTORATION COMEDY: CRISES OF DESIRE AND IDENTITY

RESTORATION COMEDY: CRISES OF DESIRE AND IDENTITY

Edward Burns

Lecturer in English
University of Liverpool

MACMILLAN

First published in 1987

Published by
THE MACMILLAN PRESS LTD
Houndmills, Basingstoke, Hampshire RG21 2XS
and London
Companies and representatives
throughout the world

British Library Cataloguing in Publication Data
Burns, Edward
Restoration comedy : crises of desire and identity.
1. English drama—Restoration, 1660–1700—
History and criticism 2.English drama—18th
century—History and criticism
I. Title
822'.4'09   PR691
ISBN 0-333-39747-9

Reprinted in Great Britain in 1993 by
Antony Rowe Ltd
Chippenham, Wiltshire

Contents

Preface

The stage comedy of the late seventeenth century has a curious status in English studies. As 'Restoration comedy' it has enjoyed a continuous and popular theatrical currency and a secure place in literary history – at least as school and university syllabi define it. Until recently, however, the attention paid to it by literary criticism has been sparse and grudging. An impressive body of American work has mapped out the field in factual and statistical detail, but here too the effect has too often been to marginalize the plays as objects of literary study.

What follows is an account of Restoration comedy. The introduction offers an historical definition of the form, while the following chapters make up a narrative of its development. This 'narrative' proceeds as a series of readings of individual texts and of writers' careers.

By reconsidering Restoration comedy critically and historically, I hope to open up a series of texts, some still popular, many obscure, to sympathetic and attentive interpretation, as well as to suggest a new evaluation of the form and of that larger historical phenomenon – a Restoration 'culture' – of which the plays are a part. What *is* Restoration comedy? Or, as Robert Hume would put it, '*is* Restoration comedy?' (in '*The Development of English Drama in the Late Seventeenth Century*'.)[1] What pleasures do the plays offer us, what pleasures did they offer their immediate audience, and what might such pleasures mean? Simple questions, but too rarely posed, let alone answered.

The genesis of this book was a thesis supervised by Anne Barton, whose very positive encouragement pushed the work forward at crucial stages in its tentative early development. I'm very grateful for this, and for the range of knowledge and interest she brought to bear on it. I'd like also to thank Louise Aylward, for typing early stages and for her always sensible advice on structure and clarification, and the typists at Liverpool – Cathy Rees, Joan

Welford, Tina Benson and Beryl Drabble – for their patience in constructing the final Frankenstein monster of a typescript.

The book is dedicated to my parents, my brothers and my sister.

The author and publishers wish to thank the following who have kindly given permission for the use of copyright material: the University of Chicago Press, for the extracts from Herbert Davis (ed.), *The Complete Plays of William Congreve* (1967).

Note Dates in the text are, when possible, the dates of first performance. My source is *The London Stage*.

University of Liverpool   EDWARD BURNS

Introduction

WHAT IS RESTORATION COMEDY?

To use the term 'Restoration comedy' is to posit the direct relation-ship of a historical event to a literary form. It is to suggest that this particular dramatic genre is characterized by its relation to social and political change. Otherwise the term has no meaning. If we are to continue to use it, we must establish whether this is so. The Restoration of the monarchy in 1660 established a new court and new social forms. It could not however 'restore' the ideologies and social structures of the pre-revolutionary period. Restoration cul-ture is a compromise, often uneasy, sometimes poised, an anxious and contradictory endeavour to create traditions and celebrate newness. We expect plays to 'register' the 'tone' of their period. But can these plays be said to be shaped by theirs? Are they sufficiently distinct from other plays and sufficiently like each other to constitute a literary genre?

Restoration comedy as it is generally understood had a vogue of approximately fifty years. If we take Anne Barton's suggestion that Etherege's *She Would if She Could* is the first Restoration comedy,[1] and assume, as I do, that the early plays of Richard Steele and Susanna Centlivre are among the last, then this period stretches from 1668 to the 1710s. I shall consider the status of the Etherege play later: beginnings can be dated more decisively than endings, but they contain the seed of a definition and so repay attentive argument. But it is obvious at once that in spanning the death of Charles II (1685), the expulsion of James II (1688), Mary's acces-sion, her death and that of her husband William, that the Restora-tion itself recedes into a complex sequence of political upheavals. The period could be defined as the last phase of Stuart monarchy, but if we are to argue that it makes sense to call its literature 'Restoration' we must see some lasting significance in that particu-lar moment. We must consider how and why literary forms articu-lated its meaning.

1

JONSONIAN MORALISTS, AND CAROLINE DECORUM

To put it at its simplest; Restoration comedy is the comedy of London life, and its dominant medium is prose. Armed with even so slight a definition one can find surprisingly little of the kind in the years that follow immediately on the Restoration itself. The first play to be recorded in performance was Jonson's *Epicoene*,[2] almost an ur-Restoration comedy in its investment in unlikeable gallants and an extensive use of prose. But this court performance did not establish a dominant 'Jonsonian' tradition. When the public theatres reopened it was Fletcher and Shakespeare who were revived rather than the comedy of polite society as practised by Shirley and other Caroline dramatists, or the neoclassical 'corrective' comedy still praised by theorists. Before the establishment of Restoration comedy in the late 1660s and early 1670s the most popular types of play were the mixed heroic and comic, fixed as a form by Dryden's *Secret Love* of 1667, and the 'Spanish romance' for which Tuke's *The Adventures of Five Hours* (1663) was the model. Both these forms demonstrate an attempt to escape classical precedent by creating a synthesis of romance and urban themes.

Restoration comedy is itself an escape from precedent and, in its own resiliently ironic way, an urban-romantic synthesis. The Caroline comedy of manners on the other hand can be seen as a graceful diminishment of the sphere of Jonsonian comedy, a move from the moral analysis of universals to a careful, sometimes intricate, vision of a society intent to meet disruption, whether personal or social, by an idealistic reimposition of order, a return to unquestionable rules. Plays with apparently 'disorderly' surfaces – Brome's *Antipodes* (1638) for example, or his *Jovial Crew* (1641), are actually those that offer most compellingly the formal pleasures of the *return* to order. They are political writings of the most enticing kind; the audience's enjoyment is structured for it as a precise replication of their desired assent to hierarchical notions of society. Restoration comedy however found less use for neo-classical principles of decorum, formal structuring or corrective intent, as its detractors were quick to point out. It rejects the ideal for a realism of the social moment and finds a dynamic not in the reimposition of order, but in the witty opportunism of intrigue. Jonson was admired, but his 'school' was at an end.

The prime mover in the attempt to reimpose Jonsonian models had been William Cavendish, Duke of Newcastle, 'governor' of

Charles II when Prince of Wales. Cavendish, his wife, Margaret, and the writers he patronized – of which Thomas Shadwell and Richard Flecknoe are the most notable – all write imitations of Jonson, for which the Duke's position and his eccentric wife's notoriety found a public. Newcastle, a patron and friend of Jonson's, was one of a group of writers who styled themselves the 'Sons of Ben', which presumably makes Flecknoe and Shadwell his grandsons in the kind of literary genealogy which Dryden's *Mac-Flecknoe* mocks. Reading Jonson's imitators one is aware of the centrality to his plays of a complex of moral and social attitudes unavailable to his successors, as one is of a sheer virtuosity equally out of their range. Jonson's *Magnetick Lady* was central to this revival. In it, the 'magnetic lady', the widowed Lady Loadstone, attracts 'humorous' suitors to her, a devise that Jonson exploits in a curiously static way. It is the easiest of his plays to imitate, if setting depressingly low standards for the imitator. Without Jonson's moral complexity, a Jonsonian comic mode is impossible. If its victims are reduced to the context of a comedy of manners, they cannot justify the continuous exposé and judgement implied by the form. The Jonsonian legacy of comic character drawing is a constant but unhappy constituent of later seventeenth century comedy; its dependence on the repetition and blatancy of characteristics sits ill with the suggestiveness and 'ease' of the 'Etheregean' style. More crucial to the failure of the Newcastle dynasty in the absence of the kind of privileged character to carry out that exposé and judgement. However ambiguous these critic characters are they can be distanced from the action in a way Shadwell's never are. Shadwell's early plays – *The Sullen Lovers* (1668) or *The Humourists* (1670) for example – come to devolve on a pattern of entrapment, herding and teasing that is at once formless and cruel. If the Jonsonian style now seemed restrictingly mechanical, the reason lay as much in historical change as with the limited skills of Ben's sons and grandsons. The Caroline comedy of manners could not survive those manners or the collapse of the Caroline court. In Caroline comedy a series of social distinctions function *as* moral distinctions; an exemplary picture of social relationships is developed through neoclassical comedy's essentially moral process (exposé and judgement). Behind 'manners' comedy and moral comedy – both in this case corrective – lies the idea of decorum. Horace's simple prescription – set out in the *Ars Poetica* – of a fitness of language to social rank was expanded by sixteenth and seventeenth century theorists, as Jones and Nicol have shown,[3] into a demand for exemplary social stereotypes, and that in turn became the basis for what was accepted as verisimilitude. Gentlemen behaved like gentlemen, servants like servants; the play would assume a consensus on what such behaviour should be, and deviant characters would be condemned or if possible corrected. Caroline comedy projects the social as if it *were* the moral, determined, of course, from above. Perhaps the vigorous eccentricity of the Cavendish group was the nearest it was possible to get in this climate to a moralist's independence. But after the collapse of the Caroline court, the civil war and a Restoration whose real implications were still far from obvious, it was simply not possible to revive corrective comedy. The violent upheavals of social history had destroyed the basis of assumptions on which such forms were built.

One can demonstrate this from the metamorphosis undergone by Abraham Cowley's play *The Guardian.* First acted in Cambridge in 1641 for the then Prince Charles, Cowley adapted it as *Cutter of Coleman Street* (1661), the first 'new' comedy to be presented after Charles's accession to the throne. *Cutter of Coleman Street* is set in 1658[4] and traces the fortunes of the impoverished cavalier, Colonel Jolly, in coming to terms with the newly enriched puritan bourgeoisie. As Cowley recognized in his preface, aristocracy can no longer pretend to be a moral absolute, and comedy can no longer claim to tell the truth through a neoclassical decorum that demands a moral hierarchy and a 'correct' view of class relationships practically identical to it. But his play ran into trouble. Audiences, trying to read it as a Caroline piece, that observed just such a decorum, construed it as an attack on the Royalists. According to Cowley, the author

> did not intend the Character of a hero, one of exemplary virtue, and as *Homer* often terms such men, Unblameable, but an ordinary jovial Gentleman, commonly called a Good Fellow . . . not so conscientious as to sterve rather than do the least Injury . . . if his true Metal be but equal to his Allay, it will not indeed render him one of the finest sorts of men but it will make him Current for ought I know, in any party that was ever yet in the world.[5]

Cowley's *normative* view of dramatic character, his appeal to Jolly's currency in 'any party' – presumably even the puritans – is in some ways more revolutionary than the simple satiric inversion his opponents would seem to have seen. Its realism is more startling, more of a challenge to the received ideas of that immediately post-commonwealth period. The eponymous Cutter and his friend Worm are

> two sharks about the Town (fellows merry and Ingenious enough, and therefore admitted into better companyes than they deserve, yet withall too very scoundrels, which is no unfrequent character at *London*)[6]

Cutter is thus halfway to being a Restoration comedy, to constructing its world from the uncertainty of London life. Like the social decorums deformed by wit and rascality, themselves the response to a new social order, the protocol of tragicomedy is disarrayed by Cowley's suspension of judgement, and a new realism seems suddenly possible. Perhaps the audience's dismay was a more alert response than Cowley's preface assumed. But what literary antecedents could the writers of 'new' comedy look to? One of the Duke of Newcastle's variations on the *Magnetick Lady* theme, *The Triumphant Widow* (1674) includes a scene in which a doctor treats a 'dull poet' by using the writers of the past as medicine. He rejects Fletcher, Guarini and Shakespeare, but eventually applies Jonson, with success.[7] The scene, in style and concerns is more like Shadwell than Newcastle; but whoever wrote it, it could not be said to be an accurate prescription for the times. The answer to a Restoration dramatists problem – how to write comedy from outside neoclassical assumptions – was to be found in ironic explorations of the Guarinian tradition of courtly pastoral.

'A LANTSKIP OF THESE KINGDOMS'

For Europe in the seventeenth and eighteenth centuries Guarini's *Il Pastor Fido* (1590) was the most influential and widely known work, not just of pastoral writing, but of the whole of polite literature. Recent commentators have claimed it variously for the Baroque or Mannerism; it eludes such labels in the sheer breadth and comprehensiveness of its influence. Voltaire, towards the end of its literary vogue, asks a question that immediately occurs to the English reader of Guarini, and answers it himself;

Pourquoi des scénes entière du Pastor Fido sont-elles sues par coeur aujordhui à Stockholm et à Pétersburg? et pourquoi aucune piece du Shakespeare n'a-t-elle pu passer la mer? C'est que le bon est recherché de toutes les nations.[8]

The modern critic is obliged to be more circumspect. Of the many reasons for Guarini's influence I shall limit myself to those directly relevant to Restoration comedy.

Pastoral could be defined as a literary treatment of the life of leisure conventionally embodied in the shepherd; a way of life of a certain natural rightness. This is the way classical and Renaissance usage had defined it; excluding as free an application of the ideas behind pastoral as Empson's,[9] or for that matter, any realistic treatment of life in the desert beyond High Park.[10] The objection to this that immediately presents itself in this context is that it limits the scope so drastically as to exclude Restoration comedy altogether. And yet by its very nature pastoral is theatrical, a fiction centred on roles and role playing, not on realistically observed character, or everyday life. We are looking not at shepherds but at people for whom the fictional shepherd was a suitable image, which they recognized as such. Restoration comedy is a comedy built around a central group of young men and women, and its main impetus is gained from opposition to their pursuit of pleasure, by the more sharply drawn, even satirized types, which make up the rest of its world. That central group is the cast of a kind of pastoral:

> . . . an ideal kind of leisure class, free from the compulsion of conspicuous consumption and ostentatious waste. Gratuitous interests, including such leisurely activities as hobbies and pastimes, but excluding such strenuous exercises as sports, are the main endeavours of the pastoral world – while for all other people time is money, the shepherd always has time to waste or to spare; and this enables him to put fun before duty and pleasure before business; or to follow no other will than his caprice.
>
> This contrasts the shepherd with the merchant, the man who prefers negotium to otium; and with the sailor who ventures his life for adventure and profit.[11]

A broad historical perspective allows one to see how a superficially unlikely identification of Arcadian Shepherds and town gallants could arise. The 'ideal leisure class' proved one of the more puzzling ideas that the Renaissance revival of classical pastoral brought to English writers, interested as they were in localizing the possibility of such leisure in a less than ideal world. Sidney in the first eclogues of the *Old Arcadia* suggests that the Arcadians –

> . . . were not suche base Shepheardes as wee commonly make accoumpte of; But, the very owners of the Sheepe themselves whiche in that thrifty worlde, the substancyallest Men wolde employ theyre whole care upon.[12]

Fletcher takes this idea up, in his preface to *The Faithful Shepherdess* –

> . . . you are ever to remember Shepherds to be such, as all the ancient poets and moderne of understanding have receaved them; that is, the owners of flockes and not hyerlings.[13]

The pastoral shepherds are thus conceived of as a class of proprietors. By 1717, when Thomas Purney published his *Full Enquiry into the True Nature of Pastoral*, the detachment of the pastoral from the consideration of the country 'hyreling' had reached an extreme of breathtaking callousness:

> If the toils of the country folk took my observance 'twould only be for variety – the pleasure that comes the nearest such of any, is a comick one, which delights to see the human form distorted and debased, and turn'd into that of a beast. And as for pity, the most delightful passion of all, it can't be excited by this means. For those swains are inured to labour; and acquainted with fatigue.

The Pastoral, whose governing principle can be usefully summed up as As You Like It, has built into it a tendency to reflect the life desired by its audience –

> 'We cannot be pleased with the description of any State, or Life, which at that time we would not willingly exchange our present state for. Nor is it possible to be pleased with anything that is very low and beggarly. Therefore, methinks, I would raise my Shepherds life to a life of Pleasure . . .'[14]

One might set alongside this David Piper's description of the conventions of a certain type of Restoration portrait:

> The tone in women's dress was no longer set by the Queen as it had been in the society of Charles I; it was set by the King's mistresses . . . the shoulders are bare, and in the case of the King's mistresses sometimes to the waist; but the dishabille, which is of the late supper-table if not of the boudoir, is set in other contexts, Olympian or Arcadian landscapes, and the sitter provided with a shepherdess spud or Minerva's helmet. The attribute of Nell Gwyn is not an orange, but a lamb . . .[15]

The idea of the courtesan as shepherdess is not of course a peculiarly Restoration one; there are parallels to be found in the painted Italian villas and the courtesan's pageant outfit in Nashe's *The Unfortunate Traveller*[16] or Ithamore's idyll with the courtesan Bellamira in *The Jew of Malta*.[17] One can argue that it is in such scenes, rather than in an Italian-style classicism, that English pastoral finds its vitality. The classically pastoral seemed thin in the context of the English commercial theatre precisely because it excludes the forces that form the pastoral by contradiction of it; forces represented in the court performances where pastoral traditionally flourished, by the show of riches in the audience, or indeed on the actors. (A court performance of *The Faithful Shepherdess* was given in 1670 by ladies led by the twelve-year-old Lady Mary, daughter of The Duke of York, '. . . who appeared extraordinarily glorious and covered with jewels' according to the following day's Newsletter.[18]) The comparative weakness of classical pastoral in English should not be seen as a provinciality in English writers; after all, the vogue for pastoral among the Elizabethans, coinciding as it did with the enclosure of lands for grazing, represents an artificial pre-eminence over the folk-lore of a basically agrarian culture, and from this stems an alternative and opposed tradition of pastoral within the drama which could be exemplified in two contrasting plays by Peele, the classical *Arraignment of Paris* and the folk play *The Old Wives Tale*, or for that matter between *The Faithful Shepherdess* and Fletcher's contribution to *The Two Noble Kinsmen*. Classical pastoral remains *deraciné* in English; not even the weather is right; hence the shift we have seen in the class of the pastoral characters, from that of those it originally claimed to depict, to that of its audience; hence also the theme of the pastoral within the urban which must reach its apogee in this description of a brothel, which Harry Levin quotes from *Fanny Hill*:

> The authors and supporters of this secret institution would, in the height of their humours style themselves the restorers of the golden age and its simplicity of pleasures, before their innocence became so unjustly branded with the names of guilt and shame.[19]

Thus classical pastoral goes underground – its paradoxes are sharpened to a point which approaches satire or burlesque, but cannot really be said to attain to it. Falsity is so much its *raison d'être* that pastoral is proof against satire; it is in itself, as Pogglioli points out,[20] an ironical form. The tradition of the pastoral within the urban is an analogy in drama to that of the locus amoenus in epic. If one is to discuss pastoral in Restoration comedy it is this which will claim the most attention.

Guarinian pastoral is itself dependent on the ironical superimposition of social class. As John Shearman has argued,[21] the Italian revival of pastoral coincides with the transfer of power from the aristrocracy to absolute and autocratic rulers. Pastoral records this overtly in its characteristic praise of absolutism – but seems more slyly to suggest that shepherds may well be courtly as courtiers have little more power than they. Pastoral pleasures occupy the vacuum of disappearing political business; negotium replaced by enforced otium to use Pogglioli's terms. (It is perhaps this awareness of an exile from influence that breeds the melancholy overhanging so many courtly–pastoral communities.) *Pastor Fido* is the locus classicus of an aristocratic pastoral endemic to political change. It imbues the polite culture of the seventeenth and eighteenth century on every level from the most extravagant court opera to the exchanges of amorous intrigue.[22]

In England pastoral became an official style, that both masked and expressed aspects of the Stuart monarchy, in ways fascinatingly traced by Stephen Orgel. He has this to say about the court masque:

> The Caroline productions . . . tend to resolve all action through pastoral transformations. . . . What is recorded in these productions is the growth of a political ideology. The masques of James I and Charles I express the developing movement toward

autocracy – it is not accidental that Jones' pastoral visions become most elaborate during the 1630's, the decade of prerogative rule. Monarchs like Charles and his queen are doubtless attracted to the vision of themselves as pastoral deities because the metaphor expresses only the most benign aspects of absolute monarchy. If we can really see the king as the tamer of nature, the queen as the goddess of flowers, there will be no problems about Puritans or Ireland or Ship Money . . .[23]

By 1647, when Sir Richard Fanshawe dedicated his dazzlingly rich and attentive translation of *Il Pastor Fido* to the then Prince Charles, the parallel of England to the 'gasping state' of Guarini's stricken Arcadia had an immediacy Fanshawe was careful to point up;

> . . . it seems to me (beholding it *at the best light*) a *Lantskip* of these Kingdoms (your *Royall Patrimony*) as well in the former flourishing, as the present distractions thereof, I thought it not improper for your Princely notice at this time, thereby to occasion your Highness, even in your recreations, to reflect upon the sad *Originall*, not without hope to see it yet speedily made a perfect *parallell* throughout; and also your self a great Instrument of it.[24]

The piece can thus be seen as part of the essentially political process by which Stuart culture overlayed country realities with an aristocratic pastoral; as a culmination of the Caroline process by which, 'like a new colony' as James Turner has put it 'the land is cleared of its troublesome natives and planted with a new and more loyal population'.[25] Fanshawe's determination to build on Caroline myth-making seems quixotic in the light of further events. Parliamentary victory forced a country retirement on him, which he passed in translating *Faithfull Shepherdess* into Latin. Charles was not himself so attached to the pastoral ethos. Bored by his exile in Bruges, 'He sent for Italian books to pass the time – such as Il Pastor Fido . . . "if nothing better could be found".'[26] Pastoral is nonetheless an important part of the propaganda of Restoration. Charles made concrete his father's use of a pastoral myth of relationship between the king and his country by opening up St James's to his subjects, and sharing it casually with them. Newly landscaped in the French style and equipped with a fashionable promenade in the avenue of lime and elm trees bordering the Mall, the royal deer-park was transformed into a social institution expressive of the King's desired image; it stood for freedom and pleasure, and his willingness to mix with his subjects. It stood above all for an attempt at a personal rapport with his people, that Charles hoped might obviate other more rigorous realignments of power.

As Royal Parks, these particular Arcadias could claim as tutelary god the King himself – 'the Royal Pan'[27] as Otway called him. They thus realize an aspect of pastoral's essentially absolutist political statement. Edmund Waller considered some of these meanings in his poem *St James's Park Newly Restored by His Majesty* (1664). He depicts a world of innocent pleasure, far removed from the darkly Italianate sensuality of Rochester's later vision of a park where

> Each imitative branch does twine
> In some loved fold of Aretine.[28]

Waller's picture is to be assigned to the Dutch school;

> The gallants dancing by the riverside;
> They bathe in summer, and in winter slide.[29]

In the midst of this almost naive celebration, his glimpse of the King at play has a bathetic charm that looks forward to Betjeman, through McGonagall.

> His shape so lovely, and his limbs so strong,
> Confirm our hopes we shall obey him long.[30]

Rochester's parody marks the distance between high Restoration nihilism and the trustingly sanguine view of monarchy that Waller records. Waller, a veteran of the court of Charles I and Henrietta Maria extends its pastoral dream of itself to their heir.

> Here like the people's pastor he does go,
> His flock subjected to his view below;
> On which reflecting in his mighty mind,
> No private passion does indulgence find;
> The pleasures of his youth suspended are,
> And made a sacrifice to public care.[31]

Had these lines been written later they might have seemed almost offensively maladroit.

Waller was not the only writer to freight the Restoration with a moral meaning it did not fulfil. Flecknoe, in his *Short Treatise of the English Stage* (1664), dedicated and addressed to Newcastle, adds to an exposition of the neoclassical tenets of his patron an attractive variation on a familiar comparison – a play 'shu'd be like a well contriv'd, Garden, cast into its walks and counterwalks, betwixt an Alley and a Wilderness, neither too plain, nor too confus'd' – and a rather hopeful attempt to link the idea of decorum thus made concrete to a reform of the stage by the King himself – who, he claims, 'after his happy Restauration, . . . took such care to purge it from all vice and obscenity'.[32] As late as 1668, Thomas Shadwell, in *The Royal Shepherdesse*, produced an insistently moralistic pastoral that points uneasily both back and forward. The play is an adaptation of John Fountaine's *The Rewards of Virtue*, published in 1661. In centring on the transcendant virtue of the Queen of Arcadia it may be taken to look back at the pre-revolutionary court. But its celebration of a post-war peace, and the admonitory tone it takes in the conversion of a once adulterous King point to the contemporary situation. In the context of the public stage, and after eight years of Charles's rule had dashed hopes of his personal reform, *The Royal Shepherdesse* looks very much like an attack on the court circle. Shadwell's musical additions take the opportunity of rubbing this in. At one point the Queen attempts to distract her consort from his philandering with a 'Dance with Gittars and Castaniettas'[33] – an Iberian touch to put spectators in mind of the home-life of their own dear Queen. The court attended the first performance, but Pepys found it a 'silly' play and wondered why people didn't go to the currently revived *Faithful Shepherdesse* instead.[34] And in the same year the basic situation of *The Royal Shepherdesse* was repeated at a performance of *She Would if She Could* in circumstances only marginally connected to the play itself. Gatty, one of the play's witty heroines, was played by Moll Davies, a mistress of the King, and when it came to her 2nd act jig, the Queen left the theatre.[35]

The moral of this is clear. Fountaine, like Waller, was out of date. The moralistic tendencies of Renaissance pastoral were dangerously inapposite. But the pastoral myth remained a useful expression of the King's relationship to a peaceful kingdom, a relationship which the parks embodied. The park-scene is of crucial importance in understanding Restoration comedy: the Royal Parks, The Mall, private gardens and the public pleasure-grounds are aspects of the urban pastoral that I shall discuss as they recur throughout this book, with some indication of the different connotations that attach at different times to each of these centres of the quasi-pastoral world of gallant society. Their chief use within the plays is, in structural terms, to frame nodes of action and character that parallel or often quite specifically derive from the pastoral drama, which is as much as to say that their source is *Pastor Fido*.

THE SCENE LONDON; THE TIME EQUAL TO THAT OF THE PRESENTATION

When, in 1668 the two companies then in operation decided to split the repertory between them, the King's Company were awarded the rights to Fletcher's *Faithful Shepherdess*. The Duke's company were awarded 'Faithfull Shepheard', presumably *Pastor Fido* in one of several stage-adaptations of Fanshawe's translation. The same year Pepys saw it performed at the 'nursery' where actors were prepared for a career in either of the patent companies.[36] Like *The Spanish Tragedy*, seen here by Pepys the day before as *Jeronimo is Mad Again*,[37] the play's use in training actors was in tracing to their source the staple characters and situations of contemporary drama.

Guarini's play devolves on the rivalry between the virtuous Amarilli and the worldly Corisca, whose trickery causes Amarilli to seem unfaithful. Guarini uses the pastoral setting with its images of the cave, of darkness and light, to give his comedy of mistaken identity a neo-platonic gloss. One of the women represents physicality (in Fanshawe's translation Coridon describes Corisca as 'a carcasse of affection')[38] while the other is almost transcendantly virtuous, and the final *éclaircissement* shows a distinction between 'false' infatuation, and the apprehension through love of a spiritual real. Jonson uses this plot in *The Sad Shepherd* – both he and Fletcher expand the mechanics of Guarini's philosophical and static drama to the more theatrically effective ploy of magical impersonation; the hint may be taken from Spenser's Una and Duessa[39] though it does parallel devices in the adaptation of academic pastoral into popular drama as seen in the commedia dell 'arte.[40] Corisca in particular – 'so perfect a mistress of intrigue' as Pope put it[41] – was an invention of Guarini's, carefully expounded in his own theory and much imitated both in type and function by later dramatists. She instigates events of greater moment than either she or her concerns would seem to justify. The treacherous message by which she negates the image of her more positive anti-type can be refined into a letter, made as implausible as accident or as blatant as magic. Often Guarini's seriousness in effecting the tragicomic balance is impugned by an imitator's decision to use her as the kind of self-erasing *donnée* that Hitchcock has called 'the McGuffin';[42] Shadwell, in his later plays, uses what one may well call 'The Corisca' to, in effect, de-emphasize plot.

Corisca's attractiveness as a type tends to counteract de-emphasis. Guarini moralizes his three women characters to set up a pattern that was obviously useful to playwrights now writing for actresses. To quote Perella's summary 'the three women of the play are expressions of three kinds of love; natural, honest (or honourable) and impure. Dorinda, acting according to her natural feelings, speaks and acts spontaneously and with a natural sort of purity. Corisca loves bestially, being motivated by a fury that is not only shameless and lustful but even wicked and cruel. In Amarilli we find the true idea of widom and of womanly virtue'.[43] These three ladies, involved in a series of variations on a standard mistaken-identity plot and associated almost always with the park-pastoral setting are familiar from even the skimpiest reading of Restoration comedy. Corisca in particular is the source of a series of ladies of intrigue whose function, sometimes coloured by that of the baroque enchantress or (conversely) the disruptive classical termagant, is to set in motion the temporary entanglements of an elegantly self-erasing plot. Too petty for tragedy, too large in effect for comedy, the plot device in which the heroine is slandered (or somehow replaced) by an anti-heroine is given a classic status by *Pastor Fido*. It sums up the controlled ambiguity of response extorted by the form Guarini had claimed to invent. When detached from Guarini's neo-platonic moral scheme, and his careful aesthetic theorizing, it becomes the basic model of the kind of plotting the seventeenth and eighteenth century called 'intrigue'.

Intrigue plotting bears in itself no moral weight. It is developed only to be undone. This is pleasurable in itself; in the more ambitious plays it also serves to articulate the social conflicts and personal need that underly a casually understated language of fashionable self-presentation. Restoration comedy is to be distinguished from its two rival forms of intrigue play – the 'Spanish' play and the tragi-comic romance – not simply by its insistence on a contemporary London setting, but by the social and psychological contingencies that accrue from this limited and apparently contradictory claim on the real. The Spanish play has as its basic, very nearly its only, plot dynamic the idea of the imprisoned girl, denied, but eventually gaining, the right to love whom she pleases. The characters are formed from a convention of hispanic psychology. The male head of the family, usually an elder brother, is choleric and authoritarian, his opposition to the sister's lover is based on longstanding family feuds, and the general concern for honour is played out in an intricate series of escapes, abductions and duels. This is a limited if appealingly colourful formula. It is difficult to extrapolate imaginatively out of a setting (a legendary Seville) derived from a limited number of literary sources, and to construct any great variety of roles from the principles of an entirely theoretical notion of national character. One Don Pedro is very much like another, and his distinction from a Don Fernando is only evident to the trained eye. I shall deal with 'Spanish' themes when they are juxtaposed on London comedy – in Crowne's *Courtly Nice* (1685) for example,[44] or Wycherley's charming *Gentleman Dancing Master* (1672), which would be a London comedy if it could. (It's only a Spanish play because the heroine's father, a hispanophile Englishman, has decreed it, and the play turns on her attempt to break this constricting form.)[45]

Tragicomedy as the Restoration knew it is simply the intercutting of a 'high' verse plot of courtly romance and an intrigue sub-plot, 'modish' in tone, pursued by the minor courtiers. It thus bears little relation to the careful generic integrity of Guarinian tragicomedy. It fits a native preference for mixed forms to the term Guarini made available when he claimed to invent the only dramatic genre unknown to the ancients (thus finding a space for baroque practice in neoclassical theory). The structural problems of the mixed form are obvious – the 'witty' subplot is inevitably destructive of any serious attention one might pay to a main plot pursuing opposed notions of love and honour. The problem is that the division between 'high' and 'low' manners is no longer clear-cut. Both kinds of behaviour are equally available to the participants, so the audience is free to read the implications of one plot into the other and the play's fragile structure inevitably, if sometimes amusingly, undermines itself. Furthermore, the Fletcherian Sicily in which the whole thing was usually placed was well

travelled terrain and Dryden found nothing new there. Tragicomedy becomes interesting when it lets contemporary concerns
invade it – as in his *Marriage à la Mode* (1672), which I will discuss
with other comedies of fashion. Dryden's attachment to this form
was partly a token of his distaste for purely comic kinds. Its vogue
was shorter and more tenuous than that of the Spanish play.

Setting an intrigue play in London on the other hand bred a rich
proliferation of realist connotation and stylistic paradox. Precise
evocation of a London setting was as old as commercial comedy
itself. Jonson had given it a respectability which the Caroline plays
developed in pieces like Broome's *Sparagus Garden* (1635) or Shirley's *Hyde Park* (1632). Topographical comedy set itself in a realistically mapped London, against which the social manoeuvring of
the characters could be plotted with precision. The vogue for
topography increased after the civil war, in which location and
ownership in becoming problematic became that much more immediately interesting. Charles II's personal interest in topographical painting[46] and a general aristocratic wish to record property
established and 'restored' found a theatrical counterpart in the
importation of 'moveable scenes'.[47] A number of the Dutch and
Flemish painters who met the demand for topographical work
painted for the theatres too. Scenery was painted in oils on heavy
wooden panels which slid together behind the proscenium. The
visual style would be detailed and realistic – bizarre tragic intrigues
would take place before a careful rendering of a real Morocan or
Portuguese landscape, as accurate as traveller's notes could make
it. Comedy relied on a series of stock pieces, neutral interiors and
familiar London locations. Only one detailed picture of such a set
has survived – the frontispiece to Perrin's opera *Ariadne* (1674)[48]
depicts a realistic London bridge, with three fashionable nymphs
poised rather awkwardly in front of it on a Venus-ian scallop. But
one can posit that a rather more roughly executed version of the
contemporary landscape style, and a series of Hollar-style panor-
amas of, say, Westminster, St. James's, the Exchange and Covent
Garden would constitute the visual idiom of the plays in performance.

Contemporaneity may create the possibility of an appeal out to
an immediately perceivable social or personal 'real', but it also
focuses the transience of the moment, an apprehension of impermanence central to Restoration culture's sense of itself. Both that
'real' and that sense of transience inform the Guarinian pastoral.

Taken out of its neoplatonic moral superstructure, intrigue plotting creates a series of temporary dualisms on the axis of reality and falsehood, which an overall assumption of a 'real' context – 'London . . the present' – allows Restoration comedy to develop into a complex psychological and social awareness. Moral distinctions operate in this, but the aim of the form, unlike Caroline comedy, is not to articulate or reaffirm them. Restoration comedy is a parody of Guarinian pastoral, in the musical rather than in the usual literary sense; that is, it imitates and builds on pastoral while observing an ironical distance from it. It creates a kind of town pastoral, wittily inverting the Arcadian norm to make the town the locus of pleasure fantasy and change and the country the domain of banal quotidian reality.

We are now in a position to say what Restoration comedy is. It is, as I said at the beginning, the prose comedy of London life. But we can add that it is a form of baroque intrigue comedy, with fashionable society as its milieu and personal fulfilment as its dynamic. Its plot is shaped from the conventions of pastoral intrigue, which it inverts or parodies but never entirely empties of meaning – which it never, in other words, simply burlesques. Its plotting is determined by the free interplay of the characters. 'Wit' – the ability to use social and linguistic artifice for personal ends – overrides 'decorum' – the affirmation of an intrinsically self-righting social order – and thus the plays reach their endings on kinds of contracts, not on an order re-discovered, presumed to have been somehow always 'there' and hence presented as natural. As these characteristics seem consonant with – are, as I would argue *produced* by – historical change, then it seems fair to continue to call the form after that historical event which produced it. For the rest of this book I shall call it Restoration comedy.

Restoration comedy then is a complex literary form, deriving its complexity from the relation of generic conventions to history. The relation is shifting, oblique, determined by different factors in different instances. My argument is not structured as an exercise in literary theory. It is literary criticism of a basically empirical kind. It is I hope useful as a series of 'readings' of plays and playwrights. But the context of those readings is an argument about the nature and development of a genre – about development as the nature of a genre.

I see the history of the form as having three main phases, which as my approach is broadly chronological, fall into three sections of the book. Chapters 1 to 3 describe its initial evolution by 'the wits' (Rochester, Etherege and their circle). Chapters 4 to 6 describe its adoption by professional writers, and its place in the Royalist crisis of the 1680s. Chapters 7 to 10 recount its revival by Dryden, Southerne and Betterton after the accession of William and Mary, and its eventual irrelevance to changing social circumstances. My conclusion is a reading of *The Beggars Opera*, ironic pastoral's last flamboyant flourish.

1 From 'Decorum' to 'Nature' – Etherege and the Wits

If any one writer could be said to have invented Restoration comedy in any one play, *She Would if She Could* would make Etherege the most realistic contender. But when one examines the comedies that precede it, it becomes obvious that the comic style which that play consolidates had been developed in the work of a number of dramatists, all known to each other and all working within some sense of shared aesthetic preferences. Sir George Etherege was part of a coterie of mainly amateur writers in an often equivocal relationship to the court. Sir Robert Howard, his brother James and brother-in-law John Dryden, Etherege, Sir Charles Sedley and such figures as the Duke of Buckingham and the Earl of Rochester make up a literary clique often and conveniently known as 'the Wits'.[1] This chapter describes the evolution of Restoration comedy within the work of the group whose common achievement it was.

COMEDIES OF RESTORATION

The first Restoration comedies are set in the late phase of the interregnum, as if to find a new style in events that invalidated the styles of the past. The first 'new' comedy, Cowley's revision of The Guardian (1641) as *Cutter of Coleman Street*, was set in 1658.[2] Sir Robert Howard's *The Committee* (1662), the first wholly new comedy is also set among newly rich puritans and cavaliers in defeat. Its events are given a definite date – 10 April – but the year is left vague, perhaps so that one can read the history of the whole interregnum and the gradual return of the Royalist party into the play's close.

Howard's play, (unlike Cowley's), remained a repertory piece.
An unassumingly neat and finished play, it is limited to a staid
view of inflammatory subject matter. *The Committee* exists in an
ordered comic world, in which all difference can be resolved in a
dance, where the strongest image of social revolution is the mix of
ranks and persons in a hackney coach and where upsets are most
likely to be upset stomachs –

> At the very same time when this same *Ruth* was sick
> It being the first time the Girle was ever coach'd,
> The good man Mr Mayor,
> I mean, that I spoke of,
> Held his Hat for the Girle to ease her Stomach in . . .[3]

The prosperity of the puritan Mrs Day is ludicrous and wrong;
she has stepped out of her class as an ex-servant and must be
balanced by the 'good' servant, the enthusiastically menial Irishman, Teg. Decorum demands that the cavaliers think twice before
admitting attraction to the puritan women; it demands that when
the attraction proves unconquerable, the girls should turn out to be
the daughters of gentlemen after all. Decorum may seem an odd
rationale for a situation that only allows sexual feeling to exist
between Careless and Ruth, if it can be seen to degrade her –

> C.Car. . . . but by the way of Matrimony honestly to encrease
>   your Generation; 'tis to tell you truth is (sic) against my
>   conscience.
> Ruth Yet you wou'd beget right understandings.
> C.Car. Yes, I wou'd have 'un all Bastards.
> Ruth And me a Whore.[4]

The strength of *The Committee* perhaps unexpectedly, lies in its
adroit placing of these women characters. Howard manages to
create figures who challenge the formula-bound, coercively ordered concept of comedy that he inherited. Mrs Day's disruptive
energy is a revolution in itself. She has made her own amalgam of
manner in her ascent to the bourgeoisie, a wonderfully ripe con-
coction of haughtiness and vulgarity. Ruth's social ambiguity at
least liberates her from the dilemma of the moping cavalier lady,

Arbella, found attractive by her lover only when in tears.[5] Like Etherege's Harriet she demonstrates her ability to mimic and to woo by the book; like Harriet she will not accept a man who cannot let himself be laughed at.[6] Perhaps she stays so long in her puritan disguise to tease Careless into breaking the invisible barrier of the class-war. There is certainly an overtone of seriousness in her declaration that

> When the quarrel of the Nation is reconcil'd you and I shall agree; till when Sir . . .[7]

The conflicts of these retrospective comedies were not confidently resolved within a single play until Sedley's *The Mulberry Garden*, of 1668. The change in the political fortunes of the cavaliers creates the comic peripeteia of the last act. When the lovers are finally reunited, and dance, Sedley has the stage direction 'after the Dance a great shout within'.[8] It is to greet the news of Charles's return. The effect is almost as if the Restoration were generated by the success of the lovers' intrigues. *The Mulberry Garden* belongs with Etherege's first play *The Comical Revenge* (1663) as a study of the stress of the times on 'peaceful families and warring states'.[9] They both attempt to reorganize comic style on the most intimate as well as on the most broadly public scale. Like *The Committee* and *Cutter of Coleman Street*, they are comedies of Restoration.

Retrospective historical placing, and the exploration of a broad social spectrum set *The Comical Revenge* apart from Etherege's other two plays. *The Comical Revenge* is less explicitly located in the world of *The Committee* than Sedley's play, but it demands an awareness of the same social events. Sir Nicholas Cully is described by a maid at one point as 'one of Oliver's knights . . . his mother was my grandmother's dairy-maid'.[10] The pivotal figure of the aristocratic, or 'high', main plot, the cavalier Bruce, is in prison; presumably for his loyalty to the royalist cause. But public events only have meaning in this play as they impinge on the personal; Bruce's eventual release is unexplained. *The Comical Revenge* reflects the experience of civil war in a high-plot formed in language and psychology by fear of division. Bruce's part in the King's party gives him a status to which the aristocratic Bevill family respond in different degrees of adulation and guilt. But Etherege is surely justified in his modest insistence on the play's stylistic contemporaneity.

Our author therefore begs you would forget
Most Rev'rend Judges, the records of wit,
And only think upon the modern way
of writing, whilst y'are censuring his play.[11]

'The modern way' as both Etherege and Sedley pursue it, is a mode of comic writing whose innovatory effect is to be seen in its disturbance of received ideas of stylistic decorum.

The breakup and reorganization of society within *The Mulberry Garden* and *The Comical Revenge* is mirrored by the playwrights' occasionally hazardous stylistic experiment. Their rhymed scenes develop themes of love, loyalty, insecurity and change in a way that encapsulates and makes static the conflicts played out more fluently in comic prose. To this extent the device attaches a 'serious' label to apparently frivolous action. But the effect of the whole is more complex, particularly in Etherege, who is able to control a sequence of scenes in a way Sedley is not. The mock funeral in IV.vii is funny, because one might presume when the bier is brought in that it belongs to the high plot, and is possibly Bruce's. Then, precisely because this plot is capsized by an eruption of the lowest kind of physical comedy – Dufoy in his tub – one can accept in the subsequent scene that Bruce is still alive. Etherege is thus able to exploit differences of mode to carry through one train of ideas, or to juxtapose them to subvert one's preconceptions of the characters involved. The correspondence he sets up between verse high plot and comic prose pushes at the barriers of literary decorum. The witty Sir Frederick Frollick's free and equal contest with the widow overlaps oddly into the garden the aristocratic ladies use to plot strictly diagrammatic shifts of feeling. The play's thickening sense of social chaos is expressed in a series of duel scenes, variously comic and heroic, but consistently disordered. The methods of farce resolve division; in the last two acts in particular Etherege creates a sort of fugue of intrigues on all social levels, and it is Sir Frederick Frollick who masters its technique and thus emerges as the play's true hero – his witty marriages, like the harmonious marriages of Sedley's *Mulberry Garden* bring the end of the play to a restoration. The play belongs to those who gain their ends by wit and disguise, a kind of commedia-dell'arte morality which works throughout the play's model of society. An anonymous footboy, looking for a 'stray gentleman', his master Sir Nicholas Cully, is forced to try and lug him drunk offstage –

If I do not get this fool clear off before he comes to himself, our plot is quite spoiled; this summer-livery may chance to hover over my shivering limbs next winter . . .[12]

But the prize falls to a stronger servant, able to lift Cully up in his arms; a rather touching vignette of two of the play's losers, one quite lost in the furious intrigue, the other just missing his opening in it. It is all to the good that this swamps the verse-plot, and its basically 'Spanish play' types of moping lovers and statutory heavy brother. Land-locked by the prose plot, they achieve a kind of Caroline melancholy, aptly overtaken by the spirit of a new age.

Sedley on the other hand tries to invest too much of our sympathy in his Eugenio, Philander, Horatio, Althea and Diana – the ladies are distinguishable from one another in that Althea is the more unlikeable, but the gentlemen are not. The exquisite scenes between Olivia and Wildish, and the interestingly handled rivalry between the puritan Forecast and the cavalier Everyoung, detach themselves from a high-plot fixed inextricably in an alien imaginative world. Again, the moral is that wit and disguise are the spirit of the new age and win out, even when, as in Sir Samuel's case, they are involuntary. Tricked first by love and then by chance, he emerges better off by the Restoration than his faintly ridiculous cavalier brother.

To this extent the play sums up themes present in earlier plays. But the history of Dryden's first play *The Wild Gallant* suggests a crucial breakthrough effected by *The Comical Revenge*. Performed in 1663 it shares with *The English Monsieur*, James Howard's play of the same year, that first popular formula for the economic and social triumph of wit, the contest between the penniless witty suitor and his rich prize. But when the play was printed in 1669, Dryden felt constrained to revise it. He points out in a rather bitter prologue, that fashions in vice have changed –

He thought him monstrous leud (I'll lay my life)
Because suspected with his Landlord's Wife:
But since his knowledge of the Town began,
He thinks him now a very civil man . . .
'Tis some amends his frailties to confess;
Pray pardon him his want of wickedness.[13]

From a literary point of view, this is more than just a temporary change in fashion. When Dryden added the scene where Loveby entertains two whores, and, one may presume, planted other references to the gentlemanly diversion of whoring, he was responding to the collapse of neo-classical concepts of comedy. Like the plays of the Howards, and like the Caroline comedies, *The Wild Gallant* in its original form observed a restricting decorum. Neo-classical comedy is a comedy of manner in a sense different from that suggested by later application of 'the comedy of manners' as a lable for 'high' comedy. (The plural makes a lot of difference.) Manner in what one might call the Horatian sense is observed propriety; a gentleman behaves in a gentlemanly 'manner', a servant like a servant. Etherege broke through this; Shadwell, initially hostile to the new style, reflects on it in the preface to *The Royal Shepherdesse* (1668):

> I shall say little more of the play, but that the Rules of Morality and good Manners are strictly observed in it: (Vertue being exalted and Vice depressed) and perhaps it might have been better received had neither been done in it; for I find, it pleases most to see Vice incouraged, by bringing the characters of debauch'd People upon the Stage, and making them pass for fine Gentlemen, who openly profess Swearing, Drinking, Whoring, breaking Windows, beating Constables etc . . . .[14]

This sounds suspiciously like Etherege's riotous Sir Frederick Frollick – though as we shall see, Shadwell's relationship to Etheregean comedy was to become infinitely more cordial. Dryden's attitude remained ambiguous, but on the whole he merely dabbled in the form, and then apologetically. He may have adapted his comedy for a world where 'the best Heraldry of a Gentleman is a Clap deriv'd to him, from three Generations'[15] but *The Wild Gallant* remains at base an old-fashioned piece, whose female and minor male roles are routine reproductions of an outdated model. Indeed one of his elaborations of the theme places the new-style gentry with a brutality that leaps ahead of its context. When the Justice, Trice, is told of a man on trial 'for getting a Wench with Childe' he asks 'Is he a poor fellow, or a Gentleman?' –

Servant: A very poor Fellow, Sir
Trice: Hang him, Rogue, make his mittimus immediately; must such as he presume to get Children?

Loveby, the wild gallant, approves – 'A poor lowsie Rascal, to intrench upon the Game of Gentlemen.'[16] The degree of irony in this is difficult to place. Some residual decorum operates in all comedy. Random injustice coexists uneasily with the cosy world of the rest of the play. The new *Wild Gallant* is simply a cosmetic job in reverse; the warts are painted on. Once Sir Frederick had broken the mould of genteel comedy, the wits were left with the task of remaking it, into a form in which intrigue, wit, and a cycle of roles for the new actresses, could expand in a way that rehashed Caroline formulas denied them.

PARK AND PLAYHOUSE

The first play to explore this new style seems to have been James Howard's *The English Monsieur*. Though not published until 1674, it was first recorded in performance as early as 1663, and then periodically in the intervening years. Whether the 1674 text is the same as the acting text of more than a decade before must be open to doubt. But as it stands, *The English Monsieur* is the first surviving all-prose comedy of fashionable London life. Howard succeeds in characterizing the town-world of his play as the world of Restoration comedy. It is this world, bounded on one side by country oddity and simplicity, and on the other by the inanity of the merely fashionable that emerges in his work for the first time. It is the world of amorous intrigue which Vaine, on 'hearing the Orange Wenches talk of Ladies and their Gallants'[17] was seized by an insane desire to pretend himself a part of; a pretence that, when he is finally invited to Lady Wealthy's ball, prevents him from participating in the reality, lest he be found out. Vaine's 'humour' exists not in psychological isolation, but is equally a product of the world of fashion as Comeley's weariness or Frenchlove's affectation. 'The reason why *London* is more pleasant to live in, than the Country . . .' Wellbred explains to Lady Wealthy, '. . . is because all sorts of fools come to it'.[18] While one may wonder whether the town's population of fools and lovers wandered the parks and pleasure grounds in Howard's first version of his play, there is no doubt that it would be placed there in the comedy to which *The English Monsieur* seems such a large step. It would certainly be nice if the unnamed location where Comely meets Elspeth looking for the place 'where the king and the queen do walk'[19] were St James's itself.

In its implied opposition of the foppish Frenchlove, the 'Monsieur' of the title, and the fresh country-girl Elsbeth (especially in the context of Comely's accidie of the heart) *The English Monsieur* deals tentatively with the themes of Etherege's *The Man of Mode*. But while Elspeth may look forward to the country heroine of the later play in function, her firmly placed clumsiness and oddity suggest that she looks back as a type. Elspeth is quite impervious to London and all it has to offer. There is so little suggestion of her conceiving ideas unsuited to her station that one wonders if Howard brought her and William to London, so impregnably sealed in bucolic innocence, simply to avoid the violence to the neo-classical unities of place involved taking Comely to the country and back again. Howard's ladies and gentlemen are insipidly ladylike and gentlemanly. There can be no sense of subtly shifting roles, of chaotic pursuit and desire as in Etherege, only a clash of behavioural dodgems. Howard defines the fashionable world with brilliant acuity, but this is an end in itself for him, not a medium.

The best of these scenes of clashing social convention is the competition of compliment Elspeth holds between Comely and her country lover William. William scores highly with a speech that makes up in physical immediacy what it lacks in elegance.

> I could lick thee all over as our Cow does her Calf . . . I could tear the cloths off thy back, smock and all, my heart does leap and caper when I do see this leg and they Coats truck't up as thou coms't home from Milking Vathers Kine.[20]

But Comely's attempt at courtly rhetoric gets tangled in platonic refinements, despite William's helpful nudgings –

Comely: Come fair soul
Will: Nay, if thou hast a mind to speak, speak of her body.[21]

Elspeth puts an end to it as kindly as possible, and they depart to the country in pitying incomprehension. Again, no setting is given for this little pastoral contest. But the games of language and disguise played elsewhere in the piece come to the centre on the commercial pleasure-ground of the Spring Garden. The link with *The Mulberry Garden* and *She Would if She Could* is clear, even if the chronology of influence isn't. All three plays use the pleasure gardens as a mock-pastoral setting, a playground of the kind, Huizinga describes in *Home ...ens*, set apart for essentially serious games. 'The arena, the cardtable, the magic circle, the temple, the stage . . . are temporary worlds within the ordinary world, dedicated to the performance of an act apart.'[22]

For Sedley the games of true and false played out in the pleasure ground scenes of *Mulberry Garden* are primarily language games. These encounters between Olivia and Wildish have as much in common with Etherege's play of the same year, *She Would if She Could*, as the rest of the play has with the earlier *Comical Revenge*. They also bear a close resemblance to *Sedley's* lyrics. The Restoration love lyric offers a small-scale formal parallel to the intrigue play. It presents the conventional 'Petrarchan' relationship as a contest of changing roles, and is perhaps another product of the Wits' modification of received forms. Sedley in particular presents distinct (though not 'characterized') speakers, anchoring speech in a context where it becomes a kind of action. This dramatic poise suggests a provisionality of language. It explores the limits and evasions, the blanks and overstatements of the conversational style.

The lyric is a space out of, an escape from 'life', like the pastoral, or Huizinga's 'playground'. The Restoration lyric, like the drama, exploits pastoral by foregrounding its contradictions. We can see this in a Sedley lyric (I shall quote more or less the whole poem) which by drawing on town-pastoral also illuminates this aspect of his play. The song which begins 'Smooth was the Water, calm the Air . . .' places its action carefully in time

> The Evening-sun deprest,

and moves in from its initial 'elemental scope to a patterning of people who imply places, a city landscape created out of what inhabits it;

> Lawyers dismist the noisie Bar,
>   The Labourer at rest,
>
> When *Strephon*, with his charming Fair,
>   Cross'd the proud River *Thames* . . .

The location is named within a topography defined as a mesh of social relationship. While the city-scape prepares us for '*Thames*', elements of a pastoral style of description prepare us for '*Strephon*'. The first stanza presents an implied harmony of art and nature, the human and the elemental, within which social roles are relaxed and simple. One only has to compare this to the huddled 'listing' of conventional descriptions of the town to bring out its closeness to the pastoral model for composing place.

The next two lines 'place' the reader.

> . . . And to a Garden did repair,
> To quench their mutual Flames.

'Garden' sets up collusion, by reserving a name which the reader can be expected to supply – the New Spring Gardens, a pleasure ground near Vauxhall. Our knowing relationship to this social topography renders the last line of the stanza suspect in a way which infects the lines preceding it. 'Charming' 'proud', did repair/to quench their mutual Flames' denote a dangerously knowing choice of diction.

In the next verse the 'crafty waiter' who serves them also colludes; the mechanism of pleasure falls faultlessly into place around Strephon. The 'Garden' 'works' as harmoniously as London did in the first stanza. The 'Cream and strawberries' offered express the waiter's interpretation of the scene (he 'soon espyd/ Youth sparkling in her Eyes;/He brought no Ham, nor Neat's-tongues dry'd,/But Cream and Strawberries). They thus become a language, a set of symbols, with which he 'prompts' Strephon.

> The amorous *Strephon* ask'd the Maid,
> What's whiter than this Cream?

The girl 'could not tell' 'I know not, she reply'd', when questioned similarly about the strawberries. The poem *allows* her to reply – as Sedley's other lyrics don't. The shepherd seizes his 'pretty Lamb' as prey. His voice takes over the poem, swamping not only hers but the narrators, the voice which constructs our dramatic and scenic perspective.

> What's redder than these Berries are?
>   I know not, she reply'd;
> Those Lips, which I'll no longer spare,
>   The burning Shepherd cry'd,
>   And strait began to hug her;
>   This Kiss, my Dear,
>   Is sweeter far
> Than Strawberries, Cream and Sugar.[23]

'Burning' answers the 'quench' of the second stanza; or questions it, retrospectively. Pleasure gives love a new language, a language that bursts decisively out of the stanza form to end the poem by beginning the action to which it tended.

In *An Allusion to Horace* (1675–6) Rochester praised Sedley's poems as acts of seduction – acts that depend on the 'mannerly obscene',[24] a smuggling in of sexual allusion allowed for in the suggestiveness of an elegantly imprecise social language. This is certainly one way of describing the process of the poems – but one may ask whom they are supposed to seduce. Their dramatic placing sets up an ironic deflection of aim: they exhibit the seducer, engaged in teasing, bullying or tricking language into complicity with desire. Language, perhaps, is the seducee.

The poem I analysed is unusual in its careful use of setting. it makes explicit a contradiction basic to the park and pleasure garden scenes of Restoration comedy. Pastoral 'places' its characters in a world with its own rules. The reader, who can neither contribute nor participate is thus 'displaced'. But topography, drawing on a knowledge of the real which the reader is assumed to share 're-places', puts the reader into collusion with a fictional world to some extent continuous with his or her own. The pleasure gardens in the plays are both fictional and real, both pastoral and topography. This double nature makes them the apt locale for playful oppositions of 'reality' and 'illusion.'

The Mulberry Garden in Sedley's play is seen to have a quasi-magical effect. 'Sure the air of this place is a great softener of men's hearts'[25] exclaims Victoria. While Modish claims that the effect is natural and tends toward truth – 'How can it choose, having so many lovers' sighs daily mixt with it?[26] – she more cautiously characterizes it as a place where rules of true and false are temporarily relaxed.

> Truth is a thing merely necessary for witnesses and Historians, and in these places doth but curb invention and spoil good Company, We will only confirm 'um to what's probable.[27]

The language and conventions of romantic love are dissolved, in a process which neatly parallels the playwright's own search for a language of feeling that yet bears some resemblance to the manners of a real world where the deepest emotions are expressed elliptically, if at all. Althea's emotions seem shallow because copiously and glibly expressed, and meaningless, because isolated by characterless verse. Olivia's instincts are obviously right in pulling her sister back from the temptations of metre – 'Fye Sister, leave this Ryming at least!'[28] – temptations into which her lover Hippolito has already strayed; indeed it is the obvious falsity of verse-emotions which allows one to accept his bald reversion to Victoria. What he has done during the rest of the play has been devalued by its medium. A fluctuation of genuine feeling is traced beautifully in the long scene between Olivia and Wildish in Act II, from Olivia's protestation –

> What' men have Liv'd years in desarts for their Mistresses sake, and yet have trembled when they spoke of love . . .[29]

to the authentically abrupt nonsequiturs of their embarrassed parting. Their truth of feeling becomes apparent in the gap of sense between his 'As your Beauty bred my Affection, so let your kindness nourish it'[30] and her 'Mr Wildish you have been so pleasant upon this new Argument, that I had almost forgot my Visit to Diana.'[31] It is against the trivia of everyday life, not against terrible vows and portents, that love must be measured –

> your true Lover leaves all Company when the Sport begins, the Table when the Bottles are call'd for, the Gaming-house when the Cards come up . . .[32]

Its strength is seen in the dent it makes in a way of life.

Sedley's prose love-scenes have a touch of the Forest of Arden about them, a romantic anti-romanticism. Their superiority to the verse is symptomatic of a new approach to the problem of dramatic language, explored in Robert Howard's preface to his *Four New Plays* (1655). The question of verse leads him into the proposition that a character's speeches must be presumed to be his own invention. Thus rhyme becomes as ludicrous in conversational contexts –

> When a Piece of Verse is made up by one that knew not what the other meant to say . . . so that the smartness of a Reply, which has its beauty by coming from sudden Thoughts, seems lost by that which rather looks like a Design of two, than the Answer of one.[33]

– as it is in the context of everyday life – 'When a Servant is call'd, or a Door bid to be Shut in Rhime.'[34] When Howard refers to 'Verse' he means rhymed verse, as opposed to 'Blank Verse', a term he evidently finds unhelpful ('A hard Expression').[35] But that, he suggests, is only a lesser evil, and he defends his criterion of naturalism in a suggestive analogy:

> Some may object, That this Argument is trivial, because, what-ever is shew'd, tis known still to be but a Play; but such may as well excuse an ill Scene, that is not naturally painted, because they know 'tis only a Scene, and not really a City or Country[36]

A drama more reliant on the beauty of 'sudden Thoughts' than on the expressive richness of verse, more committed to painterly naturalism than to the formalism of the revered Elizabethans, is present in Howard's work in theory only as he himself is the first to admit. It is the drama that, half-realized in *The Comical Revenge* and *The Mulberry Garden* argues destructively against the half that remains in rhyme. Howard was not an ambitious dramatist, as he admits with an engaging insouciance in defending his practice against his theory.

> While I give these Arguments against Verse, I may seem faulty that I have not only writ ill ones, but writ any; but since it was the fashion, I was resolv'd, as in al indifferent things, not to appear singular, the danger of the vanity being greater than the error; and therefore I followed it as a Fashion, though very far off.[37]

One cannot believe that writing was an 'indifferent' thing to either Etherege or Sedley. Both *She Would if She Could* and the prose scenes of *The Mulberry Garden* are an ambitious attempt at a new dramatic language. They are both comedies of manner, in a sense rather different from Shadwell's in condemning the stage rake for the lack of it. for Etherege and Sedley, manner is an ambiguous language, but it is also the material of day to day relationship. They work from a tension between conventional behaviour and implied emotion with the park a space set out for the exploration of this kind of duality. It is still perhaps a product of courtly neo-platonism, but translated into a more valid convention of everyday

behaviour; or, manners. Sedley shows his lovers coercing manner
into an expression of feeling; the effect is charming but somehow
diminutive, like the pair in the mock-pastoral lyric, looked after by
an attentive waiter. *She Would if She Could* is a much tougher play.
Etherege is genuinely afraid of the deceits of manner, the risk of
missing those golden opportunities that comedy throws in its
participants' way. The foot-boys little scene in *The Comical Revenge*
offers just such a vignette of failure. The central image of *She Would
if She Could* is of the ladies masked or in disguise, its basic movement is pursuit. Etherege almost seems to go too far in his avoidance of directly expressed feeling. Not until the final duologue
between Arianna and Gatty does the play reach a bed-rock of
acknowledged emotion; and even there the girls discover the
distinctness of their feelings, a subtler and more fragile effect than
similar scenes of intimacy in, say, Vanbrugh. And the circumstance that holds over the scene a farcical sword of Damocles also
offers a parody of it. The two gentlemen that Lady Cockwood has
bundled into her closet have found out the coincidence of their
own aims.

The status within the play of these sceptically presented gallants
marks the final break between Restoration comedy and the politer
drama that precedes it. There are no verse-speakers in *She Would if
She Could*, no stratified scheme of social behaviour. Freeman and
Courtall are the nearest thing in it to normative characters; they
evoke from the start that world of polite vice only intermittently
apparent in previous comedies, and the articulate scurrility of their
comic prose is the medium of the play. 'Well!' Courtall remarks . . . .

> this is grown a wicked town, it was otherwise in my memory; a
> gentleman should not have gone out of his chamber, but some
> civil officer or other of the game would have been with him, and
> have given him notice where he might have had a course or two
> in the afternoon.[38]

The town is a region of projected pleasures, plotted on the play's
imaginary map as a complex of pleasure-grounds, eating houses,
temporary lodgings and theatres. For the characters who arrive
from the country it represents a freedom and anonymity which
soon tighten into a comic mechanism of concealment and coincidence as their first flurry of exploration reveals farcical sameness of
intent.

Courtall and Freeman almost miss Arianna and Gatty in the Mulberry Garden; Courtall, who exhibits a diffidence to belie his name, is disinclined to pursue them as they enter 'with vizards, and pass nimbly over the stage'.[39] In fact Gatty has already matched his recurrent hunting metaphor with her own more combative conception of the freedom the town affords: not only an emancipation from familial control – the choice 'not to feed their pride, and make the world believe it is in their power to afford some gallant or other a good bargain'[40] – but a freedom to challenge men on neutral ground. Arianna is won from a conventional praise of 'the fresh air, and the delights of wandering in the pleasant groves',[41] knowingly mocked by its context, to recruitment in Gatty's campaign – 'Upon these conditions I am contented to trail a pike under thee – march along girl.'[42]

But in the pastoral contest the masked ladies are outpointed by the gentlemen's flair for a language of polite deceit. The scene may end with their oath never to speak to a lady till the four of them meet again, but they arrive at the Cockwood's in the very scene, to be faced with Arianna and Gatty once more. They explain in terms of the paradox of gentlemanly behaviour;

Courtall: Fie fie, the keeping of one's word is a thing below the honour of a gentleman.
Freeman: A poor shift! Fit only to uphold the reputation of a paultry citizen[43]

Freeman detaches both language and the social language of behaviour from commercial considerations of exchange and evaluated trust. Gatty shows her paces for her prospective suitors as Sir Joslin bids her, but the scene is now spiced with a sense of a new more personal game. Song and dance, like language and 'manner', are the tools of those who have the wit to explore. As far as the lovers are concerned the first half of the play is an exposition of the same problem posed in Sedley's Mulberry Garden.

The second half is dominated by Lady Cockwood who copes with the disparity of personal need and social language in her own dottily self-deceptive way. If there seems something pathological in her hysteria of desire and trepidation at the start of the hint is confirmed by Sentry, and maids are after all a touchstone of truth in this kind of play;

This is a strange infirmity she has, but I must bear with it; for on my conscience, custom has made it so natural, she cannot help it.[44]

And the cause is surely revealed in the chaos in the end of the act, when Sir Oliver tells Freeman –

I have had a design to break her heart ever since the first month that I had her, and 'tis so tough that I have not yet crack'd one string on't.[45]

Lady Cockwood has lost herself in a policy designed to hide her feelings as much as possible and the responsibility is Sir Oliver's. It is in this light that her callous attitude to the other characters must be seen; she has withdrawn into almost total psychological isolation.

And yet by the end of the play Lady Cockwood has not only gained a measure of control over her own situation, but, accidentally, broken the ice between the pairs of lovers. The language of self martyrdom, the awesome self-abasement of the Cockwoods in the tavern scene, made concrete in his 'suit of penitence' and her self-induced fits, marks a low point from which Lady Cockwood retrieves a freedom her husband, conventionally enough, sees as an attempt to dominate him. It seems almost tautologous to speak of her concern for language and 'Honour', given the emotional investment she has made in the power of language to deceive, to replace not only honour but all other forms of self-presentation. It is this complex of ideas that finds expression in the park-pastoral plot. As a type-character she has an honourable ancestry going back to Virgil's Juno, and the shadowy Eris of the Troy story; but the lady whose sexually inspired malevolence prods plot-complications ever onward is a figure whose centrality to Restoration comedy requires a further explanation that the idea of park pastoral helps to focus.

Guarini's Corisca is the prime comic archetype of the female plotter, and the slanderous message which disrupts apparent 'honour' only to reveal true 'virtue' is as I have argued in my introduction an important point of reference in this kind of comedy. Etherege does not treat the motif referentially, (as Wycherley does in *Love in a Wood*[46];), it is woven subtly into Lady Cockwood's ironic self-presentation; it emanates from her own consciousness of Love and Honour, those basic themes of courtly pastoral.

Etherege's brilliant use of locale points up the irony. It is the play house to which she sends her message, and the New Spring Gardens in which her plot comes to unexpected fruition. Park and Playhouse are closely linked on the imaginary map of Etherege's London of pleasure, the town pastoral of disguise and self-realization to which the country gentry come so eagerly. The New Spring gardens stood apart from both the west end and the city, on the other side of the Thames. The easiest way to represent it on stage would be with the familiar panoramic view of Westminster.[47] It may well have suggested a summation of the whole town-world.

When the lovers met in the Mulberry Gardens, Gatty picked out Courtall for her own, and he reciprocated in admiration of her wit. Freeman and Arianna joined in rather hesitantly; no one actually made a move towards pairing off. Lady Cockwood notices the real state of affairs and unwittingly sorts them into couples. It is her medium of linguistic deceit that ironically liberates the lovers' true feelings. They reach *éclaircissement* through the false idea each has been given of how the other speaks of them; and Gatty finally trumps her Aunt's command of the treacherous medium of verbal declarations, by using the pretence of a forged contract to raise the idea of marriage. As for Lady Cockwood, she wins Freeman – not only more efficient to her purpose than his friend, but more appreciative in the language he uses of her – and replaces her mask of ironic self-confidence. Her rebuff to Courtall is elegantly turned.

> Certainly fortune was never before so unkind to the ambition of a Lady.[48]

One gets the impression of an ironic reversal of expectations; while one might expect the two gallants to comically exploit her, she has in fact retained a crazy kind of integrity and broken down their relationship instead. There is after all a certain ambiguity in the title. Does it imply a farcical pattern of endlessly thwarted desire, or could one take it to mean that Lady Cockwood has adapted her aims to the possibilities? As far as we can tell she is satisfied with what she gets. Courtall's fear of a design on his particular person seem heightened by vanity. She is playing a game of pursuit. The same could be said of both her husband and her nervous gallant. Sir Oliver's pursuit of the notorious Madam Rampant propels him through the play. When she finally arrives chez the Cockwoods, only to be shooed out immediately, she is dressed as a man, to make up a pair of 'suitors' for the girls. This final theatrical joke discovers the essential sameness of those 'lineaments of gratified desire'.

A subtler aspect of Etherege's art allows him to create the remarkable sense of contingent lives of the final scenes of the play. The Cockwoods continue an existence off stage that owes something to our continued sense of the lady's unknowability. I began my discussion of the play with the scene between the two girls; it seems to me to bring to a head a vein of feeling that underlies the piece as a whole, a kind of melancholy intrinsic to public pleasure grounds. The play is riddled with images of trivial but disproportionately nagging loss, like Freeman's remark in the Spring Garden scene –

I have observed thee prying up and down the walks like a citizen's wife that has dropt her holyday pocket-handkercher.[49]

It is picked up in the solitary orange that Sir Oliver drops and lets roll across the stage, or in Arianna's pensive observation;

'Love, like some stains, will wear out of itself I know, but not in such a little time as you talk of, sister.'

Gatty's reply casts a retrospective glance over the action of the play.

It cannot last longer than the stain of a Mulberry at most . . .[50]

COMEDIES 'À LA MODE'

Different places on Restoration comedy's imaginary map derive their meaning from different kinds of connotation. The New Exchange and the Strand, for example, were by this time a centre for the would-be fashionable country ladies, and the modes they purchase there are subtly mocked in the parody language of Etherege's saleswomen. Manners like Lady Cockwood's are as much a manufacture as those 'ribbons, gloves, and Essences'.[51] And Courtall is just as much her commodity. Other locations override reference out to a social real by a certain literariness, a focusing of language in itself, a playful foregrounding of conventional plotting. The commercial pleasure gardens, the New Spring Gardens and the Mulberry Garden provide as I have suggested a blank space, like the space of lyric. This does not place it in simple opposition to a busy London world, as the model of the classical 'locus amoenus' might suggest. The 'business' of the exchange is only recorded in so far as it can function in intrigue. The pastoral reference creates a pause, sometimes realized topographically, sometimes not, in which the perpetual motion of a society of individuals can gel into pattern, can become readable to the audience, and to itself.

In the 1670s this essentially literary space was realized by the plays as St James's Park, and its adjacent 'Mall' or fashionable promenade. This is in a sense a movement into a culturally central, ironically 'official' terrain. Royal associations multiply the possibilities of political connotation, as Otway for one was aware. But for the 'Wits' and their now numerous imitators it would seem to represent a consolidation. The apologetically proffered 'modern way' became comedy 'à la mode'.

The 'modish' comedy of the early 1670s (often to be identified by the 'mode' or 'fashion' tag in its title) takes its response to the social moment seriously. A comedy whose linguistic medium is determinedly conversational, whose sense of history is repressed and then restated within an attention to the moment, whose milieu is chosen by the fantasy and gratuitous choice of fashion, is primarily a comedy of surfaces. This most confident phase of Restoration comedy articulates its surface with the play of true and false ironically encoded in pastoral. The key words of Restoration fashion are 'ease' and 'nature'. '. . . All he does and says is so easie and so natural'[52] says the admiring Bellair of Etherege's glass of fashion and mould of form, the dazzling Dorimant. But, as Harriet knows, such 'nature' is only achieved by art. It is the aim of 'high' art as well as of fashion, a part of the Restoration society's enterprise to render itself solid, to make itself relaxedly, unquestionably *there*. The plays do not mock or moralize upon fashion. But their play of opposites, their pastoral game of artifice and nature expose it as the signal of a vulnerability it denies. They stylize the idea of fashion into the material of an English baroque, aesthetically lightweight, finely attuned to an awareness of its own fragility.

Marriage à la Mode (1672) is not a London comedy, but it is Dryden's nearest approach to the Etheregean style. The part of the play that most obviously resembles contemporary comedy is the pair of witty couples. Two pairs of lovers are enough to suggest a model of society. As late as *The Confederacy* (1705) Vanbrugh was to use the paired couples to demonstrate the beneficial effects of free love on a consumer economy, but there the context is bourgeois. In the world of Dryden's play the dissolution of the courtiers' trust of each other and respect for social institutions would have larger implications, as Rochester slyly hints –

> . . . whilst th' insulting wife the breeches wore,
> The husband took her clothes to give his ____(sic)
> Who now maintains it with a gentler art;
> Thus tyrannies to commonwealths convert.[53]

The reinstatement of the lost prince Leonidas marks it as the last of the comedies of Restoration. But the echo of this high plot in modish intrigue raises a delicate query. Can the compacts of government last any longer in this society than the compacts of relationship? Dryden takes care to bind the lovers, Rhodophil, Palamede, Doralice and Melantha, into the same structure of court life that determines the outcome of the high plot. The little scenes which dovetail the halves of the play place them in social roles which point up their ignorance of the politics that determines their standing. The progress of their intrigues is curtailed as the duties of the court diminish them gracefully into the on-stage audience of events of greater moment. The famous double plot is a single action, with disproportionate emphasis on four of its walk-on roles.

Setting an intrigue plot in Fletcherian Sicily effectively quarantines it from the social and even the psychological contingencies that accrue so satisfyingly to London comedy. And to show that Leonidas is dependant on the likes of Rhodophil and Palamede – who neither know nor care about the rights of his case – is to diminish the scope and seriousness of his heroic pretensions. Outside the self-regulating world of heroic drama, or the richer but no less autonomous territory of London comedy, the characters of *Marriage à la Mode* have only so much meaning as can be conveyed by an attention to surface.

In that this is the conscious method of the play it is a strength, not a weakness. The high plot is romance rather than tragedy; an exploitation of literary convention, or, less aridly, a game of pastoral ironies. In concentrating on the recovery of the thing long lost

Dryden wittily uses the resolution of a conventional romance plot to launch a baroque flight into doubling and disguise. The characters themselves play at the ironies of pastoral;

Hermogenes:	Why, Nature is the same in Villages,
	And much more fit to form a noble issue
	Where it is least corrupted.
Polydames:	He talks too like a man that knew the world to
	have been long a Peasant.[54]

By endowing them with a consciousness of the fiction in which they participate, Dryden takes one step further the emotional manoeuvers of his tragedies. Octavia in *All for Love* (1677) has proceeded from control over her emotions, to the realization that what one controls, one can exploit. Kings and princes control, and exploit, the pastoral fiction. The tyrant Polydamas, in transferring his court to the country and starting the hallowed game of establishing an heir, has set going a version of pastoral that expands with its own crazy logic to engulf a usurper no longer able to prevent the disparity of real and desired power from becoming ridiculous. Leonidas on the other hand undergoes a radical rediscovery of identity that places him in the strongest position of creative will imaginable.

Tis true, I am alone;
So was the Godhead ere he made the world,
And better Serv'd Himself than serv'd by Nature.[55]

He takes control of the pastoral fiction, wins the game, and is crowned King.

The end of the play posits a triangle situation. Leonidas has out-manoeuvered his lover Palymyra's attempts at sentimental blackmail, but at a cost measured by the hardening towards the end of the play of the language they use of each other. The court environment tends to calcify those emotions it calls into play. Once innocent enough not to notice the princess Amalthea's desire, he is able now to control his recognition of it. Such a mistress would after all be politically to his advantage. Thus the ironically shaped high plot ends at the point from which an intrigue play might begin.

To some extent the prose scenes make an overt generalization of these issues. Doralice no more receives the attention she would seem to merit than Amalthea does;

Doralice:	Hold, hold! Are not you two a couple of mad fighting fools, to cut one another's throats for nothing?
Palamede:	How for nothing? he courts the woman I must marry.
Rhodophil:	And he courts you whom I have marri'd.
Doralice:	But you can neither of you be jealous of what you love not.[56]

The play's idea of marriage is the product of its limited concept of love, of whose inability to comprehend a whole Doralice preserves a secret knowledge. The underplot moves by a cyclic logic in which she loses both husband and lover to a woman too inane to be unlikeable. Palamede's shallowness is engagingly farcical at moments of crisis, but he is so utterly the creature of light comedy that he comes to love Melantha for the songs and silliness he must use to woo her. The circle is complete and it excludes Doralice, for it has become clear that it was for a song that she too was first loved.

Melantha moves between both the play's worlds and they move in turn according to her conception of the necessary fiction of behaviour. Her great comic scenes in act III are central to the play in every sense. She demonstrates on a mundane level both the willed self-realization that strengthens Leonidas, and the dedication to the social fiction that holds the society of the play, that single plot, together and overriding the double. Like other great comic creations, her apparent extravagance is a shrewder assessment of reality than the compromise of the normative characters around her. Rhodophil's court post aligns him with his mistress as one who spans private and public life and trusts himself only to make very limited demands on the former. The men's preference of Melantha to Doralice has more of a sting than Millamant's ousting of Mrs Fainall. It is placed in the play's own compromise world with an elegantly precise cynicism.

One might characterize *Marriage à la Mode* in terms of Doralice's description of the French poetry for which Melantha would 'sacrifice her life', 'the very Wafers and whip'd Cream of sense'.[57] But that fragility of artifice, that wafer-thin pastoral plot and its whipped-cream intrigue, is expressive of the tenuous stability of the society from which the play comes. The 1670s, the 'high' Restoration, seem a peak of social confidence, at least in the hindsight of the next decade and the exclusion crisis. While there is a balance and clarity in the comedies of mode – to be shattered spectacularly by Wycherley's *The Plain dealer* (1676) – the possibilities of dissension are acutely marked out. The plays are informed by a sense of strictly temporary agreement.

Etherege's *The Man of Mode* (1676) is the most ambitious of these comedies, a summation of their style – 'ease' and 'nature' are ideals equally apt to the niceties of conversation and the aims of art, and it is in the fullness of his response to them that Etherege could transmute 'the mode' to a dramatic form of some suggestive weight. *The Man of Mode* fulfils Etherege's earlier attempts at a minimalism of dramatic language, in making of the everyday a peculiar subtlety of dramatic form. The movement towards a conversational prose style is a movement towards a new kind of stage realism. *The Man of Mode* extends this to plotting and to the definition of scenes. It is his fullest attempts to formalize the mundane into an expressive convention. Etherege crystallizes day-to-day situations into plot units, into the basis of set scenes.

One must take care when using the word 'realism' of seventeenth century art. 'Realism' as such is a nineteenth century phenomenon, a moral impulse to objective and engaged perception. But when Renaissance and neo-classical ideas of artistic decorum broke down, as they did in this period in almost every art-form, then the practitioners of that form have to redefine the real and their modes of representing it. Decorum, as Madeline Doran has argued,[58] is the means to an ordered, philosophically selective version of 'the real' – to what the Renaissance called 'verisimilitude'. Late seventeenth century or baroque art can often seem to have a double aim, to render its object as substantially as possible as a material object, but to offer an overt moralized or symbolic reading of the resultant image which often seems puzzlingly inadequate or even contradictory.[59] (In the case of Caravaggio this produces shock, in that of Vermeer it creates mystery.) When 'verisimilitude' no longer seems philosophically or socially accessible there is a contradiction between a newly scientific 'objective' perception of the world, and the philosophical and moral structure of ideas which artists have inherited and not explicitly questioned. Seventeenth century artists characteristically play off the possibility of a symbolic reading of the object against the material fact of its 'nature'. Their aim is to realize, to create material presence. Symbolism becomes incidental in being embodied, or, on occasion, made too 'obvious' to signify. Its main function for the interpreter is to set up conceptual shocks and surprises in which we confront the object afresh and thus experience an effect of 'the real'.

Taken on the large scale of the preceding argument, Restoration comedy is undoubtedly a minor form, but the same shift, from decorum to 'nature', is perceptible in it. Etherege's stylistic daring in *The Man of Mode* makes these points especially relevant here. The admiration academic critics have expressed for the play is often compromised by an attempt to reduce it back to symbolism.[60] But its religious imagery is a necessary step to its materialism, and attaches quizzical labels to it. Keeping Lent for a mistress in hope of a happy Easter to come is a lightly blasphemous concept, a joke with the serious overtone of perspectives awry. Dorimant is primarily a material thing, his physicality stressed by dressing and undressing on or just off stage, by the whole brilliant exposition. He is a donnee of mundane sensuality to whom moral questions attach like jokes. One must describe Dorimant, one cannot analyse him. The whole play moves towards realization.

Dorimant's personal casualness artfully disrupts the structure of the exposition. We begin the play as Dorimant starts his day. Any information we are given comes to or from him. The device confers on him an unearned authorial status; it leaves us dependent on his expository whim. The scene was much imitated in its presentation of willed disorder of the libertine-hero's arrogant unconcern in confronting his audience in an 'undress'. It establishes the stage as a place as much his own as a dressing-room. Etherege's remains the best in so effortlessly establishing a milieu. A whole social world is caught in the orange woman's altercation with the shoemaker, and the smaller world of the play is nicely placed in relation to it. The play proceeds through the family party, the marriage contract, Medley's gossip, Lady Townely's *belle assemblée* and, of course, the park as a series of social occasions, of realities, and rites.

This is true even of the scenes with Mrs Loveit. The overall tone of the play contains them as social rites in themselves. Dorimant and Loveit both plot what they'll say; their quarrels are collaboratively staged, and Bellinda and Pert remain on stage as our representatives, as audience. Loveit is herself a richly baroque conception; she sees herself as a martyr to love – Dorimant is indeed her 'God Almighty'.[61] He deflates her by robbing her fury of meaning. 'What,' he exclaims on finding her pacing about the room, 'dancing the galloping nag without a fiddle',[62] and the abruptness gives it a kind of structural weight; an unearned authorial status. He forces us to see her as an object, a thing in motion, with a mock-seriousness joke on her obviousness.

> 'I fear this restlessness of the body, madam (pursuing her) proceeds from an unquietness of the mind'[63]

The first flash of his 'Mr Courtage' characterization, in fact. He points out her attempt to realize her feelings; that he can make her funny by isolating her as an object is in this context a sign of her intrinsic funniness, of the incongruity of those feelings to the dignity she gives them. Loveit is not who she thinks she is. She claims to be unintelligent in language whose balance and control proclaims the opposite.

> The man who loves above his quality does not suffer more from the insolent impertinence of his mistress, than the woman who loves above her understanding does from the arrogant presumption of her friend.[64]

Her love for Dorimant is described by him in hard, man-made images;

> Love gilds us over and makes us show fine things to one another for a time, but soon the gold wears off, and then the native brass appears.[65]

'Nature' in this scene becomes a paradox of bewildering, insulting complexity.

> Good nature and good manners corrupt me. I am honest in my inclinations and would not, wer't not to avoid offense, make a Lady a little in years believe I think her young, wilfully mistake art for nature.[66]

The country heiress Harriet comes to the town-world equipped with an asperity of tongue to make the young Jane Austen blench, and the more traditionally pastoral virtues of decency, directness and innocent clearsightedness, which the enclosed society to which she comes tends to exclude. For Harriet the pastoral fiction offers an imaginary oasis of fulfilled desires, an escape not from moral, but from nakedly economic pressures for an arranged marriage of the kind that brought her to town in the first place. The two pastoral songs she asks Busy to sing are both connected to Dorimant and both lead to scenes of courtship, the first the mock courtship with Bellair that establishes her control by micmicry of self presentation and the ritualized exchanges of the world in which she finds herself. Harriet brings to London what Rosalind brought to Arden, a sense of play, as a leisurely discovery of the distinctions of true and false. It is of play that Harriet first speaks to Dorimant, a gamble in which selfhood is put at risk and real freedom is the prize. As she exclaims straight after the first song

> Shall I be paid down by a covetous parent for a purchase? I need no land; no, I'll lay myself all out in love. It is decreed.[67]

It is of course in the park that these games are most deftly played. The affable, ineffectual Bellair, increasingly nervous of her bold incursion on the Mall, to be further surprised by a comment on Dorimant's 'affectation' –

> Lord madam, all he does and says, is so easy, and so natural.[68]

Harriet replies with a literary comparison –

> Some men's verses appear so to the unskilful, but labouri' the one and affectation in the other to the judicious plainly appear.[69]

She has the measure of an aesthetic that governs the behaviour of the characters within the play, as well as its overall form.

Loveit, in contrast, hates the Mall, but manages to turn the play away from Dorimant on what might seem to be his own territory. The scene she plays out with Fopling bears an interesting resemblance to the central situation of Rochester's *St James Park*.[70] Dorimant is as much implicated by the spectatorship it forces on him as Belinda was in the quarrel with Loveit. Such moments have an intimate almost prophetic relevance to the on-stage viewer. Sir Fopling as we see him in the play is in the fullest sense self-made – his litany of the mode is the least ominous of all the play's rituals –

Lady Towneley:	The suit.
Sir Fopling:	Barroy.
Emilia:	The garniture.
Sir Fopling:	Les Gras –
Medley:	The shoes!
Sir Fopling:	Piccar!
Dorimant:	The Periwig!
Sir Fopling:	Chedreux.
Lady Towneley, Emilia:	The gloves!
Sir Fopling:	Orangerie![71]

To moralize upon him to disturb his delicate placing in the play as an exquisitely vacuous triumph of fashion over life. But he strays into the Loveit–Dorimant game as a timely reminder of the sterility of that mirror world in which he lives. Bellinda's alibi for the early morning spent with Dorimant again turns his control back on itself, unwittingly answering the peach that 'comes from the stone' of the still-life of act one, with the nosegays and nectarines ('the best I ever tasted') that hint so delicately at the real cause of her weariness.[72] The experience of the play dwindles into tokens of its insufficiency; a valet tying up bed linen, a pinched out taper, Fopling's redundant mask.

When Harriet sends Loveit packing, she demonstrates the nature of her 'rescue' of Dorimant in a tough public moment to balance a private exchange with her mother, in the middle of the tumult but not overheard;

Lady Woodvil: . . . you would marry this Dorimant.
Harriet: I cannot deny it! I would, and never will marry any other man.[73]

The play's most open emotional statement is, unsurprisingly for Etherege, its most private; less expectedly it is its most final. Etherege objectifies cruelty within the Loveit–Dorimant relationship as a force over which they have forfeited control in, simply, acting up to each other. Here he objectifies love. The end of the play attains an emotional purity that one knows none of the characters will ever reach again. Dorimant will marry Harriet, keep Belinda, avoid Loveit, pursue Emilia (who may well be so bored with Bellair, and so teased by his father as to yield); or not. One doesn't really want to know. The play leaves its characters on a brink from which they can see an ideal happiness, but never acceed to it. Never, because the play ends, and because the effect of its ending is to cast one's attention back over its span, to create a final mirror image; Harriet goes back to the country, but Dorimant and the others go back too, recede from this point of illumination. Etherege's development could be seen as an attempt to accommodate perceptions of individual desire to a comic structure tending persistently to the collective experience of farce. Farce rests on a basically comfortable assumption that pleasure is always public however privately we pursue it; that we all in fact have one objective. In these terms Etherege is not primarily a farceur. There is always a tension in his work between the individual and that society whose leisurely rites make up the surface of his plays. Each character is conceived in terms of strictly personal needs; there is a sort of freedom in their interaction that creates a pattern of opportunities lost or grasped, of partnerships breaking down or closing up, of desires modified and attitudes changed. The endings of Etherege's plays are provisional of necessity, as it is only by accident or incidental trickery that his lovers become aware of each other's feelings. Sir Frederick's contest with the widow, or Dorimant's with Harriet, are shadowed by a constant fear that one party only shows emotion when the other cannot perceive it. Etherege's pursuit of a face behind the mask is compromised by a fear that there may be none there.

'. . . I must confess', Etherege wrote in a letter, 'I am a fop in my heart; ill customes influence my very senses, and I have been so us'd to affectation that without the help of the aer of the court, what is naturall cannot touch me. You see what we get by being polish'd as we call it.'[74] There is a plural identification behind the ambiguous title of *The Man of Mode*. Sir Fopling is the man of mode, certainly, so is Dorimant, but so too is the author. Etherege wrote a masterpiece because he was the right man in the right place at the right time. The melancholy humour of his letters from Ratisbon becomes a wonderful pathos when the accession of William and Mary leaves Etherege so much the wrong man in the wrong place at the wrong time, that his traces simply disappear. But within three plays he had already consolidated the experiments of the Wits into a reshaping of comedy to a form expressive of its period, into a 'Restoration' style. The idea of 'the mode' or 'modishness' is, at its most refined, an impulse to capture the moment, to relocate comedy's claim to the real in a fluid presentation of 'nature' – as opposed to te ordered verisimilitude of classical forms.

'The scenery is very light, capable of a great many changes and embellished with beautiful landscapes', an Italian traveller wrote of the comedies he saw in 1669; '. . . The comedies which are acted are in prose; but their plots are confused, neither unity or regularity being observed; the authors having in view, rather than anything else, to describe accurately the passions of the mind . . .'.[75] This is a very adequate description of the form as Etherege left it; one might set it against Heinrich Wolfflin's attempt to define Baroque style, in *Renaissance and Baroque;*

> Perfection is the exact means between excess and deficiency. But the formless art knows no such limits, no consummation or finality.[76]

A similar idea is developed more elaborately in Walter Benjamin's observation that 'the baroque knows no eschatology. . . the naturalism of the baroque is "the art of least distances. . . . The most vivid and concrete actuality is sought as a contraposition from which to revert . . . into formal elevation" '.[77] In its sense of continuous irregular movement, in its manipulation of surfaces, in its drawing back from 'consummation', in its paradoxical naturalism, Etheregean comedy is a Baroque form.

2 William Wycherley

Wycherley's first play, *Love in a Wood* (1671) is subtitled *St James's Park*, a location hailed by the play's three gallants with a litany of its unrespectable functions:

Ranger.   Hang me if I am not pleas'd extreamly with this new fashioned catterwauling, this midnight coursing in the Park.

Vincent.   A man may come after Supper with his three Bottles in his head, reel himself sober, without reproof from his Mother, Aunt, or grave relation.

Ranger.   May bring his bashful Wench, and not have her put out of countenance by the impudent honest women of the Town.

Dapperwit.   And a man of wit may have the better of the dumb shew, of well trim'd Vest, or fair Perruque; no man's now is whitest.

Ranger.   And now no woman's modest, or proud, for her blushes are hid, and the rubies on her lips are died, and all sleepy and glimmering eyes have lost their attraction.

Vincent.   And now a man may carry a Bottle under his arm, instead of his Hat, and no observing spruce Fop will miss the Crevat that lies on ones shoulder, or count the pimples on ones face.

Dapperwit.   And now the brisk reparty ruins the complaisant Cringe, or wise Grimace, something 'twas, we men of virtue always lov'd the night.

Ranger.   O blessed season.

Vincent.   For good-Fellows.

Ranger.   For Lovers.

Dapperwit.   And for the Muses.[1]

This is Rochester's St James's, not Waller's. 'In a Wood' means lost, confused, mad. The play's action, to use an image Ranger picks up from *Pastor Fido*, is 'Blind-mans Buff'.[2] 'St James's Park at Night' is not the same place as Etherege's civilized Mall; it stands for an anarchy of desire wiser than self-conscious wit. *Love in a Wood* is often found diffuse. I intend to answer the charge that the play is centreless by pointing out, not, I hope, wholly unpredictably, that its centre is the park.

Wycherley's first attempt at the recreation of Etheregean comedy reduces a cast that previous playwrights would have arranged in careful social and stylistic layers to an equal footing of muddled desire and botched emotional contact. He not only deprives Valentine and Christina of verse but involves them despite themselves in a comic world where the clearest outcome of Christina's cloistered devotion is a lifestyle of alternate mopings on the balcony and squabbles with her maid, where Valentine's passion becomes peevishness and an ignorance both of himself and its object. The dizzy game of blindman's buff is to draw them into its pattern despite their determination to stay aloof; the disguise plot drags them from their own custody as it is to drag Margery from Pinchwife's. Christina and Valentine, Lydia and Ranger, are lost 'in a wood' of self-created fears and doubts, the witty couple levelled from a potential Etheregegean poise in Wycherley's disordered version of the choreography of pursuit and unmasking. *'They all go off together in a huddle, hastily',*[3] as one of the stage directions puts it, aptly summarizing the effect of the equalizing darkness of the park.

Disguise and the doppleganger plot fascinate Wycherley, for they pose in its most flamboyant theatrical from a crisis of desire and identity. His characters cannot have what they want without betraying their sense of who they are. But by the end of the play – and this belies the idea that Wycherley's are dark comedies – they rediscover that identity, having established it for themselves. In so far as Hippolita, for example, or Margery, is the butt of the plot, their 'innocency' is open to question. But the shape of the play transforms them from object to subject, from prize to plotter, and a new paradoxical innocence is discovered. Horner alone of Wycherley's major characters becomes, bewilderingly, the object of a plot he has set in motion himself.

Wycherley remakes the conventions of Etheregean comedy into

a personal comic style. As a consequence, he takes care to measure the distance between himself and his predecessors. In *Love in a Wood* Flippant and Dapperwit are a parodistic version of the widow and the wit. The lady is perfectly willing to pursue wit-combat through to a marriage she affects to abhor, but the gentleman deliberately fluffs his cues. At the end of Act I Flippant and the inconstant Ranger are put in suggestive apposition.

> Flippant: . . . pray tell me is your aversion to marriage real?
> Ranger: . . . As real as yours.
> Flippant(aside) If it were no more real than mine.[4]

But in the last act Ranger has come to propose marriage, surprising Lydia into doubts that have not apparently slowed her pursuit of him in the past.

> Cou'd you find in your heart to quit all other engagements, and voluntarily turn yourself over to one woman, and she a Wife too? Cou'd you away with the insupportable bondage of Matrimony?[5]

Ranger, who has earlier nudged Valentine into proposing a completion of the line of married couples that span the stage at the end of Act V ('Our Ladies, Sir, I suppose, expect the same promise from us'),[6] ends the play with a reply that seems to me to touch on Wycherley's central concerns.

> You talk of Matrimony as irreverently, as my *Lady Flippant*;
> the Bond of Matrimony, no –
> The end of Marriage, now is liberty,
> And two are bound – to set each other free.[7]

Wycherley's prose style links ideas by analogy. His characters are similarly disposed in a pattern of doubles, thus freeing each other from an emotional solitude that may seem heroic to Christina and Valentine (or Alithea) but is in fact the most despairing kind of farce. These characters must find a partner; society is too precarious and cruel a mechanism to answer their needs. The early plays and some of the casts of the later tend towards a freedom found in pairing.

Ranger's romantic adventure with Christina comes to a head just after he tells Dapperwit that he makes '. . . honourable Love, meerly out of necessity; as your Rooks play on the square rather than not play at all'.[8] Woman-chasing is a compulsive, and up till now, a harmless game. It is entirely fitting, when the 'Blind-mans Buff' gets out of hand, that he should choose to give it over. When the 'honourable' romance with Christina dissolves it reveals the reality of his need of Lydia, to which those final lines bear witness. Like wit and heroic virtue, game-playing is a behavioural trap sprung in the night-park.

The resolution of *Love in a Wood* is imaged not, as in classical pastoral, by dawn, but by a shared enjoyment of those private pleasures the characters have tended to pursue, a feast at the Mulberry Garden in which the whole cast takes part. The comic villain of the piece is the niggardly Alderman Gripe, for in aiming to take his pleasure cheaply he contradicts the pull towards a generous and honest acknowledgement of appetite that is the real ethos of the park. His mean self-indulgence is the physical equivalent of the other characters' treasured neuroses, and it is when Mrs Joyner succeeds in lugging him to the Mulberry Garden that the end of the play is signalled. Every character however resistant is pulled into the park; it reforms the entire cast of unlovely individualists into a society of couples, of matches not only just but practical. The end of the play posits not an ideal, but a reality, unrespectable but festive.

The Gentleman Dancing Master (1672), in marked contrast, limits itself to the scope of a single household. Hippolita and her maid Prue may lament their exile from the pleasures of the town, but it does enforce a discipline on the playwright that might well have seemed a necessary curb on the inventive exuberance of his first play. In *The Gentleman Dancing Master* Wycherley shuffles and re-tests aspects of his dramatic style that seemed to run out of control in *Love in a Wood*, but become crucial to the effect of the two last great plays.

Love in a Wood markedly lacks the kind of double-entendre that makes the style of *The Country-Wife* so lewdly buoyant. Only the mock-innocent Lucy uses the arts learned as Dapperwit's mistress to entice the ponderous lust of Alderman Gripe.

Are you a Dancing-Master sir? . . . I don't see your Fidle,
Sir, where is your little Kitt?[9]

In *The Gentleman Dancing Master* Hippolita's 'innocency' is itself a double meaning at which the other characters probe. She teases her aunt Caution with an account of dreams bred by the lack of a man –

> Hippolita: But I did not only dream Ih . . . (sighs)
> Caution: How, how! did you more than dream! speak, young Harlotry; confess, did you more than dream? How could you more than dream in this house? speak! confess.
> Hippolita: Well! I will then. Indeed, Aunt, I did not only dream, but I was pleased with my dream when wak'd.
> Caution: Oh is that all? nay, if a dream only will please you, you are a modest young woman still; but have a care of a Vision.[10]

Hippolita is too sensible and forthright to join the frustrated dreaming heroines of the period, – Lee's Princess of Clove, for example, or the heroine of Rochester's *Valentinian* – but the parallel is suggestive when one bears in mind 'fair Chloris' of Rochester's mock pastoral, 'innocent and pleased'.[11] Isolation and stress are themes of the times, and the self-sufficient Chloris provided an extreme model of one way of resolving them. The passage from *The Gentleman Dancing Master* is interesting as an example of the way the characters in this piece pick up words carefully as if to see what is lurking underneath. Even in *Love in a Wood* a single word can hammer through a speech, till its meaning becomes almost ominously doubtful. This is characteristically Wycherleyan, in a way that makes him of all Restoration dramatists the most nakedly theatrical, the closest to the bone of dramatic situation. While for Etherege speech and action are 'manner', a mask behind which one deduces a fully imagined reality, for Wycherley they are alive with a theatrical electricity, a potently treacherous communication to whose shifts of meaning one must be continually alert. There is an impulse basic to Wycherley's plays in this sense of the dramatic language as a risky but vital medium of his characters' aims and selfhood. The linguistic double meaning is complemented by the ambiguities of performance, and it is in isolating the idea of performance that *The Gentleman Dancing Master* proved so valuable. *Love in a Wood*, like so many first plays, describes what it cannot enact. Betrayal is an idea implemented by the cast to a mindboggling cumulation of social chaos but it is not yet implicit in the language. Similarly, those crucially Wycherleyan scenes where x watches y encounter z and makes a very private deduction of what happens between them are all arrived at by accidents, with an undeniably, though to my mind not unappealingly, flustered effect. In *The Dancing Master* Hippolita, by disguising her lover Gerard as the 'master' of the title, involves him in a performance whose meaning is gracefully worked out from act to act. Only the aunt understands what is happening between them, but the fiancé and the father restrain her from revealing it. It is a very funny, rather cruel variation on the process of distanced, botched comprehension that is the best Wycherley's characters can usually manage. Caution knows what is going on in the same way that she felt she understood Hippolita's dreams – '. . . I know by experience what will follow'.[12] Like Olivia at *The Country-Wife*.[13] Caution is exposed by her understanding of the performance, and criticized for her meanly hypocritical reaction.

A firm and sympathetic judgement of Wycherley's work is impossible unless one can characterize a distinctly Wycherleyan mode of comic writing. Perhaps that requires a larger scope. But it is worth pointing out how badly Wycherley comes off even in as sympathetic an account as Anne Righter's, if he is presumed to be attempting to write comedy in the style of Etherege or Moliere. Only *The Gentleman Dancing Master* is left unscathed; other, in many ways more ambitious, pieces come to look like the result of subtle material filtered through a coarse and uncomprehending sensibility.[14] Alithea and Harcourt do not seem to me (as they do to Dr Righter) to be Etherege characters in whom Wycherley cannot believe; I don't believe in them as Etherege characters either. One should see them in the light of what Wycherley was doing in *Love in a Wood*, a play which *The Country-Wife* (1675) to some extent remakes.

The Etherege characters whom Alithea most resembles are those of the 'high' plots. She has a simple 'heroic' concept of love and marriage.

Love proceeds from esteem; he cannot distrust my virtue, besides he loves me, or he wou'd not marry me.[15]

But, like Christina and Valentine, Alithea is flung into a vigorously prosaic comic world in which ideals are not safely packaged in that

cotton wool of Restoration blank verse. The play's intrigues equal-
ize her with Sparkish and Harcourt; they all live in the same
town-world, whose delights Alithea finds herself increasingly
called upon to pay for by marriage to Sparkish. That is one view of
her predicament, and in that it is her maid Lucy's one can accept it
as thoroughly realistic. Alithea's own is that to betray his trust
would be to betray her own identity. Like Manly she has found a
mirror for her virtue, her 'truth',[16] and like him she finds that
mirrors are brittle things that one must learn to do without. Her
heroic self-sacrifice is, like his heroic love, self-indulgence and, in a
way, cowardice. She has to learn to trust the hazards of intrigue,
and to face, sharply but temporarily, the loneliness of slander, of
the loss of that externalized 'truth'. Alithea functions deftly, even
wittily, in the fashionable world, but she is much less of a heroine à
la mode than Etherege's. There is something statuesque and old-
fashioned about her. One wonders if she is not a little nearer her
brother's age than, say, Arianna and Gatty's. Her wistfully retrospective correction of Pinchwife's 'greasie' comparison puts a personal rather fragile sheen on the plot device that is to bind her
story and Margery's together.

> I had a gentle Gallant, us'd to say, a Beauty mask'd, like the Sun
> in Eclipse, gathers together more gazers, than if it shin'd out.[17]

Harcourt too is significantly unlike the Etheregean norm, but in
rather the opposite direction. He is too light, too playful, for those
gentlemen's serious dedication to pleasure. For Harcourt -

> Mistresses are like Books; if you pore upon them too much, they
> doze you, and make you unfit for Company; but if us'd dis-
> creetly, you are the fitter for conversation by 'em.[18]

The wit games with which he tries to break Alithea's contract to
Sparkish, like the game in which Hippolita coaches Gerard, are a
medium of contact which, like conversation, bridges the gap between wary personalities. Harcourt moves from Horner's world to
Alithea's, remaining amicable to both. He has none of the egoistic
drive of the Etheregean male; rather, like Ranger, Gerard and
Freeman, he offers a shallow, slightly opportunistic, but just and
humane companionship, that effectively rescues others from neurosis, or virtue. The point in which he announces his trust in Alithea

is scarcely a great leap of faith, though it does outjump Sparkish – after all Harcourt was one of the first to know of Horner's 'impotence'. Wycherley is content to reduce Harcourt and Alithea back to the compromised truth of the town-world. Their resolution is personal and, characteristically, he refrains from pointing a moral, however delicately Etheregean.

It may seem perverse to start a discussion of the play at Alithea, but I want to stress Wycherley's method of linking his characters by relationship into a kind of lateral, unstratified scheme. If literary critics seem not to realize this, then neither do the play's performers. Wycherley very deliberately put Sparkish and Alithea into relationship, and yet they are always acted in flamboyantly divergent style. To link Alithea, Harcourt, Margery and Horner into the change-of-identity plot is to force opposites into analogies.

Horner is not, I think, a libertine; libertines do not specialize in concealment. He does possess a heightened intelligence, even moral consciousness, of a kind that detaches itself from the rest of the play. The contempt he has for Pinchwife is a case in point. One might characterize his plot, so vague in the infinity of its aims, as an experiment. The Quack serves to point this up. Horner's 'process'[19] is an experiment in natural science, or, more precisely, as it operates on bodies, in medicine. Horner is a true virtuoso, his experiment carried out, in the spirit of the Royal Society, as an exhibition of skill for the knowledgeable few (the assistant quack, and the audience), and as a selfless pursuit of the truth; the truth about the ladies of quality, the suppressed libertinism of his patients. He looks for a cure for 'Love and all other Women's evils';[20] in a sense the pretence is psychologically apt as Horner, though not fiercely misogynist, is eunuchoid emotionally in a way that Harcourt is not. The indulgence in woman-hating that his pretence allows him is itself to be relished. Aptly enough, when Margery finds herself to be in love with him, she soliloquizes with typical frankness in terms of her physical symptoms.

I have heard this distemper, call'd a Feaver, but methinks tis liker an Ague, for when I think of my Husband, I tremble and am in a cold sweat, and have inclinations to vomit, but when I think of my Gallant, dear Mr Horner, my hot fit comes . . .[21]

When Pinchwife is tricked into bringing her disguised to Horner, Horner enquires of the pox. For him Pinchwife's whoring has led to a kind of moral pox, and the contempt he shows him is more chilling for Pinchwife's inability to be shocked by it. But while this would seem to place the analyst of physical and moral disease in opposition to the passive Margery, by the very end of the play they have come to change places.

The ability of the society for which the town ladies stand to use people simply as things absorbs Horner into its hypocrisies; and thus Horner finds himself a wondrous necessary man to those whom he had seemed to challenge. He becomes a double meaning. China is only the latest craze. In the games of the 'Bacchic' scene he is used among other things as 'thou representative of a Husband'[22] and the real husband, Sir Jasper, achieves what Sir Epicure Mammon only dreamed of; he has made a 'town-stallion'[23] his eunuch. Horner is the victim of a town society with which Margery eventually learns to deal and from whose representative, Sparkish, Alithea is rescued.

Wycherley's farce implodes. It leaves Margery the only character not its puppet; she has the only moral choice to make, and she chooses to lie. The final scene is curiously touching. Perhaps the first lie is the end of childhood; the end of her trust in her own pastoral simplicity, and its attendant concept of fidelity to Horner in an unattainable ideal of a relationship of mutual satisfaction, without economic pressures or social ties; the beginning of responsibility. The reality of rural life to which she returns, to play endless card games, to tell her neighbours of the sights, is as real for us as that of Harriet (another Hampshire girl) but a little more attractive. Margery has the sturdiness to function well in her own world, even, in better times, with her own husband – 'You are mine own Dear Bud, and I know you' she says, 'I hate a Stranger.'[24] If the play puts her in apposition to Horner, it is as the reality that the virtuoso seeks. When the play ends, she is liberated into ordinary life and compromise; he is boxed in by the demands of deceit. Just how much china *can* he produce?

Wycherley builds *The Country-Wife* out of the contradictions and tensions in pastoral ideas, with a deepening apprehension of the unattainability of real escape. The play is at once more farcical and more despairing than anything that went before. Margery is herself a *locus amoenus*, an enclosed pleasure for Pinchwife, as Horner is at the end for his three ladies. When their paths cross in Act III they act out within the enclosed environment of the room off the New Exchange the pastoral game of Orlando and Ganymede (though it must be said that Margery is less of a Rosalind than a Mopsa). The event is enclosed again by her narration of it to the obsessed Pinchwife within their bed-chamber.[25] *The Plain Dealer* (1676) takes this process of enclosure a step further. In exploring pastoral ironies in an increasingly interior and private way Wycherley instigates the pattern to be followed by Congreve, Farquhar and other writers of a limited comic *oeuvre*, who gradually eschew flamboyance and burlesque for a sober, even static discussion of the issues that inform the mode. This is how Olivia in *The Plain Dealer*, expresses her responses to *The Country-Wife*.

Olivia.	. . . does it not give you the rank conception, or image of a Goat, a Town-Bull or a Satyr? nay, what is yet a filthier image than all the rest, that of an eunuch?
Eliza.	What then? I can think of a Goat, a Bull, or Satyr, without any hurt.
Olivia.	I, but, Cousin, one cannot stop there.
Eliza.	I can, Cousin.
Olivia.	Oh no; for when you have those filthy creatures in your head once, the next thing you think, is what they do; as their defiling of honest Men's Beds and Couches, Rapes upon sleeping and waking Countrey Virgins, under Hedges and on Haycocks . . .[26]

Pastoral ideas exist within it as prevalent fictions in the characters' world; they serve to expose a mental landscape. Against the dissembled libertinism of Olivia's satyr-haunted description of her reaction to *The Country-Wife* – thus one play may even enclose another – one must set the fantasy world of Manly, the 'plain dealer' of the title;

Therefore I raher choose to go where honest downright Barbarity is profest; where men devour one another like generous hungry Lyons and Tygers, not like Crocodiles . . [27]

Between the two of them Wycherley places Fidelia, the girl disguised as a boy, the embodiment of that goal pursued by the other characters, a world to satisfy their inner world. She sums up the problem in a blank verse soliloquy;

O Heav'ns! is there not punishment enough
In loving well, if you will have't a Crime;
But you must add fresh Torments daily to't
And punish us like peevish Rivals still,
Because we fain would find a Heaven here?[28]

Fidelia's unreality is the unreality of this ideal.

The Plain Dealer is a pivotal piece in the history of Restoration drama. Were it not for its expansive literary energy, figures like Crowne and Otway might not have been interested in writing comedy at all. It is the watershed between the gentleman amateurs and the professional dramatists who dominate the 1680s. The play is innovative in the relationship of the protagonist to the world it depicts. Manly is goaded into a moral aggression; he is dispossessed and resentful; he makes demands that the world he lives in cannot satisfy. If he is indeed normative in the way his name suggests, it is as a modern hero. This was enormously influential on subsequent comedy, to at least Southerne and early Congreve. Perhaps most important is the way the play redraws the groundplan set out by Etherege. Gambling, used in *The Man of Mode* as a graceful metaphor for kinds of emotional commitment, becomes the way of a relentlessly acquisitive world. For Wycherley the metaphor devalues what it images. 'We women . . .' says Olivia,

like the rest of the Cheats of the World, when our Cullies or Creditors have found out, and will, or can trust no longer; pay Debts, and satisfie Obligations, with a quarrel; . . . for oftentimes in Love, as at Cards, we are forc'd to play foul, only to give over the game; and use our Lovers, like the Cards, when we can get no more by 'em, throw 'em up in a pet, upon the first dispute.[29]

When in the third act the play moves to Westminster-Hall, the law acquires the image for its own.

. . . 'tis like one of their own Halls, in *Christmas* time, whither, from all parts, Fools bring their Money, to try, by the Dice (not the worst Judges) whether it shall be their own or no.[30]

Love and law are not gambles in metaphor only, real money is involved, and the play admits money as a ruling factor in the comic world. The effect on later comedy is obvious. Even such a dissimilar play as *The Way of the World* (1700) owes its slightly bitter worldly wisdom, as well as its tangled property-motivated plot structure to the *Plain Dealer*. The idea of a densely plotted pursuit of money and love through law, ending in a measured judicial finale, is the new and clearly more ambitious model that Wycherley sets up for the comedy of the next two decades. The play deliberately and finally strips off the glamour of the early Restoration to show the well-oiled financial wheels underneath. As the prologue states, its aim is to cut through the flattering self-image of the age.

> Pictures too like, the Ladies will not please;
> They must be drawn too here, like Goddesses.
> You as at *Lely's* too, wou'd Truncheon wield
> And look like Heroes, in a painted Field.[31]

Its method is almost excessively literary, a return to classical satire. Oldfox, with his 'feign'd Friend in the Countrey'[32] to write epistles to is a witty image in little of the process by which the author hopes to achieve his hard, Roman disabused view of city-life. But this also points to its claustrophobic futility.

Manly and Freeman stand apart from the life of the town. To put it in simple practical terms, they have no money; but Freeman, he tells us, 'chose to cheat the King, than his subjects'[33] and thus left the law, and Manly realizes (as Horner did not), that 'he that is the Slave in the Mine, has the least propriety in the Ore'.[34] *The Plain Dealer* catches a moment of social disillusion with prophetic acuity. But its claims to be a successful political play are jeopardized by the looming detachment of its hero. As the prologue announces;

> I the *Plain-Dealer* am to Act to Day;
> And my rough Part begins before the Play.[35]

Roles like this are exciting emotionally; this too is Wycherley's legacy to future writers. But he is not, as Otway and Crowne are, primarily a psychological writer, and Manly's outbursts can seem like effects without causes. The fantasy of the Indies creates a

pastoral of innocent savagery that links up suggestively with the
pre-moral landscape of early heroic tragedy. As an heroic figure
Manly has emotional roots in the realm of Zempoalla. But the fact
that the only contact he has with a character for whom he can
admit fellow feeling is the little scene with Vernish near the end
wraps him in an isolation that encourages one to see the play as a
kind of blusterer's concerto. Wycherley's approach to character in
this play seems very literary, a classical wordy gloss on those
patterns of performer and critic, of the self-imprisoned, of meaning, double-meaning and misunderstanding that come to such
gorgeous fruition in *The Country-Wife*. To this extent the play fails.
The step towards a redefinition of character is made by Otway.[36]
But a failure to top *The Country-Wife* is scarcely a disgrace. If one
pushes Manly back into the play, a lot of its power reasserts itself.
Manly after all is a plain-dealer only till the end of the second act.
The discovery that moral outrage and a wounded ego do not in
themselves cure love – a step out of childhood, like Margery's –
trap him into the dissembling he despises in others. It is a discovery that the brittle Olivia makes before he does; all she need do to
counter his outburst is to echo the last curse:

May the Curse of loving me still, fall upon your proud hard
heart.[37]

Olivia has his measure in more ways than one. She has acquired
his affection by acting up to his narcissism, and retains it by
playing with a sadomasochistic urge he is unaware of in himself.
'He has Cruelty indeed' she remarks to Fidelia, '. . . which is no
more Corage, than his Railing is Wit.'[38] That Wycherley lets him
see through her as soon as they meet in the play indicates where
his true interests lie. It is the emotional tie between these two that
gives the play its great tension.

Olivia is something of a generalised figure, like the ladies in *The
Country-Wife*, she too has no single identity, as Novel's comparison
of her to a mirror suggests; '. . . she stands in the Drawing-room,
like the Glass, ready for all Commers to set their Gallantry by her;
and, like the Glass too, lets no man go from her, unsatisfi'd with
himself'.[39] And like those ladies she tends to the allegorical, in her
case by her identification with money. Its influence on her language is curiously elevating in effect.

I . . . think you do not well to spirit him away to Sea, and the Sea is already but too rich with the spoils of the shore.[40]

She may see Fidelia here as 'spoil' but she needs a glamour on the idea that partly identifies her as an aspect of the 'shore', as a cold but convincingly attractive embodiment of the town and its need for such as Manly for support. Like all Wycherley's misers she is harshly judged. In a brutally witty parody of *Twelfth Night* it is Olivia, not Malvolio, who exists vowing revenge.

Fidelia is another of those problematic heroic figures who deal so ineptly with the comic world and create such problems for Wycherley's critics. The implied comparison with Viola seems deeply unfair, but, though one might point out that male disguise is as much as a convention of Restoration comedy as of romance, that the voyage had only been a short one anyway and that such things happened not infrequently, one must remain dubious not so much of Fidelia herself but of what Wycherley does to her. Like all those other heroines, 'romance' is her grimly farcical trap. As a boy Manly finds her a snivelling bore and is too overbearingly bad-tempered to allow her to explain herself. As she realizes, he would probably be even more bad-tempered if she did. She takes refuge in a Viola-like reliance on time, but the scenes with Olivia in that favourite Wycherley locale, the darkened room, explode into a confusion of sexual identity that not only breaks up Olivia's new marriage but convinces both partners that she is of the opposite sex. Viola has wandered into Orton's *What the Butler Saw*. The problem with Fidelia is an unevenness in the writing; the malice in some of her scenes with Manly brings her much closer to us than the woozy verse or the unearned rhetorical seriousness of the end. To say that this might be resolved in the theatre is not to say it away. I feel sure myself that Fidelia could be taken through the Wycherlean progress from the heroic to the farcical to the real by a sympathetic actress, but it is not in the writing – the most obvious example of Wycherley's ambitions cracking the bounds of his dramatic skill.

Fidelia is baulked of her chance to rescue Manly. The exorcism of his love for Olivia, comes, uncompromisingly, in the playing out of its meaning. Her stature at the end is kept inviolate by her striking away of the jewels, though soured by her observation that now the whore's fee goes to Fidelia.[41] Manly's rescue is his coaxing by Freeman into a realization of the existence of the real world and the necessity of our compromises with it. His last lines are not merely cynical, they resonate back over the play as a formulation of that problem of desire and identity I mentioned earlier.

> I think most of our quarrels to the World, are just such as we have to handsom Woman; only because we cannot enjoy her, as we wou'd do.[42]

After all, there is one real Plain Dealer in the play, Eliza, and she is cut off from almost everything that goes on in it. Like Vincent in *Love in a Wood* (with a trust in women that no other man in the play shares) or Horner with his hard-won knowledge of the Ladies of quality, she is a lonely, and ultimately, a mysterious figure. If there is an ache at the heart of Wycherley's plays, it is the fear of isolation. Vincent is consoled by his bottle; Horner by his taxing pleasures; and Eliza by the plays of the writer she so admires, the author of *The Country-Wife*.

3 'The Wits' Garden' – Court Forms and Libertine Philosophies

Carolean myth-making is a much more improvised and ironically shaded business than its Caroline antecedents. The history of court entertainments under Charles II is patchy and irregular, characterized by false starts and half-hearted ambition. There is no equivalent of the coherent and idealistic enthusiasms of the court of Henrietta Maria. The hierarchical platonism of the Caroline court gave place to a materialist philosophy associated with Lucretius and the new science. Epicureanism in this sceptical 'libertine' form could scarcely provide a framework of ideas for court propaganda to match the elaborate constructions of neo-platonism. Instead, the patronage games of courtiers as intent on furthering their own careers as those of their protégés produced an ambiguous, often ironic, set of mirrorings between playhouse and court.

The Earl of Rochester's complicity in this was both active and passive, as patron and writer, and (as libertine) as a kind of exemplar of personal style. He is in a sense more potent as absence than as presence. His death in 1680 became an iconic moment in the career of Restoration 'wit', redefined and reinterpreted by a series of plays that allude to it. A posthumous presence seems to suit a writer set in his own work on a willed negativity of vision. Rochester is only superficially a 'comic' or 'dramatic writer'. The elaborate and justly praised structure of his epistolary poem *Artemisa to Chloe*,[1] for example, is generated by his failure, or refusal, to sustain a voice. The poem becomes a series of voices, each phased into nothing. His method is essentially anti-dramatic, using theatre to explode theatre, smashing through jokes into a vacuum. His one play, *Valentinian* (1684), is a brilliant demolition and restructuring of a Fletcher piece into a personally anarchistic vision. Rochester's presence/absence links many of the pieces I shall deal with in this chapter, plays that move towards the limit of generic definition, none more subversively than Lee's 'Farce Comedy Tragedy or meer Play', *The Princess of Cleve* (1680), with which the chapter ends. The interaction of court ideologies with the Epicurean scepticism of the Wits produces uneven, sometimes chaotic work in which ironic intention is often apparent if never developed fully and explicitly.

Many dramatists owed the beginning of their fashionable careers to Rochester's patronage. John Crowne was to become the most openly political writer of Restoration comedy, the closest in some ways to the king's personal favour. His *Calisto* (1675) was perhaps the most ambitious court entertainment of the period, certainly the best documented. Rochester's implication in it suggests ironic purpose, in particular when one bears in mind an apparent preference for bad verse from his protégés. As Eleanore Boswell points out in her study of the staging of Calisto,[2] Crowne's earlier dramatic work was undistinguished. Rochester could fear, or hope for, the worst.

In fact the verse is light, with puckish echoes of Shakespeare. It is the subject that initially intrigues. 'Resolving to choose the first tolerable story I could meet with' he writes in his introduction, he 'unhappily encountered this. . . . I employed myself to . . . write . . . a clean, decent, and inoffensive play on the story of a rape . . . ,[3] a task further complicated by his all female cast, including the future Queens Mary and Anne as the virgins in jeopardy.

Crowne, of course, doth here protest too much. At times the play can seem a chaotic private joke. It lacks an overview of the kind essential to pastoral; or rather, the formal split between the play and the masque interludes presents two contradictory views. The masques were written for male and female professional actors and create a pastoral image out of Tasso rather than Guarini, an emphasis on love satisfied. As the first interlude argues, with a guileless eye to the ecology:

> Kind lovers, love on,
> Lest the world be undone,
>   And mankind be lost by degrees
> For if all from their loves
> Should go wander in groves
>   There soon would be nothing but trees.[4]

This is in obvious opposition to Diana and Calisto's championship of virginity, and the shepherds tend to celebrate the nymphs' discomfiture.

The disparity is bridged by that vital element in court entertainments, an awareness of the identity of the participants. The prologue is the familiar allegorical river scene. The Thames was impersonated against precedent, as Crowne notes, by a woman, Moll Davis, the King's mistress;[5] another mistress, Mrs Knight, played Peace. They try to allay the fears of the City, Augusta, by evoking the relaxed Arcadia of Charles II. As Europe remarks

the mild power of this happy place
                  . . . is inclined
to make the world as peaceful as his mind[6]

If one sees peace as an erotic state, as the imagery of this kind of thing clearly does, then this characterization of Charles carries over to the bountifully sexed Jupiter of the play

You but in part my kindness can enjoy,
My ocean must a thousand springs supply.[7]

It is a familiar association of ideas where the King is concerned. Crowne maintains the delicate balance of allusion basic to his play's meaning by moving in and out of a playful sense of amateur theatricals. The pomposity of this masque is charmingly deflated at its close. After all the mythological personages have departed, two anonymous singers give us a glimpse back-stage –

Now the play, the prologue is done,
The dancing is o'er, and the singers are gone.
The ladies so fine, and so fair, it surpasses,
And dress'd and have all taken leave of their glasses.

There follows 'An Entry of Carpenters'.[8]

Jupiter gets his disguises past the other characters by blinding them with science.

Now, you cool atoms, from your ranks disband,
Flow to loose air again at my command.

Mercury thinks he sees 'the atoms loyally obey' but Jupiter corrects him:

> Poor god! No shape at all thou didst descry;
> I only graved a figure on thy eye.[9]

It's cheating really (and wouldn't fool a pantomine audience), but Crowne offers, instead of spectacle, a play of ideas, a tongue-in-cheek juxtaposition of science and mythology. In this play Arcadia and the Royal Society overlap; the wood of *A Midsummer Night's Dream* is scrutinized with the cruel eye of one of Shadwell's virtuosi. It is riddled with scientific language. The earth for Jupiter is one big sexual laboratory, and Juno in her pursuit of him threatens a gruesomely apposite train of enquiry –

> And I will Jove too in his thefts detect,
> Or I'll each bird and beast I meet dissect (Exit)[10]

Crowne's up-to-date scientific and raffish Jupiter is seen gradually to corrupt the ideal of Diana's wood. It becomes a sensual nightmare, like Rochester's *St James Park*; in a sense it *is* St James's Park. The sequestered hunting ground of its earlier owner is opened up to marauding gods.

> The spreading trees are not so full of birds,
> The caves of beasts, as all the woods around
> Of wanton gods who ev'rywhere abound,
> Waiting to make our chastities a prey,
> And gins and toils do for our honours lay.
> On our occasions we can no where move,
> But straight we fall into some trap of love.[11]

Diana is moved to exclaim

> What! I am turn'd a Venus, and my groves.
> Private retreats and nurseries of loves.[12]

In obvious allegorical terms (the terms of Dryden in the *Secular Ode*) the Caroline Diana *had* become the Restoration Venus.[13] The wood had been her laboratory also; a laboratory of platonized spiritual alchemy – 'Now where's your chymistry – your beaten gold?' taunts Psecas. 'Your spiritual flesh and blood?', Diana replies in an image of summed up emotion, typical of Crowne's later verse.

> Treacherous love has rob'd my paradise,
> And pluck't the fairest fruit that there did grow;
> The gods in vain plant virtue here below,
> It ripens not by any sun or time,
> This world for virtue is too cold a clime.[14]

But the hard-won victory for chastity at the very end of the play is peculiarly satisfying. After all, in the royal princesses there is a covert hope for Crowne of the return of virtue to public life. Calisto has a tiny victory; Jupiter begs her to 'accept the small dominion of a star', and the play reserves spectacle for a final emotional punch:

> *Calisto* and *Nyphe* enter under a canopy, supported by *Africans*; immediately upon their entrance, a heaven is discover'd filled with gods and goddesses.[15]

I shall return to Crowne in two later chapters. *Calisto* has in it the seeds of a complex series of plays, a lifelong exploration of typically 'Restoration' themes by a dramatist at odds with his context. In *Calisto* Crowne displays an ideological bias to Jupiter, as a figure of absolute patriarchal rule, but conveys also a sense too of Juno's wrongs. The question of absolute power, above both the law and morality is a question that hangs over incarnations of Jupiter as libertine as Charles II; the married couple's final exchange has some of Crowne's typical strength –

Jupiter.	And are you weary then of empire grown?
Juno.	I am, and of my life! — And to be free
	Desire no blessing like mortality;
	That my own hand might pour out with my blood
	My sorrows and my life!
Jupiter.	I wish you could!
	That both of us and all the world some ease
	Might find of your eternal jealousies.
Juno.	Who is in fault?
Jupiter.	Your folly is the cause,
	For I will not be limited by laws.[16]

If one puts together the operatic ventures of the end of Charles's reign – Dryden's *Albion and Albanius* (1685), *King Arthur* (1691) and *Amphitryon* (1689) Blow's *Venus and Adonis* (1682?) and Purcell's *Dido and Aeneas* (1689) – one can I think see the development, particularly in Dryden's work, of a royalist imagery, first to carry the propaganda of absolutism, then to state the implications of its failure. *Albion and Albanius* both states and enacts a revival of concern for the issues surrounding the Restoration, a reaction to the anti-Catholic crisis and the King's subsequent determination to rule without parliament. It is part of a body of operatic work inspired by an attempt to reassert the power of the monarchy. Of course the very existence of opera would enhance the King's prestige. A process of doubling is aptly central to English Baroque; it is itself a doubling of the modes of the French court.

Dryden's preface to *Albion and Albanius* offers a summary of the dramatic scope of opera.

> The suppos'd Persons of this musical Drama are generally supernatural, as Gods and Goddesses, and *Heroes* which at least are descended from them, and are in due time, to be adapted into their number. The Subject therefore being extended beyond the Limits of Humane Nature, admits of that sort of marvellous an surprizing conduct, which is rejected in other plays . . .[17]

When Dryden says that when 'Humane Impossibilities' are depicted by an opera they are accepted 'Because where Gods are introduced a Supreme Power is to be understood; and second Causes are out of doors . . .'[18] he is perhaps, not entirely disingenuously, putting the cart before the horse; it is not that music is allowable because gods are depicted, but that gods are depictable because music allows it. It is because a musical statement cannot be challenged that it cannot be said to lie. If the tradition of English spoken drama did not allow of classical pastoral, then music might. If it was difficult to argue the kingly virtues of James II, one could at least sing about them. The very first English Opera, D'Avenant's *The Siege of Rhodes* (1656), with music by Locke, Lawes and Cook), had been reprinted in 1663 with a dedication to the Earl of Clarendon, arguing the role of the theatre as an incitement to 'complacency to Government'.[19] It is partly the expense of opera which aligned it to court, rather than popular attitudes. And yet, while *Albion and Albanius* scarcely claims attention for its literary merits, it does illustrate the failure of opera to extricate itself from town-comedy completely. In 1674 the French *Ariadne* (Perrin/ Grabut) was performed by the 'Royall Academy of Musick' (an institution of which nothing else is known) at the Theatre Royal, with a newly written prologue, a dialogue of rivers, perhaps owing something to the prologue of *Pastor Fido*, spoken by the river Alfeo. Tyber, Seine and Po join to congratulate Thamis, who announces in terms echoed by the anonymous preface, and later in Dryden's King Arthur, that

> Everything here doth seem to smile!
> *Cupid* himself raignes in this Isle:
> E'r since *Venus* resolv'd to quit
> Her Native Throne, to come and dwel in it.
> Fair *Albion* now will new *Cythera* prove
> And must be call'd, The sweet Island of Love[20]

There follows an illustration of the stage setting in which the three naiads (Po is yet to enter) have evidently just disembarked from a shell that bears a strong resemblance to Venus's own scallop. Behind the shell stretches London Bridge. The King's greatness is the country's and the country's greatness is seen in the Preface in the terms of the London of the comedies – ' . . . You have made this Queen of Cities to become also the Center, the Source of Love, Pleasures, and Gallantry . . . '.[21]

Albion and Albanius asks for similar effects; Ilii represents ' . . . a Prospect taken from the middle of the *Thames*; one side of it begins at *York-Stairs*, thence to *White-Hall* and the *Mill-Bank* etc. The other from the *Saw-Mill*, thence to the Bishop's-Palace, and on as far as can be seen in a clear day'. On to this scene comes Augusta, or London, to be tempted by the hypocritical Zelotia and Democratia, to unfaithfulness –

> Maintain the seeming duty of a Wife,
> A modest show will jealous Eyes deceive,
> Affect a fear for hated Albion's life,
> And for imaginary Dangers grieve . . .[22]

In juxtaposing heroic opera in the French style with contemporary comic types (like the unfaithful citizen's wife), Dryden burlesques opera as he writes it. It is no step at all from these characters to 'Fraud a female Quaker'[23] in Duffet's *Mock Tempest* (1675), a burlesque of one of Dryden's earlier operatic ventures. This lays a trap for opera at its very inception – the myth of the King's beneficent rule has already been developed and embodied by the comedies, for the Arcadian myth, with its connotations of peace, ease and fertility, the myth of a land of pleasure, is by its nature concrete, and therefore much better seen in the terms of social actuality than those of allegory. Mythological opera is thus lumbered with a subject all too likely to evoke the observed particulars that would reduce it to burlesque. *Orphée aux Enfers* is much more likely to result than *Orfeo*.

In *King Arthur* (1691), Dryden reverts to a native tradition, that of the masque, as his musical vehicle. His earliest exercise in this form is *The State of Innocence* (1674, though not published til 1677), a dramatization of *Paradise Lost* which helps define some characteristics of his use of the operatic masque. Magic and ritual provide a dramatic context for music in Dryden, almost exclusively, and this context defines and perhaps qualifies its meaning. The masque tends to be associated with evil or – as the circumstances of other plays may modify this – at least sinister forces. Lucifer creates a full-scale masque to tempt Eve. The derivation from *Paradise Lost* is itself interesting, and possibly influential as far as later comedy was concerned. It establishes the pair of lovers as the measure of moral or social values in the operatic/pastoral mode, or at least provides a very strong rationalization of it, and it sets out in the most emphatic form possible the sense of a world at stake; as the little world of Britain is in King Arthur, or the New World in *The Indian Queen* (1664) and *The Indian Emperour* (1665). It also takes back to its origin the Dryden heroine – metaphorically or even literally 'blind'. Seeing and not seeing, knowledge and ignorance are the poles of Dryden's dramatic imagery. His characters are accused by their critics within the play of blindness, and often we see that this is so, and yet the loss of their blindness is the loss of their innocence, and so of the world they think they live in. This is Dryden's tragic nexus, and explains part of his enduring distaste for traditional comedy, where these themes are not only treated lightly, but in such a way as to suggest that the return of true sight is in fact a *happy* ending. It is perhaps our awareness of this tradition that puts Dryden's tragedies in the constant peril of becoming not derisively, but wholly and happily comic. Dryden uses the imagery of neoplatonic enlightenment to suggest an overriding fear that the light might be something worse. Heaven, in *The Tempest*, *King Arthur* and, sublimely, *Tyrannic Love* (1669),[24] is a bad joke of not-knowing, a blinding light as it were – it is his characters' tragedy that they can only temporarily withdraw from it. A materialist's nightmare, perhaps; Dryden's thought is a complicated business largely because these sorts of imaginative fears persistently curtail it.

Emmeline, the blind heroine of *King Arthur* is, of course, excruciating, as she persistently mixes up sight and hearing, but it is fitting that the heroine is literally blind in his major opera. It is by seeing that his characters trap themselves in the actual; the supernatural must manifest itself in sound. The most operatic scene in Dryden – in other words, that where music takes one right to the nub of the dramatic situation is IIIii of *The Indian Queen*, both in its original and expanded form. Zempoalla seeks counsel of the spirits, who refuse to give it to her; were it not for the centrality of this to Dryden's thought this would be simply anticlimactic, but especially in the operatic Purcell version it is an oddly powerful scene, which could serve to sum up the state of any of Dryden's tragic characters at this sort of dramatic midpoint –

Seek not to know what must not be reveal'd;
Joys only flow where Fate is most conceal'd[25]

In *King Arthur* too the problem of what kind of credence one gives musical statements remains unanswered. When the final patriotic masque is over Arthur casts doubt on its validity in a way that restates the whole issue of the masque-form's ability to state truths –

Wisely you have, whate'er will please, reveal'd,
What wou'd displease, as wisely have conceal'd[26]

Unlike Zempoalla, he is satisfied with partial knowledge.

The masque in *King Arthur* sums up the myth of England as the rich new isle of Venus. Pastoral is a very practical kind of myth, in that its tenure in England coincides almost exactly with the preeminence of the wool-trade.

For Folded Flocks, on Fruitful Plains,
The Shepherds and the Farmers Gains,

Fair *Britain* all the world outvyes;
And *Pan* as in *Arcadia* Reigns,
  Where Pleasure mixt with Profit lyes.

Though *Jason's* fleece was Fam'd of old,
The British Wool is growing Gold;
  No mines can more of wealth supply:
It keeps the Peasant from the Cold,
  And takes for Kings the *Tyrian* Dye.[27]

It was Milton's Comus, of course, who gave the definitive statement on sexuality as Nature's capitalism, but the deity's appearance in Dryden's masque is in a much reduced form as a peasant
harvest god. Here Dryden steers near political realities. His picture
of a loyal peasantry as an ignorant and irreligious peasantry seems
self-defeating, but it recognizes the importance of intellectual and
religious ideas to possible revolutionary action; the peasants (kept
warm by their woollies, one supposes) are depicted by Dryden as
sensible, down-to-earth fellows interested only in their stomachs,
a condescension Purcell cheerfully compounds with an appropri-
ately hearty setting –

We ha' cheated the Parson, we'll cheat him Again;
For why shou'd a Blockhead ha' One in ten? . . .

  . . . For Prating so long like a Book-learned Sot,
Till Pudding and Dumplin burn to Pot . . . [28]

It is perhaps odd of Dryden to bother including them at all. That he
does so shows his desire to make an inclusive statement of, or
ritual plea for, peace and prosperity. They are the ante-masque to
Venus's coming. She states Britain's honour in terms similar to
those discussed earlier, of love and gallantry, and then a pair of
lovers act out an ideally free and 'kind' pairing; to contrast perhaps
with the steamier ideal of the forest scene ('How easie his Chain,/
How Pleasing his Pain?').[29]
  In the *Secular Masque* and *Epilogue* to Vanbrugh's *Pilgrim* (1700)
Dryden was to characterize the court of Charles and James II as the
era of Venus, contrasted to Charles I's era of Diana, and the Interregnum as of Mars. In the famous chorus he rejects all of them –

All, all, of a piece throughout;
Thy Chase had a Beast in View;
Thy Wars brought nothing about;
Thy Lovers were all untrue.[30]

It is the source of a sense of transcience hanging over Dryden's visions of Charles II's court, that Venus's lovers will not remain true, or at least, not young. But Venus, as Aeneas's mother is by tradition the ancestress of the British, as well as of Rome. Furthermore, the power she represents is actual as well as legendary, in that successive embodiments of Venus serve to symbolize wealth; her beauty is always that of a status-symbol. Unlike Athene or Diana, Venus is not the representative of an absolute. There is always a tension between incarnation and ideal as Dryden cruelly reveals in his Epilogue –

Whitehall the Naked Venus first reveal'd.
Who standing, as at Cyprus, in her Shrine,
The Strumpet was ador'd with rites divine.[31]

This is just the kind of reduction awaiting the personages of the King's opera. King Arthur circumvents it – in the ritual context of the masque disbelief is suspended to evoke the goddess wholly seriously. Venus and Adonis (1682), in which Moll Davies took the title role, makes an interesting contrast, a masque for a king more interested in entertainment than ritual. Cupid addresses the Court outright ('Courtiers, there is no faith in you')[32] when, the onstage shepherds ask him about it. Played by Lady Mary Tudor, Davies' daughter by the King, he is a sort of master of ceremonies between the two worlds, and effects an easily playful sort of pastoral convention, in which the double nature of Venus, and of the whole entertainment can easily be taken for granted. Here opera has at least created a court-pastoral; placing its Venus in Whitehall the opera identifies the huntsmen as those who 'slothful city-pleasure hate . . . '[33] the pleasures of Venus that is – and thus creates the same kind of inversion to town-pastoral and country-reality as shadows contemporary comedy. Better than any other dramatic work of the period, it sums up the prevailing idea of the London of the late Stuarts as Cytherea.

Burlesques of opera, like Duffet's *Mock Tempest* and *Psyche Debauch'd* (1678) are accurate and occasionally funny, but somehow, unnecessary. *Psyche Debauch'd* parodies the vogue for pagan rites –

'the invocation'
2 Priests: James Naylor, Pope Joan, Wat Tyler, Mall
                       Cutpurse, Chocorilly
All Answer: Help our *Opera*, because 'tis very silly. . . .
2 Priests: Hocus-pocus, Don Quixot, Jack Adams, Mary
                       Ambry, Frier Bungy, William Lilly
Answer: Help our *Opera* because 'tis very silly . . . . [34]

But its source, Shadwell's *Psyche* (1675) opposes a vein of philosophical argument to its elaborate, detailed, pseudo-catholic ceremonial. *Psyche* contains, in the princes Nicander and Polynices, a pair of stout rationalists insistent on arguing away all the heavenly manifestations Betterton's stage machinery can produce.

If, Priest, by Means not nat'ral Heav'n declares
Its will, and our obedience so prepares;
The Gods by this their weakness wou'd confess,
What you call Miracles wou'd make them less.
If something without Nature they produce,
Nature is then defective to their use . . .

Apollo thunders at the impiety, but to no avail –

'Twas nothing but a petty cloud did break;
What, can your Priesthoods grave Philosophy
So much amaz'd at common Thunder be?[35]

Unsuccessful rivals for Psyche's love, they leap into a river hand-in-hand, but reappear in Act V to tell her that, like Stoppard's Rosencrantz and Guilderstern whom they somewhat resemble, they find death quite nice. Shadwell's strenuously (and probably deliberately) self-defeating rationalism points some of the cause for this failure; English drama in this period is almost wholly materialist in outlook. Opera could be criticized as mindless, in that it worked outside the dominant philosophical assumptions.

Scientific materialism, as explored by the Royal Society, provides a fashionable, intellectual context for what contemporary writers perceive as an essentially moral debate. Lucretius's poem *De Rerum Naturae* provided a literary codification of a materialist philosophy traditionally associated with the Greek philosopher Epicurus. Its assumptions – that the metaphysical is outside the scope of human knowledge and, if it can be said to exist, is irrelevant to man, that men and nature alike are 'matter' and that morality is a human construct – offer an attractive rationale of 'libertine' behaviour. Creech's translation of *De Rerum Naturae* (1682) was welcomed with a chorus of praise that bears witness to the attractiveness of Lucretian Epicureanism to a society at once post-revolutionary and incipiently scientific. Verses by Waller and Aphra Behn, are particularly interesting in combining their praise of Creech with lamentations for the recently dead Rochester. Behn hails Creech as the 'Unknown Daphnis', from the same pastoral retreat (i.e. Wadham College) as the great Strephon himself. Wadham also saw the beginnings of the Royal Society, so Behn's extravagant verse is not as silly as it seems, the revival of Epicureanism in England must seem to stem from here. Her poem turns into an elegy for Rochester –

> Strephon the Great, whom last you sent abroad,
> Who writ, and lov'd and look't like any God,
> For whom the Muses mourn, the Love-sick Maids
> Are languishing in Melancholy shades . . .

The literary influence of Epicureanism was the doing of Rochester and his circle, and for Waller, who lived long enough to contribute a dedicatory verse, Creech's poem marks the end of that era; for now, 'the Wits Garden is o'errun with Weeds'.[36]

The plays that discuss these issues most explicitly are, perhaps surprisingly, Shadwell's. His fragmentary spectaculars on philosophical themes are central to the history of opera and semi-opera. They are perhaps *too* fragmentary to be usefully discussed as arguments. But they suggest a realignment of fashionable philosophy (from the platonic to the epicurean) and a parallel realignment of Shadwell's literary allegiance – from the Jonsonists, to the Wits.

At the start of the *Virtuoso* Bruce (even the name is Etheregean), a gentleman 'of wit and sense', quotes in Latin the lines of Lucretius of which there exists an undated translation of Rochester's.

> The gods, by right of nature, must possess
> An everlasting age of perfect peace;
> Far off removed from us and our affairs,
> Neither approached by dangers or by cares;
> Rich in themselves, to whom we cannot add;
> Not pleased by good deeds, nor provoked by bad.[37]

Shadwell had come a long way from *The Rewards of Virtue*. By the time of *The Virtuoso* (1676) and *The Libertine* (1675) Rochester is actually using Shadwell (in the *Allusion to Horace*) as part of his shortlist of approved wits and poets.[38] The Epicurean rakes in *The Virtuoso* are pitted not only against the virtuosos, and the Caroline Snarl, but against the Stoic Formal Trifle, and, needless to say, prove their greater wit and sense every time. In *The Libertine*, Shadwell's semi-operatic version of the Don Juan story, Don John and his fellow rakes enact what amounts to a black comedy of Epicureanism;

> In spite of thee we'll surfeit in delights,
> And never think ought can be ill that's pleasant.[39]

The legendary Seville of *The Libertine* is a sort of nightmare inverse of the real London of *The Man of Mode*. Shadwell's apprehension remains at base disapproving, insofar as his images of unleashed nature within the city call up this sense of the monstrous and the claustrophobic. As Maria says –

> More savage cruelty reigns in Cities
> Than ever yet in Deserts among the
> Most venemous serpents, and remorseless
> Ravenous Beasts, could once be found.
> So much has barbarous Art debauch'd
> Man's innocent nature.[40]

Yet his delight in monstrosity forces him to suspend criticism. Shadwell's imaginary stage architecture always has a rather Piranesian quality to it. *The Libertine* takes his favourite dramatic motif – the trap – to its spectacular limit. The plot persistently traps even itself. Each act is taken to a pitch of bad taste from which Shadwell must force the play into wilder and wilder stratagems of escape. Eventually, when the bulk of the named characters have met their ends, we reach a pastoral lull, in which two shepherds and two shepherdesses tell off the usual cliches with a four square solemnity funny in itself. They sing "Nymphs and shepherds come away' – is the determinedly sprightly Purcell setting *intentionally* parodistic? – but their revels are interrupted by the incursion of the rakes, who carry off the shepherdesses.[41] Their swains soon join the rout of nuns, cavaliers, and outraged relatives that sweep on in the Don's wake, always a little too late. The next scene is the graveyard, arranged as a large banquet for all the ghosts and all the libertines; a 'collation'[42] to parody comic endings.

Libertine figures in most versions of the Don Juan story are seen in sharp opposition to a society intent on reaffirming conservative moral values. The libertine is thus in a formally uneasy relationship to the pastoral or mock-pastoral society of pleasure. Libertine behaviour has the same philosophical roots as a kind of golden age pastoral; Tasso's world of guiltless pleasure can be internalized as personal licence. But when libertime behaviour is a group characteristic, when it becomes conformity rather than opposition, the heroic libertine, the Don Juan or legendary Rochester, becomes a meaningless or impossible figure. 'Libertines' in pastoral, like Fletcher's Sullen Shepherd or Jacques in *As You Like It* are marginal figures, whose libertinage is ambiguous, left ominously obscure. (Guarini's libertine, a satyr, is marginal to the extent of half-human status.) Libertine ideas inform a kind of pastoral but the libertine can never inhabit pastoral – he must be expelled, converted, killed, buried, memorialized.

Jove in Crowne's *Calisto* and Strephon/Rochester in Nathaniel Lee's *Princess of Cleve* are both libertines in perfected absence – godhead, in Jove's case, death in Strephon's. The Lee play is perhaps best approached through Rochester's other mode of influential absence, as patron. Rochester's patronage seems irresponsible as much in what he chose to promote as in whom he neglected to support. His involvement in the more gauche extravagances of Lee, Shadwell, Crowne and Elkanah Settle suggests a negative patronage, holding up distorting mirrors to the court, manoeuvring his protégés into ambivalent positions. Settle's *The Empress of Morocco* (1673) first performed at court and then commercially was an enormous and influential success. A dazzlingly silly, extravagantly entertaining piece, it established a vogue for the so-called 'heroic' play, a style already worked out in more complex ways by Dryden.

Tragedy is outside the scope of this book. But a brief examination of *The Empress* and of Dryden and Sir Robert Howard's *Indian Queen* suggests ways in which the conventions and concerns which I have discussed in comedy tend to replicate themselves, often in reversed or contradictory forms, in this almost uniquely extroverted and unreflective tragic form. Many commentators see an irreconcilable divide between the tragedy and comedy of the period, though actors, and indeed many dramatists, moved from one to the other with ease. They obviously feel that the intelligence needed to follow, say, a comedy of Southerne's would militate against the success of blood-and-thunder tragedy.[43] I think myself that this misrepresents the genre: they are plays of intrigue rather than of action and demand a similarly knowing response. The best of these plays combine the stylishly bizarre with an acute sense of social behaviour, of the dry tone of power politics. Their sense of humour is often that of imposing a formal couplet or a dry, understated exchange on outrageously violent emotions.

More importantly, the apparent gap between Restoration tragedy and comedy is bridged by a continuity of subject matter and dramatic convention. Park-pastoral finds its equivalent in the tragedies in a kind of prison-pastoral. Parks and prisons are obvious opposites; in that they are both public symbols of confident power, they are polarities on the axis of authority. (In the best known of all authoritarian structures they are Hell and Heaven.) Restoration writers set the cruxes of their tragic plots in prisons over and over again, so the simple formal equivalence would justify comparison with the park-scenes, without any attempt to link their role in the plots. But their use is often more exactly equivalent; the veiled Zara is mistaken for the virtuous Almeria, Montezuma must choose between Zempoalla and Orazia, Cortes between a much less virtuous Almeria and Cydaria – the intrigues, the disguises, the unexpected confrontations are all the familiar stuff of Etheregean comedy. They are in fact working out the same set of assumptions. I would suggest that prisons owe their popularity in these plays to the range of erotic metaphor they afford, and that this in being basically neo-platonic, works out various strains of Petrarchan erotic imagery into a more cogent and ruthless statement of the ideas behind the comedies. The prison has two basic meanings; as a symbol of oppressive power, and as Plato's cave, (pastoralized, of course, by Sidney and Guarini) of earthly misconceptions.

Acacis, at the beginning of *The Indian Queen*, prevents Montezuma from killing the Inca when he refuses to hand over his daughter. Acacis, a captive, explains that he too loves Orazia.

> . . . Yet to my freedom, shou'd my chains prefer
> And think it were well lost to stay with her.[44]

This in effect announces the play's intertwining of captivity and eroticism; it is a lesson the childishly direct Montezuma has yet to learn. When the tables are turned, and Montezuma is imprisoned, Zempoalla reacts at once in the terms of the metaphor –

> Does he command in chains? what wou'd he do
> Proud slave, if he were free, and I were so?
> But is he bound ye Gods, or am I free?
> 'Tis love, 'tis love, that thus disorders me . . . [45]

The conflicts that inform the play crystallize in the prison scene in a way that invites parody, and was to receive it from both Sheridan and Gay. Traxalla and Zempoalla take each other's beloved hostage and the resultant impasse makes a splendid piece of baroque echo form that culminates in a dance like change of partners. The stylization is apt. It frames a point in the lovers' development, the sacrifice neoplatonic forms associate with the ascent from the cave. It is the nature of the sacrifice that seems questionable.

> Forgive my passion (says Orazia) . . . I had rather see
> You dead, than kind to anything but me[46]

This is where Polly and Lucy come in.

Lucy: Hadst thou been hang'd five months ago, I had been happy.

Polly: And I too – If you had been kind to me 'till death, it wou'd not have vex'd me – and that's no very unreasonable request (though from a wife) to a man who hath not above seven or eight days to live.[47]

Dryden answers his own doubts about Orazia's ideals in *The Indian Emperour* (1665). Cydaria in a similar situation makes less fanatical demands,

Cortes: Can you imagine I so mean could prove
               To save my life by changing of my Love?

Cydaria: Since death is that which naturally we shun
               You did no more than I perhaps had done.[48]

He continues this implicit criticism by returning Montezuma to the
pre-conscious state from which *The Indian Queen* had seen him
develop. In the context of the coming of Christianity, the Indian
world becomes an image of a lost age of innocent instinct. In
Empress of Morocco (1673) the lurid vices of the wicked Empress are
balanced by a Platonic ascent through love – the same pattern as in
The Indian Queen, but more extravagantly realized. The masque of
Orpheus and Euridice more than symbolizes the spiritualization of
the hero and heroine's love; in a sensational plot-twist it comes to
effect it. The Empress Laula tricks the Queen (Euridice) into stabbing
the King (Orpheus).

[. . . the Dance ended, the King offers to snatch the Young
Queen
from the Company, who instantly draws her Dagger and stabs
him.]
Y Q: Take that, Ravisher[49]

The ascent from hell in the masque parallels the movement of the
King and Queen from the dungeon to 'pure' love:

Then with a gentle gale of dying sighs,
I'le breath my flying Soul into the Skies
Wing'd by my Love I will my passage steer,
Nor can I miss my way when You shine there.[50]

One could fill out this account of the play by following the progress
of the characters' emotions as I did for *The Indian Queen*, but as the
masque in Settle's only real addition to the pattern the effect would
be rather repetitive. The intriguing thing about it is how far the
masque stems from an echo of England's own Dowager Queen,
Henrietta Maria. The dramaturgy resembles that of a Caroline
piece like Shirley's *The Ball* (1632) (with a masque of Diana),
subverted startlingly by Laula's Jekyll and Hyde personality
switches.

Both Rochester and Mulgrave wrote prologues for the play which exploit the erotic metaphor as an appeal from the women of the audience to the King:

Nor can you scape our soft captivitie;
From which old age alone must set you free.[51]

At least up till Rochester's death, when the court-wits cease to concern themselves with drama, tragedy can parallel the circumstances of court life with almost indecent closeness, particularly in the series of plays of which Rochester's own *Valentinian* (1684), is by far the best, about the courts of lustful tyrants. As Dryden points out in his dedication to the Duke of Monmouth of The Indian Emperour, 'Heroick Plays' were a court taste, at this time almost exclusively so. The 'Heroick' play is about power; as if it was only after the Revolution that it became apparent as an abstract thing. 'Princes are sacred' Traxalla says, objecting to Zempoalla's attempt to sacrifice the Inca.

. . . True, whilst they are free;
But power lost, farewell their sanctity . . .

is her reply, and she goes on to shrug off advice in an attempt to maintain her own power; when dependent on the opinions of their subjects –

. . . Princes but like publick pageants move
And seem to sway because they sit above.[52]

These questions must have been uppermost in contemporary assessment of the monarchy. The sex-power nexus so obsessively explored by Rochester is one newly apparent aspect of a desanctified reign, even had Charles not chose to exploit his virility as part of the propaganda of rule. How the court understood these plays, and how the Wits, as patrons, intended them, is the subject of a study in itself.

The knowing response one might ascribe to the spectators of a play like *The Empress of Morocco* is implicit in the writing of Nathaniel Lee's 'Farce Comedy Tragedy or meer Play',[53] *The Princess of Cleve* (1680). Lee makes the courteous Nemours of Madame de Lafayette's novel into an extreme type of the libertine of his own time. He thus splits his play into two halves, a libertine comedy and a domestic tragedy, and pits them against each other. Nemours bridges the two effortlessly 'No more . . . ' he exclaims on being told of a possible meeting with the Princess,

> if I live I'll see her tonight, for the Heroick Vein comes upon me – Death and the Devil, what shall become of the backstair Lady then . . . [54]

Nemours exercises a more flurried and yet more absolute control over the styles and plots of the play than Dorimant does of his. He can play the 'Heroick Vein' well enough, but he carries over into it an outrageous ironic consciousness.

Like Dorimant, Nemours is, obliquely, an avatar of Rochester. Nemours quotes some lines from *Valentinian* and ascribes them to Ronsard, one of a series of rather equivocal tributes to the then dead shepherd.[55] Lee silently borrows much more from Rochester's play; the Princess, who exists wholly within the 'Heroick Vein' is the most alarming example of the 'dreaming heroine' I talked about in connection with Wycherley, and is derived in particular from the wronged heroine of Rochester's *Valentinian*, the virtuous (and very young) Lucina.

Lucina is plagued by feelings she cannot understand; Rochester uses the pastoral fiction to express these in a dream sequence. Her innocent meditations and a flippant half-overheard conversation between her attendants are distorted in her dreams by a dance of satyrs,[56] and her conscious innocence, for which the pastoral retreat stands, is intensified into a struggle between internal forces she cannot recognize. But where Lucina's integrity is respected by the play, Lee's savagery exposes the Princess as a monster of self-repression and prudish coquetry. The pastoral dream is intensified into a psychotic narcissisism. She is an addict of the pastoral fantasy, with a particular fondness for images of lonely caves and dark grottoes that strikes ominously on both the Platonic and the Freudian awareness. Shortly after her wedding she tells her attendant of a dream of the libertine Nemours –

> I slept, and dreamt I saw
> The bosom of the Flood unfold;
> I saw the Naked Nymphs ten Fathom down,
> With all the Crystal Thrones in their Green Courts below,

Where in their busie Arms *Nemours* appear'd
His Head reclin'd, and swoll'n as he were drown'd,
While each kind Goddess dew'd his Senseless Face
With Nectar drops to bring back Life in vain;
When on a sudden the whole Synod rose
And laid him to my Lips – oh my *Irene*!
Forgive me Honours Duty – Love forgive me,
I found a Pleasure I ne'er felt before,
Dissolving Pains, and Swimming Shuddering Joys,
To which my Bridal Night with *Cleve* was dull . . .[57]

The poor Prince enters, typically puppet-like, on cue. In her dream the Princess at once phallicizes Nemour's face – it is 'swoll'n' – while transferring the responsibility for its stimulated state to the Nymphs. Her ecstacy on kissing it picks up an obscenely suggestive tangle of ideas from the underplot earlier in the act –

For my part, I'll serve my Damn'd Wife as *Tantalus* was punish'd
the Fruit shall bob at her Lips, which she shall never enjoy.[58]

If the Princess, whatever the gulf in social ranks, seems closer to fair Chloris than Lucina in her sexual practices, she is simply the most notable sufferer from a general malady. The play opens with a song apparently in praise of the wetdream; its comic plot climaxes in a juxtaposition of sleep-walking and cuckoldry. Though the Prince is treated with a little more dignity, unrespectable puns lurk in his use of the word 'expire' –

. . . I each night will see thee softly laid,
Kneel by the side, and when the Vows are paid,
Take one last kiss, e'er I to Death retire,
Wish that the Heav'ns had giv'n us equal fire
Then sigh, It cannot be, and so expire[59]

Sleep, Death and frustrated sexuality continually interweave in the imagery of the play. Cleves is upstaged in death by a character not even in the play – Rosidore/Rochester, one of the signs that mark the picture of this corrupt court as an image of another closer home. They share a funeral song; Strephon is Rochester's pastoral synonym, and this is the name used in the mourning song of V.iii.

Mrs Barry, who acted the princess, had also notoriously acted with Rochester in 'Loves Theatre, the Bed'.[60] (The pun is a crude one, I know, but both 'act' and 'part' are favourite puns of Rochester's own.) And yet the image of Rosidore singing 'in the urn' is not an unqualified burst of nostalgia. His death is claustrophically emphasized. He becomes a *memento mori* in a court lush with decay. Nemours becomes placed by Lee in a way that contradicts an easy alignment of him with Rochester, or of Lee with the cult of Strephon. The speech of Nemours that begins –

> . . . thus wou'd I have Time rowl still all in these lovely Extreams, the corruption of Reason being the Generation of Wit . . .

ends with 'thus sang Rosidore in the urn',[61] both as an imposition of quotation marks on a sentiment not the speaker's own, and as a slightly ironic bathos. Such singing counters neither time nor corruption; they claim it for their own.

Nemours himself is remarkable for the sense of sanity with which Lee has endowed him. True, he has an exhibitionist tendency – he imagines for a split second Vidam watching him 'leap'[62] the Princess – but in the world of this play that's an almost healthy alternative. he is in his own way representative of an ethos of 'nature' comparable to that of another mirror of Rochester's career, The Man of Mode. Lee, in his manic imaginative fluency, imbues the play at every level with images that attest to it. Nemour's pansexuality seeks rather to extend the bounds of nature than to transcend them. His bedmates, real and imaginary, include not only the youth Bellamore, but the devil, in the guise of Marguerite. But this too he can naturalize, even domesticate.

> . . . don't you think a feat Devil of yours and my begetting, wou'd be a prettier sight in a House, than a Monkey or a Squirrel? Gad I'd hang Bells about his neck, and make my Valet Spruce up his Brush Tail ev'ry Morning as duly as he comb'd my head.[63]

The masquing scenes in which Nemours comes to his own are games of repressed identity. The various couples find out truths about their partners, themselves and their desires. It is a manic process, but of a salutary humour from which the 'Heroick' vein exiles our neurotic Prince and Princess. Nemour's outrageous banter with Tournon and Marguerite, his real friendship with the former and admiration for the latter emerge out of the extremes of apparent corruption as exhilarating positives that mock the real corruption of the virtuous Princess. Tournon admires Nemours for the stoicism of Petronius, as real as the stoicism of Seneca evoked in Valentinian, and rather more so than that of Rosidore/Rochester/Strephon. The death of Rochester recurs as a mock-pastoral topos in both pro-'wit' and anti-'wit' writing of the next two decades. Only the more simple-minded playwrights use it without ambiguity.

Nemours admires Marguerite, for qualities which Dorimant found in Harriet. This is, to say the least, unexpected. Marguerite is a Loveit who saves herself by consciously using disguise. Her description of married life, sarcastic though it is, reveals qualities of awareness and wit which make marriage suddenly possible. Nemours plays off her with light, mock-civil banter, but his 'I swear most natural and unaffected'[64] is a tribute to qualities that allow his mistress to turn the emotional tables. His marriage to her is scarcely the repentance he claims it to be. But then, how real was Rochester's repentance? Repentance on marrying has stronger if more risky possibilities for reform than repentance on point of death. And it will certainly be a healthier union than that of the Cleves. The Princess rather slyly admits to Nemours a recipe for passion that condemns her personally, as it elevates her into an astonishingly acute symbol of the nexus of passion, repression and the bourgeois marriage ethic that looms so in the literature which the play at once forecasts and demolishes.

> You have a sense too nice for long Enjoyment.
> Cleve was the Man that only could love long:
> Nor can I think his passion wou'd have lasted,
> But that he found I cou'd have none for him.
> 'Tis Obstacle, Ascent, and Lets and Bars,
> That whet the Appetite of Love and Glory;
> These are the fuel for that fiery Passion,
> But when the flashy stubble we remove,
> The God goes out and there's an end of Love.[65]

Nemours plays the scene impeccably, but he is quite right to explode it after she leaves –

Believe that you shall never see me more – she Lyes, I'll
Wager my state, I bed her eighteen months three weeks
hence,
at half an hour past two in the Morning.[66]

The quartet that make up the underplot, and occupy the park-
scene are themselves a parody of wit comedy cliches; it is to this
that they may aspire, but their version of the London wit that the
travelled Poltrot so admires reveals simply coarseness, cruelty and
greed. The mode of ironic mirroring is tragedy's, as is the outrageous contempt of good taste: the vivacity is partly comedy's,
and partly Lee's own. The breaking and juggling of contemporary
formulae is the effect of his explosive creative energy. Lee's parody
is unexpectedly rich.

Lee spent his time in and out of asylums; he offers an extreme
image of the pressures and exploitation undergone by the professional dramatists in this period. *The Princess of Cleve* belongs as
much to their world, perhaps, as to the semi-tragic cruelties of the
seventies. A Prologue added for a revival in the reign of William
and Mary reduces the play to order, retrospectively. The world of
decayed trust and spreading disorder, has now been reformed by

William the Sovereign of our whole Affairs . . .
Our Guide in Peace, and Council in the Wars.[67]

But *The Princess of Cleve* survives to cast an ironic eye on the
plays of marriage and the new stability with which this reading
would align it. Lee seems to me to exploit the ironies and extravagances of a court, and its favoured entertainment, both more
chaotic than to lend themselves easily to rational political comment
of this kind. Between the plays of the seventies and the aesthetic
flowering of the nineties, a comedy of conflict and stress evolves to
which Wycherley's *Plain Dealer* was the crucial development.

4 Professional Dramatists – Shadwell and Crowne

SHADWELL AND THE WITS

Shadwell was McFlecknoe in more ways than one. The heir, in Dryden's poem, to 'all the realms of Nonsense'[1] succeeded Richard Flecknoe not only as the protégé of William Cavendish Duke of Newcastle, but also, more relevantly perhaps to Dryden's scorn, as the second professional writer to work regularly for the Restoration stage. The distinction between professional and amateur is important to the four writers whose work I discuss in the next three chapters. Flecknoe, the author of *Love's Kingdom* (1664) and *Demoiselles à la Mode* (1668) – the first play, incidentally, to use the 'à la mode' tag in its title – is every bit as undistinguished as Dryden claims, and his short career seems of little interest. Shadwell, Behn, Crowne and Otway on the other hand, provide an impressive roster of still underrated plays. More complex and ragged than the products of the Wits, their occasionally botched or compromised form is compensated for by an energy and ferocity all their own. A Restoration revival on the contemporary stage could well start here.

A lack of the gentlemanly virtues of poise and perfect finish puts these plays outside our preconception of Restoration comedy. Apart from Otway's mysteriously foreshortened career, the span of creativity of a professional dramatist was necessarily longer than that of an amateur. Many of the assumptions of literary criticism effect a bias toward the gentleman writer, able to stop when his interest dies, not condemned to the hazards of unevenness by the necessity of regular production. A Restoration dramatist would not, of course, have the options by which a modern writer might compensate for the apparently endemic short windedness of a

87

dramatist's career with a withdrawal backed by royalties, film money or a theatre post. I spell this out as the most obvious reason for these dramatists' neglect; the effort to exhume the good from the less good is daunting in the face of Behn's or Shadwell's enforced prolixity. Crowne seems to me an exception to this professional unevenness; in some ways a throwback to the eccentric moral seriousness of the Jacobeans, he commands in each of his plays an attention not always justified by Shadwell or Behn. His career seems as much that of a 'lost' great dramatist as Otway's, though the reasons are less blatantly external. But for all these dramatists, the circumstances of professional writing cut oddly across a genre formed by ideas of wit, 'ease' and leisure. The contradictions that result inform the writer's work at base; at the level of economic and social identity, of his image of himself *as* writer. 'There seems to be a strange affectation in authors', Johnson comments in his life of Congreve 'of appearing to have done everything by chance.'[2] But this is simply a sign of Johnson's distance from the pastoral fictions of a pre-Augustan age. A Restoration writer's fictions about writing carefully preserve the illusion of a spontaneity of wit. Ease and elegance are values so pervasive to writing that the act itself must not be seen to be impugned as paid labour. Thus Congreve or Vanbrugh must project their first efforts back to periods of enforced idleness; illness in Congreve's case, or in Vanbrugh's, a stay in the Bastille. The town-pastoral ethos renders ridiculous the ungentlemanly effort of a professional writer, whose burlesque opposition to the courtly ease of his social superiors is perhaps an aspect of the opposition of the labourer to the shepherd in the pastoral fiction. Like 'the toils of the country folk' in the passage of Thomas Purney's that I quoted in my introduction, the attention the professional attracts seems only to be the 'Comick'.[3] In pastoral all effort is ridiculous. Dryden was no more exempt from this than the victim of his MackFlecknoe. The grotesquely busy little Bayes of Buckingham's *Rehearsal* (1671), the dirty minded litterateur of Rochester's *Allusion to Horace* – unable that is to be *elegantly* dirty –

> But when he would be sharp he still was blunt;
> To frisk his frolic fancy, he'd cry 'Cunt'.
> Would give the ladies a dry bawdy bob,
> And thus he got the name of Poet Squab.[4]

– is as much the object of the Wits' amusement as Shadwell was of his.

I wish to argue throughout this and Chapters 5 and 6 that the contradictions between the conventions these writers accepted from the amateurs of the 1660s and early 1670s, and their own position as outsiders of the court ethos, fed all the best plays of the 1670s and 1680s: that, in other words, an anti-wit turn to Restoration comedy propelled the form through the crises of the end of Charles's reign and thus incidentally preserved it till the Etheregean revival of Southerne and the 1690s. Otway and Aphra Behn would seem to demand a self-contained treatment and will receive it in the next two chapters. In this chapter I want to return to two dramatists whose earlier work I have already discussed. Shadwell and Crowne had unusually long careers, whose most productive middle periods involved them in the complex issues of the Restoration settlement's newly apparent failure.

Satire of Shadwell offers the best record of the shifts of interest that sustain his long career. MacFlecknoe grants Shadwell a pedigree sired by Jonson himself. The patronage of the Wits however influenced a movement away from the neo-Jonsonian formal precepts of his early comedies. In Rochester's *Allusion to Horace* (1675–76), a kind of poetic roster of true and false wits, he is praised for 'Great proofs of force of nature, none of art.'[5] His work in this middle period breaks extravagantly out of the bounds of decorum or indeed, of any canon of taste. Shadwell parallels Flecknoe's belief in decorum, and its implied link to Royalism, in his Preface to *The Royal Shepherdesse*.[6] Yet in *Epsom Wells* (1672) he came so close to the Etheregean mode that Dryden can claim Sedley collaborated in the writing.[7] There is nothing in the verbal style of the piece to point to his co-authorship; though I will argue later that Sedley is a close influence on *A True Widow* (1678) and Shadwell's career at that particular point. But *Epsom Wells* does move decisively out of the private town house of Jonsonian comedy, to the mock pastoral pleasures of a fashionable resort. It moulds the action to a leisurely exposition of the social rites of the place; and it takes over the plot of *She Would if She Could*.

This last could be said of almost all his subsequent plays. But Shadwell's variations on the pattern of paired couples and the interfering 'other' woman – usually played by Anne Shadwell, his wife – implies a kind of distance from it. The 'Aunt' figure is often minimized or made self-parodistic, while the pairings of the men and women of wit tend to involve an ironic snag that implicitly criticizes the values those couples normally stand for. The plots tend to trap or trip up those characters who seem to represent 'wit' values. In addition, his use of plot conventions and character types from the Etheregean plays can be almost contemptuously sketchy, in a way that both draws attention to them as quotations from a different tradition, and shifts the centre of the play elsewhere. Shadwell's repetition of this plot is itself a sign of how little plot mattered to the kind of comedy he set out to write. Jonson is invoked in *The Virtuoso* – in a dedication to Newcastle, as well as in the prologue – with incidental remarks on the impossibility of emulating his polish within the limits of a Restoration dramatist's career, limits Shadwell sees defined by economic pressures.[8] The primary function of the Etheregean plot is to replace the too slender wooing-the-widow plot of *The Magnetick Lady* and its imitators as a self-effacing but commodious and symmetrical grid on which to plot satirical targets. All his plays after *Epsom Wells* are informed by an attempt to combine the skeleton of the Etheregean form, the patronage of the Wits, and a dialogue style to some degree endebted to theirs with his own persistent impulse to judge his characters with an un-Etheregean ferocity. He never lost a sense of comedy's corrective mission. It is indeed the basic impulse of his style. Theatricality for Shadwell is show, and show is exposé, often of a kind that overwhelms the critical faculty it means to engage.

There is a moment at which the ethos of Restoration comedy begins to change; or, rather, one can identify a contradictory evaluation of marriage, perhaps always inherent, but teased out in the plays of the professional dramatists to the point where it seems to criticize earlier wit comedy, by simply invoking within it a contrary impulse of feeling and moral judgement. One can locate this in *Epsom Wells*. In the last act Shadwell initiates the divorce ending, to be brought to an oddly exhilarating perfection in Farquhar's *Beaux Stratagem*. Shadwell has the same sense of almost physical release – a wittily inverted use of the traditional metaphor by which a dance makes concrete the marriage ending –

Woodley: How easie and how light I walk without this Yoak:
                methinks 'tis air I tread — Come let's Dance,
                strike up.[9]

Dance is the most transitory of performing arts. It is thus an ideal vehicle for the paradoxes and provisional contracts of the comic ending, the unfulfillable bargains, the attempts to affirm continuity in the act of conclusion. Shadwell ends his play with a speech by one of the comic cuckolds, exhorting the audience

> . . . for Heaven's sake take the first occasion,
> And marry all of you for th'good of the'Nation.

> Gallants, leave your lewd whoring and take Wives,
> Repent for shame your *Covent Garden* lives.[10]

The plea for marriage and the family is oddly placed, but worded strongly; its emphasis on the problems of property and succession is particularly interesting. Shadwell has sent throughout the play a current of ideas contradictory to the values that inform his models. The very youth of his protagonists implies a kind of criticism.

> Raines: O let me kiss that hand; he must be an illustrious
>   Man whose hand shakes at 22.

> Woodley: You are pleased to say so, but faith I take pains
>   and live as fast as I can, that the truth on't[11]

The Woodleys have arrived at the Cockwood's state with alarming precocity. Fast living at the Wells would seem to accelerate the ageing its waters retard.

The gentleman heroes of *The Virtuoso* are introduced as the representatives of the Wits' epicureanism in a play of intellectual humours. But Bruce and Longvil do not triumph quite so smugly over the Virtuoso as the philosophical labels attached to them might lead one to expect. The agent of their discomfiture is the *She Would if She Could* plot: the ladies choose differently from the gentlemen – a possibility hinted at by Etherege[12] – and then it is the gentlemen who in the end agree to be chosen rather than choose. Clarinda and Miranda are, furthermore, the least likeable of all Restoration comedy heroines. They combine the self-righteous mischief-making of the Jonsonian arbiter with a flair for vicious experiment that seems to be a family trait. Gentlemen of 'Wit and Sense'[13] though they be, Bruce and Longvil seem to have got more than they bargained for.

Lady Gimcrack, the female intriguer, is herself a very funnily shopworn creation, as wearily mechanical in her pursuit of the usual objectives as Shadwell is in the prose he gives her.

That's Mr Bruce, a fine, straight, well-bred gentleman, of a pleasing form, with a charming air in his face. The other, Mr Longvil, who has a pleasing sweetness in his countenance, an agreeable straightness, and a grateful composure and strength in his limbs. I am distracted in my choice on whom to fix my affection.[14]

Her arts are exercised in a garden setting, a diminution and enclosure of the pastoral characteristic of all the professional dramatists, for whom the park implies a freight of values to which Otway and Crowne for example are hostile, or at best indifferent. It is of a piece also with Shadwell's own interest in closed situations, tending to laboratory conditions, and thus distinguishable from Wycherley's oddly introverted passion for the boxed in. Lady Gimcrack's experiment is as unexpected in its outcome as the courtship games of her 'Gentlemen of Wit and Sense' but it parallels her husband's in its distinction of the 'speculative' and the 'practic';[15] thus the platonic language of love is translated into the scientific. Bruce and Longvil are tripped up in their laborious tracking of the ladies' 'cross-love' by their aunt's interventions. The high seriousness of their mood at the opening is soon brought down to the Etheregean norm by the thought of their two apparently interchangeable loved ones. The intrigue plot at its very inception effects a levelling not unlike scientific objectivity, and when the apparatus of traps, grottoes, cupboards and masquerades is set into an ever more frenetic operation on the characters one can begin to see that in the sameness of their impulses all the various 'humours' are reduced to the 'ants, flies, humble bees, earwigs, millipedes, hog's lice, maggots, mites in cheese, tadpoles, worms, newts, spiders'[16] of a grand experiment in the practic and the speculative. Shadwell expounds a minutely detailed cross section of his society's pursuit of pleasure, teeming with unrespectable life.

The problem with most of Shadwell's plays is the short windedness of his inventions. Scene after scene coalesces into one simple comic shock, a staccato effect which the wanness of the love plot can do nothing to smooth out. *The Virtuoso* is perhaps alone in allowing a correspondence between 'humour' farce and Etheregean comedy. Science and philosophy infuse with the conversational style (like the blood of sheep and lunatics to evoke one of the play's less happy monstrosities)[17] to create an idiom in which both halves of the play can be seen to be aspects of each other. Shadwell, at last a virtuoso, has bred a Jonson-Etherege hybrid. His next play, *A True Widow* (1678) is an even more ambitious synthesis of the available comic styles. The play is dedicated to Sedley, who has, according to Shadwell, 'in the *Mulberry Garden* shown the true Wit, Humour and Satyr of a Comedy'.[18] The triple categorization is interesting, and I think, exact. Wit comedy, humour comedy and satire are distinct styles rather than simply discrete objectives, and Shadwell uses them in a more conscious and organized way than the Sedley of the *Mulberry Garden*.

The play begins, conventionally enough, with a trio of witty gallants. Their description in the Dramatis Personae indicates the use Shadwell intends to make of them;

Bellamour – A Gentleman of the Town, who had retired some
            time into the Countrey
Carlos   – A Gentleman return'd from Travel, with Wit
            enough left to love his own Countrey
Stanmore   – A Gentleman of the Town.[19]

In approaching the town-world from such carefully drawn angles the three men provide an instrument of analysis and comment to deal with every aspect of its manners. But at the end of the act Shadwell springs on us his other prime comic device; a Jonsonian 'magnetic lady', the Widow Cheatley. He sets up the formula in a way that not only multiples and confuses the opportunities for satire, by operating as a different level of satirical device, but would seem to threaten the witty gallants themselves –

Lump.   Have a care of Wits at this end of the town; Wits are good
        for nothing, of no use in a Commonwealth, they under
        stand not Business.

Lady.   The better for my purpose. They value pleasure, and
        will bid high for't[20]

The amusements of the town skate over a sense of nothing; in this play all the characters share an odd angst. The 'humours', Shadwell's funniest, are all motivated by an anxiety of organization. Prigg's genealogy of his hounds, Lump's methodical diary-in-advance –

> Lady Cheatley: What do you do on the sixth of May come fifty year?
>
> Lump: This book will tell you – May – May – 6th – 6th, Let me see – 6th – I take Physick, and shave myself.[21]

are all one with Young Maggot's poetry, as ways of encompassing a frightening blank of time. Only Cheatley, wit and widow is one, can reveal, at the end of the play, the 'nothing' of her fortune – she's only, after all, a fake magnetic lady – and still find a way of turning nothing into something. She goes into banking.[22]

The wits and their world are the primary subject of the play. Shadwell gives indication of its ambition and scope, and of its literary self-consciousness, by including a detailed play house scene and a play within a play. It is here that the change of identity plot is placed; here also that the widow, at the wonderfully complex climax of the play's structure, demonstrates her mastery of the play's theatrical idiom in the most literal way. She calls upon the machinery of 'mock-devils' and flying chairs to dispose of her entourage of humourous suitors when they wander after her back stage.[23] Thus the flair of Shadwell's operatic style is layered on to the manic fullness of the play's theatricality. Thus, more crucially, the use of the theatre itself as a frame-device for the peripeteias of the two intensely conventional dramatic modes, holds a kind of mirror to the material from which the play itself is made.

Whatever the private meaning of the play – it would be difficult to deny a darkening of Shadwell's talent in this period – its public meaning is firmly placed by the introduction, and the collaboration on it not just of Sedley but of Dryden himself, whose prologue is a defense of 'Wit'.[24] Wit is the subject of the play, a subject which form must enact. The revival of wit is also its aim. In this the enemy was not simply the kind of farce the playhouse scene satirized, but the contemporary political crisis:

In troubled Times, like these – the Ancients chose
T'exhibit Feasts and Plays and publick Shows . . .
If they did well then, now your Mirth to raise
Were of such merit, you th'attempt should praise.
But 'tis a task too hard for Comedy,
Which ne'r again expects good Days to see.[25]

The defeatism of Shadwell's epilogue was to some degree answered by the commercial failure of his play. Shadwell's critical distance from Etheregean comedy was less marked than that of Otway or Crowne; the contradictions it implied were more easily accomodated within his eclectic theatrical practice. Where other professional dramatists exploited aspects of both wit comedy and matrimonial farce to build a comedy of social critique, Shadwell's commitment to the Wits involved him in their attempt to revive a wit comedy exclusive of the factional interests so crucial to the other writers of the time.

One source of a new direction is evoked in the Dedication of *A True Widow*[26] the Roman comic dramatist, Terence. Etherege, writing from his diplomatic exile in Ratisbon, noted the success of both Shadwell's *Squire of Alsatia* (1688) and Sedley's second comedy, *Bellamira* (1687). The two plays are linked by more than a coincidence of timing. Sedley gave the profits of his play's third day to Shadwell, and both plays use Terence as their source, the *Adelphoi* and the *Eunuchos* respectively. Etherege, considering them together and weighing them against each other is assessing an attempt to redirect wit comedy.[27]

Sedley's epilogue sets his play up against the political drama of a factional kind.

Poets of late with humane Sacrifice
Have feasted you of late like Heathen deities.
In every play they serv'd you up a man
Nay some at parties and whole factions ran.
After such fare how flat must Terence taste?
Yet his plain tales have had the luck to last
While your fam'd Authors in their life time wast.[28]

An attempt to implant the 'plain tales' of Terence is a more subtle attempt at classicism than Shadwell's Jonsonian revivals.

Contemporary French scholarship had effected a shift from classicism as tradition, founded on deducible theory, to classicism as attention to the qualities of particular texts. For the author of the preface of a translation of Terence that appeared in 1694, identified in its 1703 edition as Lawrence Echard, '*Terence* may serve for the best and most perfect *Model* for our *Dramatick* poets to imitate'; not as a source of moral or behavioural exempla in the neo-aristotelian way, but in his achievement of a liaison of formalism and realism, nature skilfully achieved as the Restoration admired it.

> He was certainly the most Exact, the most Elaborate, and withal the most Natural of all Dramatick Poets; His *Stile* so neat and pure, his *Characters* so true and perfect, his *Plots* so regular and probable . . . [29]

Moral questions are nowhere mentioned in this ambitious opening essay. In 1694 Echard proposes Terence as an antidote to the shapelessness and extravagance of the plays of his time. It is at least arguable that his challenge is taken up in the scrupulously well-crafted and unified plays of Congreve. For Sedley and Shadwell Terence represents a return to realism.

Shadwell's dramatic ideals at this point in his career can be deduced from his preface to *A True Widow*; the scene he himself singles out as the most worthy of memory and imitation – in that sense the 'classic' scene – is that where the bawd figure tries to persuade Isabella, with her mother's and sister's encouragement, to become a kept mistress.[30] It is a segment of realist action, in the loose sense, in which I used the term in talking about *The Man of Mode*, but the moral label attached to it is entirely unambiguous. (It's more like nineteenth century narrative painting than a Dutch genre piece.) Shadwell has abandoned the flamboyantly spectacular for a tough moralized realism. Characters become types; in *The Squire of Alsatia* the Termagent is called simply that, and the unfairness of her treatment is made as overt as the hints of violence and even insanity that shadow the role;

> Term.:   I am become desperate; Have at thee. *She snaps a Pistol at* Belfond, *which flashes in the Pan, the Ladies Shriek.*

> Belf.:   Jun.;   Thank you Madam: Are not you a Devil? 'Twas loaden, twas well meant truly. *Takes the Pistol from her*

Sir Edw.: Lay hold on her: I'll send her to a place where she
   shall be tam'd, I never yet heard of such malice.[31]

We are not asked either to approve or disapprove of these hap-
penings, but we can draw a moral from them. Stock characters and
situations are fraught with fixed and rather obvious meaning,
which Shadwell can order into statements of a smooth, consciously
'masculine' objectivity. This is a classicism of a kind and it is the
dominant mode of the rest of his career.

For Sir Charles Sedley, 'realism' is a return to the aesthetic of the
first wit comedies. The years between his *Bellamira* and *The Mulberry Garden* are measured by historical events evoked within the
play; even those events whose memory Restoration comedy conventionally represses:

There was a plague in Sixty-Six, but what is that to *London* now?
there was a fire too; but it is since new Built, and more beautiful
than ever.[32]

Bellamira's world is carefully placed as the outcome of the comedy
that preceded it. The busy action and essentially disorganized cast
of characters of *The Comical Revenge* and *The Mulberry Garden* belong
to a London as yet unrefined by fire, a London prior to the
elegantly organized map of pleasure of a play like *She Would if She
Could*. The moment of social panic and fluid class relationships at
which *The Mulberry Garden* is set has coalesced to a new stability
whose anomalies the servant Smoothly, once himself a gentleman,
is given a scene to expound.[33] Despite the gap in time *Bellamira* is a
companion-piece, or in an admittedly limited sense, a sequel.

Bellamira, unlike any of Shadwell's plays, has the leisurely plot
pace of Etheregean comedy – realism slowly explained, exposition
casually subsequent to event. Act one for example ends with a
scene between Thisbe and Bellamira that endows them with a
clearsighted perspective on the male characters, and explains the
Bellamira we see in the first scene firmly in her own terms. The
apparently relaxed dialogue, in its fluctuations of small talk, intro-
spection and prompt decisions to action, is a remarkable example
of Sedley's sophisticated grasp of dramatic language. Thisbe and
Bellamira arrive at different views of marriage; the play contains
both and within the ample purview of a generous realism they are
not at all contradictory.

As the play goes on Bellamira is firmly instated as its centre; her status as courtesan bestows a kind of knowledge on her instead of simply making her an objectifiable type. She is the most clearly dominant and sympathetic character in the whole of Sedley's oevre. She may well be Duchess of Cleveland, as Genest claimed, just as Dorimant may well be Rochester. But then the Rochester-of-gossip, the Cleveland-of-gossip are dramatic creations in themselves, summaries of event and ethos of which Bellamira and Dorimant are theatrical parallels. One aspect, of course, of the use of mock-pastoral or romance names is that they are really no names at all; they do not specify, so the character behind them might be a particular person known to the audience, or in other cases than these, representative members of the audience itself. If one is to accept the identification, then Sedley is clearly responding to the same aspect of Cleveland as Lely did when he painted her as a sly and unlikely Minerva.[34] The lady's self-confidence saves her from silliness; it is one of Lely's most adept tightrope acts. Like Bellamira, she seems to sum up her little world's knowledge of itself.

Sedley restructures the Terentian rape plot to set up ironies that reverberate back into the town-comedy world. Its protagonist, Lionel, exiles himself from this world *into* that of classical farce.

> I blot all former Faces out of my heart; I am tired with these daily Beauties of the Town, whom we see Painted and Patch'd in the Afternoon in the Playhouse, in the Evening at the Park, and at Night in the Drawing room; so that we have half enjoy'd 'em before we speak to 'em.[35]

But his disguise as eunuch disrupts his initial idealism; he abuses the opportunity it offers to be near his unknown mistress by making love to her – whether this is an impetuous or a premeditated rape is left unclear – and hits a further snag when the gentleman to whom he confides this escapade, turns out to be the lady's brother. The younger male characters are caught on a switchback of responses and rendered farcical by their own lack of irony.

These events are placed much better by the anger of Bellamira and the other women in the play than by the lady's own reaction, a sentimental relapse into verse. Her long pathetic speech is the real weakening agent of this part of the play.[36] Classicism of this kind is a masculine mode, not only in that as schoolroom texts plays like these were central to male rather than the female experience of literature, but in the convention of the plays themselves; the silence or non-appearance of 'virtuous' women. Sedley seems to refer to this in introducing the heiress Theodosia at the end of the play; much talked of, crucial to the plot and never seen. A style of plotting that however carefully handled – and Sedley, unlike Shadwell, goes to great lengths to balance out this masculine bias – effectively derogates women characters sits oddly in a play that celebrates its heroine with the warmth and equity of Restoration comedy at its best. Perhaps *Bellamira* is as much of a stylistic mismatch as *The Mulberry Garden*; the two halves come closer but still do not meet.

Sedley nonetheless finds a classicism; he sifts the materials of Restoration comedy into parallels of the roman types. Bellamira is set against Merryman, for whom Sedley delicately dramatises the 'imperfect enjoyment' convention, in a wonderful piece of generous and unconventional realism. ('Your Pennance is too severe for a sin of Omission, I like you the better for it',[37] Bellamira explains.) Merryman ends the play married to Thisbe, who in III iii rejects the ageing rake Cunningham's attempt at repartee, his gossip of the Spring Garden, for Merryman's relaxed plain talk. The scene turns into a bargain made between them – a proviso scene, which that in *The Way of the World* closely echoes. Here the trading is of a much more equal basis (I shall discuss the comparison later). Sedley finds a classicism where Congreve invents one, it is true, but the way in which Sedley's last play achieves its balance of astringency and tolerance, the way it builds on the past of wit comedy to make its own realistic and accepting statement seems to me to be the work of a real dramatist, uneven but undervalued.

Shadwell, like all the professional dramatists did badly out of the crises of the end of Charles's reign. He takes a less firmly Royalist line than most, attempting instead to combine a Whig rationality with a Jonsonian belief in the traditional values of the English gentry. *The Lancashire Witches* (1681) is the odd outcome of the two. Those particular gentlemen of wit and sense mock the credulity of the peasants who believe in witches, and yet the witches are palpably *there*, flying around on stage. On the one hand they make a masque-like statement of disorder to be set against the life of the country house, on the other to believe in them is equated with Catholicism and sedition. But how far *does* one believe in what one sees in the theatre? How far, and when, can one privilege one character's view of events above another's? Its confusions are echt-Shadwell, and it is somehow a pity to move from this to the somewhat impersonal smoothness of a play like *Bury Fair* (1689).

Bury Fair is very much a play of the nineties. After crisis subsides, the plays settle securely in privacy or provinciality and survey London and its exciting past from a safe and ambivalent distance. Shadwell marks the distance of his resolutely unfashionable locale from earlier comedy in the terms of his own career:

> The great Masters of the former Age
> Had all the Choice of humour for the Stage;
> And they that plenteous Harvest reap'd so clean,
> Their Successors can little else but glean . . .
> Our author some new humour did produce.
> But look for for an unexhausted cruse
> The task each day grows harder than before . . . [38]

Oldwit, in act I takes us back further still; 'I . . . was a Wit in the last Age: I was created *Ben Jonson*'s Son in the *Apollo*.'[39] It's an attractive play, but I feel that Shadwell mellowed is somehow Shadwell no more. The fairground is an apt place to leave him; even at his worse he has its bracingly wild vulgarity. But his theatricality is perhaps more interesting than that; of all the playwrights I discuss he seems to need the theatre to complete him. The incompatibility of plot and metaphor in *The Lancashire Witches* seems typical. It is a disharmonious pantomine, on discrete levels of meaning; one cannot read it as a whole without discounting some of the parts. Shadwell is not really amenable to conventional ways of reading drama, hence the continual temptation to dismiss him. One could not but applaud any attempt to short-circuit the round of faint praise and more vivid mockery that has been *MacFlecknoe*'s lot since his investiture. One good production could set the swings and roundabouts in motion again.

JOHN CROWNE

Crowne's career was unusually long; only Dryden, of Restoration dramatists, exceeded the span from the romance, *Pandion and*

Amphigeneia (1665), to *Caligula* (1698). His original intention in approaching the court circle was to regain the territory in Nova Scotia lost by his father.[40] The romance of prince Pandion's restoration to his kingdom, and Crowne's personal loyalty to the newly restored king of England both reflect a personal quest that was never resolved; though Crowne did eventually become his sovereign's favourite dramatist. The landscapes of *Pandion* may be labelled Arcadia and Thessaly, but the scale of their forests and plains are as like the America of Crowne's Harvard education as Sidney's Arcadia resembles England. Surely this is the first American novel.

Crowne's career was linked to the court for the rest of Charles's reign. It owed more to the King's personal interest than to the favour of Rochester, the dedicatee of *Calisto*.[41] Crowne was no more able than any other of Rochester's protegees to retain his patronage. In the *Allusion to Horace* he is attacked in company with Otway and Settle; Shadwell, praised here, was attacked soon after. Like Otway, Crowne comes to reject the pattern of wit comedy, and to attack minor characters who aspire to it. Rochester remarks on a lack of 'Wit',[42] but Crowne's own attitudes are hinted at by the title of his first comedy; *The Country Wit*. In an ironical demonstration of the closeness of town and country taste the eponymous Mannerly Shallow reveals an admiration of, among other things, heroic tragedy. His ignorance of the town leads to a long comic conceit on the idea of the park, for though Shallow thinks he is in a deer park (like Diana's) he has strayed into Whetstone Park, the notorious brothel district . . .

> . . . just as our park is all trees, that park is all houses . . . they said the park was now quite spoiled, and the best deer were all gone to the other end of the town . . . [43]

The play is set on the Mall, but it exists at a deliberate distance from the values of fashionable life. Shallow serves to devalue 'wit' and fashion.

Within this context Ramble's libertinism is seen, convincingly and even touchingly as grounded in self-doubt. He discusses it in what is surely the longest soliloquy in Restoration comedy.

> How like a barbarous villain do I use that divine creature Mrs Christina! If I were fifty Rambles bound together, I had not merit

enough for her love; and I though I am but one, yet parcel myself out every minute to fifty women; yet 'tis not for want of love to her, for the enjoyment of other women gives me not so much delight as a smile from her: and yet, I'gad the enjoyment of her would not keep me from the chase of other women . . .[44]

This is a long way from the unthinking impulse of Etherege's gallants, or the bravado of Shadwell's. Crowne sets Ramble up as a representative libertine – 'The order of Nature? the order of cox-combs! the order of Nature is to follow my appetite'[45] – but puts him into a deliberately unheroic, literally 'low' dramatic context. His eloquence is modest and attractive, persuasive as a gallant in a late Jacobean play, his inner life is persistently self-questioning and private. The whole movement of the play leads up to a secure knowledge of Christina's affection, and a secure self-confidence arising from it; farcical accident takes him over the barrier the 'married beau' of Crowne's last comedy is to find so daunting. Placing a true value on the self is the moral aim of Crowne's characters, and its opposition to wit-comedy, the celebration of self-disguise, is surely obvious.

A certain individual intransigence marks his oblique relationship to the conventions of the drama in which he worked, and limits his commitment to the Etheregean form. Crowne may in fact be characterized as the only important Restoration dramatist with a bourgeois protestant sensibility. This shows itself in a range of imagery taken from commerce rather than romance or game-playing, a dislike of populist politics, and most important in this context, in his attitude to women and virginity. Crowne's heroines are, in the main, pert little things, with none of the self-posession and initiative of Etherege's women or even Wycherley's. They never direct the plot. Crowne diminishes the change-of-identity device to implausible (though quite acceptable) accident – his women are the objects of the plotting, never its instigators. As a corollary to this, he places a positive value on virginity. If one had to sum up Crowne's favourite subject in a word, it would be 'dissension' – his plays exist as a clash between two ways of life and the most interesting characters tend to be those caught be-tween the two, often quite unconsciously. In this way he is able to explore the disparate contexts of his own career and to find in them the materials of a cycle of plays which focus more acutely than any others the public dissent and private uncertainty of the times.

The King liked *The Country Wit*, rather to Crowne's surprise, as he had meant it for less fashionable tastes; as 'an apprenticeship to the city'.[46] Charles' favour continued, in an interesting inverse relation to the decline of Rochester's. *City Politicks* is partly an expression of loyalty to the King, who on Crowne's direct application, finally got it past the censors. Crowne uses stock figures of Etheregean comedy – two gallants who cuckold older men of their unsatisfied wives – and gives it a political dimension by making the cuckolds prominent Whigs and indulging in much incidental satire on Shaftesbury and the Whigs in power in the city.

The amount of direct political potential in adultery is probably pretty low – as satire *City Politicks* is mean-minded and random. The best hits are accidental. The Governor, for example, is suavely disbelieving of the result of what had obviously been meant to create a puppet administration:

'I thought his Excellency the Viceroy had given you intimation another person would be more pleasing to him, and in this juncture more fitting for the office.'[47]

The Podesta's standard gang of uppity proles make uninspiring satiric fodder, though again the writing subverts the intention – the Bricklayer's reply to the Governor seems dignified and reasonable –

'We have a charter for the free election of our magistrate, and what we have done our charter will justify'.[48]

The whole situation is vastly too complex to be dealt with in this form. Crowne resorts to making all his Whigs hypocrites, ready to change sides if the money's better. But this in turn up-ends the meaning of the gallants' pretence at piety – if all the Whigs are also pretending, and for similarly selfish motives, then no-one is a Whig, and everybody is; the gallants have been drawn into a labyrinth of disguise. Indeed, the name of Crowne's hero – Artall – points to that sense of farcical plotting and deceit that entirely swamps political realities. The play's comic climax is the farcical chase around the Podesta's house occasioned by Artall and his friend Florio, in identical versions of the 'sick equipage', pursuing Rosaura and Lucinda under their husbands' noses. In a miracle of split-second coincidence, between one eruption and the next, Artall pads quietly across the stage, offering a key to the whole mad whirl –

'I venture boldly into the dominion of these arbitrary rogues, who have a strange absolute authority over their own consciences in lying and swearing, but love! love! love!'[49]

Anarchy is the real subject of *City Politicks*; an anarchy of self-indulgence warping the sense of reality; an anarchy that exists in the libertines as much as it does in the Whigs. At base *City Politicks* is no more political than *Duck Soup*.

Rochester's deathbed is clearly alluded to in Florio and Artall's pretended conversion, and Crowne was attacked in an alley by an anonymous bully who resented the slur. Obviously, in its own day the attack on the wits struck deeper. Those parts of the play most typical of Crowne at his best are Crafty's scenes. Crafty is a monster torn between a Whig upbringing and Tory appetites, but his attempt to make a whole out of the two halves evokes Crowne's strongest imaginative response. Indeed the Podesta's menage, a gruesome incestuous parody of the bourgeois family, is his best hit at Whig values. At the end of Act III they line themselves up complacently in the closing verse, as if for a family snapshot.

Podesta.   But are not these unhappy times,
            That I can take no joy
            In such a wife, and greate estate

Crafty.   And such a son as I.[50]

Sir Courtly Nice (1685) places the whole Whig/Tory controversy within the family structure; Hothead and Testimony are used by Lord Belguard to keep his sister under lock and key, in the hope he will be doubly secured by the eye they keep on each other. The issue of the play is whether women should be governed by their male relations and it is answered in the sub-title – 'It cannot be'. The King himself gave Crowne the Spanish play he uses as a source; the play's advocacy of 'freedom' over control links it to the prevailing ethos of the court. Crowne may well have meant the obvious implication that the theme of 'government' stood in for the government of England; the play insinuates that Charles is using

the dissensions of his ministers to exercise tighter control himself.
But Belguard remains an obstinately opaque figure, in ways that
betray the source – 'When I talk of governing women' says Belguard,

> 'I talk of a thing not understood by our Nation. I admire how it
> came about, that we who are of all nations the most wise and
> free in other respects, shou'd be the only slaves and fools to
> Women.'[51]

But the 'nation' Belguard represents is Spain; he remains the stock
heavy brother of a drama where male supremacy was still an issue.
The relentless and quite inexplicable feud he carries on against his
sister's lover has too much of the hidalgo about it.

The witty Violante is in love with Belguard, and her taming of
this priggish male shrew would seem to be the impulse of the play.
That it gets lost in the welter of eccentricity stems partly from her
being the sort of character Crowne would never have created
unprompted. Her wit and decision make her as indigestible as
Belguard's rigorous feuding, and seem every bit as foreign to the
author. There is a limited kind of success in their scenes, notably
their quarrel at the beginning of Act IV.

Bel. I think I've given convincing Proofs of Love.

Vio. When?

Bel. When I offr'd Madam, to take you for better and for
worse; those are Heroical compliments. The form of Mat-
rimony outdoes Ovid for passionate expression.

Vio. Ay, my Lord, but that's none o' your wit, and I wou'd not
have a Man o' your parts, steal other Mens Phrases;[52]

Crowne is with Belguard here, and puts his stodgy affection over
well; as one can see from his other comedies, Violante's championship of 'wit' values is an empty gesture. The play makes a move
towards the freedom represented by the eccentric Crack, and the
'Indian' masque of the garden scene, but withdraws from the
conflicts this seems to represent. Belguard remains an unshattered
idol of patriarchal authority.

Crowne works hard to translate the play into the prevailing comic mode. Between the libertine-play *The Country Wit* and the satire *City Politicks* comedy changed direction, along the route indicated by Wycherley's *The Plain Dealer*. The characters no longer have a fixed place on a system of manners dictated by fashionable behaviour, they are aggressively self-directed in a society seen as ill-managed chaos. They nurture their own quirks and prejudices and collide with each other in a kind of psychological kamikaze. Everyone in *Sir Courtly Nice* is a plain dealer, reeling off their grudges in a way that ultimately says less of their targets than it does of themselves. The play's success lies in this heavy undergrowth of 'humour'; the most up-to-date aspects of the play – those benefitted by the interests which Otway brought to the form – declare it to be about men torn between desire and a pathological fear of women. Crack propels this into farce when he invents the mad woman-hater who invades Belguard's house. It lies also in the squeamishness, the 'niceness' of Sir Courtly, who won't use salt unless he knows who touched it, lest 'they take up the wenches' coats, then handle the salt'.[53] Two stock figures, the fop and the puritan are translated into aberrant psychology; Crowne sees Testimony as the product of unhealthy upbringing:

> . . . a conscience swadled so hard in its Infancy by strict Education, and now Thump'd and Cudgel'd so sore with daily Sermons and Lectures, that the weak ricketty thing can endure nothing.[54]

His talk of religion collapses unwittingly into sexual innuendo when he's faced by Leonora, and then collapses altogether.

> They would shew you the great – great sinfulness of sin, that sin is one of the sinfullest things in the whole World.[55]

Crowne explored the imaginative link between religion and a sickness that is also a social malaise in his next comedy, *The English Friar* (1690). With the two comedies previous to it it makes up an informal political trilogy, tracing through the medium of farce the events and attitudes behind the fall of the Stuarts. It is Crowne's strictest essay in the post-Jonsonian humour play, of the kind that develops each character as a variation on a moralized theme. All its aberrant characters have a single drive in common; a drive towards conformity. This type of play at its most sophisticated springs sameness as a surprise. It reveals opposites as parallels. The court characters, nibbling anxiously at the bait of a new vogue for catholicism, and the contrary pull exercised by the riotous Ranters, father and son, are all aspects of the same insecurity, to be exercised from at least his immediate circle by the arbiter, Lord Wiseman.

Passages of the play have a suggestive richness rare in the earlier comedies. But as a whole it is flawed by the simple shaping Crowne uses to get his satire into focus. Wiseman cannot in fact be so easily instated as arbiter, nor the friar as villain. Contemporary audiences complained that it had 'no plot';[56] its plot has in fact been pushed out of kilter by Crowne's desire to make unambiguous political points. In the dramatis personae Crowne characterizes Airy, the mischievous agent of the slander plot as 'A young, gay beauty privately debauch'd and kept by Lord Wiseman',[57] a compromising description of a relationship that generates the most interesting part of the play while remaining irreconcilable to the simplicities of this private debaucher's public role. It demands, and receives, a toughness content to raise questions that have no easy answers, the toughness of *The Way of the World*. Airy enters singing, an emanation of the easy theatricality of Restoration social styles. She is a kind of modish sprite, a little frayed by her life, and like Philidel in Dryden's *King Arthur*, whom the same actress, Mrs Butler, had played just previously, a half moral being, skimming through the play over unresolved possibilities of damnation. That Wiseman is at once the cause of her situation and her would-be rescuer, that he wants to abandon her for the equally light-headed but more easily rescuable Laura, that he manages his life with a bland gravity that in no way precludes real affection in his passion for opposites; all these things show Crowne at his most typically complex, and all contradict the easy assumptions of the 'humour' scheme however much more sophisticated his basic approach is than, say, Shadwell's. In even the play's crudest scene, the unmasking of the lecherous friar, Finical is given a long speech of self-justification;

'Tis certainly most lawful to circumvent a dangerous enemy by all frauds, it has ever been a holy stratagem o'priests to pretend to more power over the flesh, than perhaps mortal man can attain in this life; thereby religiously to deceive the world into a bold contest with a seeming baffl'd foe . . . . to keep our selves in veneration (we) carry saint-like chastity or at least the image of it before us. And though, like the bearers of my Lord Mayor's pageant, we may have many a secret foul step, we must keep our pageant pure, for that is seen, we are hid.[58]

It is not merely Finical's sincerity that makes this rationale more than farcical. It is a point of contact not only with Crowne's concerns, as we have seen them from *Calisto* on, but with Lord Wiseman's.

Crowne can be seen as inventing a reforming comedy some years before Cibber; the play is no more successful than his, but the failure is of a much more honourable kind. Crowne's other comedies work better as wholes precisely because of their incomplete presentation of the issues. Crowne is able to work through a suggestiveness that sits better on the available comic forms than does a fully complex discussion. The voice we hear in his dedications and forewards has a moral passion in it that might be intuited behind the plays, but which they rarely express. He launches the *English Friar* with a devastating attack on life under the Stuarts –

It has been our misfortune to live in a vicious, degenerate age, where men were thought great Wits, that had no more wit than what wou'd serve vicious pleasures . . . virtue has been so strange amongst us, vice has past for virtue. . . . They practis'd upon us the arts of the Virtuoso; they emptied our veins of the Englishman, and transfus'd a sheepish nature into us, which disposed us to slaughter; and when they had done this, they thought they completed us . . .[59]

This bitter moral energy is finally to be harnessed by his last and greatest comedy, *The Married Beau*.[60]

5 Thomas Otway

The crises that exiled Etherege had divorced the comedy he established from its social basis. The professional dramatists took over a
form with which the court wits no longer concerned themselves.
The social ethos to which it had given expression was not of
immediate interest to a town taken up by the factional politics of
the Exclusion crisis. The Whigs attempt to exclude James, Charles'
catholic brother, from accession to the throne, brought into direct
question the always equivocal nature of the monarch's relationship
to his parliament, a relationship to be suspended by Charles'
decision to rule without parliament, but then restored after his
death by James' expulsion and the constitutional settlement with
William and Mary. The mood of the interim period could scarcely
be contained by the ironies of modish comedy. The contradictory
position of the professional writers allows them access to a darker
more disabused view of events.

Of these Thomas Otway was the most uncompromising. He
extends the range of post-Etheregean prose dialogue, going beyond surface wit into the play of allusive conversation and apparently casual ironies that articulates wit comedy's fascination with
the unsaid. Otway's characters use language to hide their reality
from themselves as well as from each other. His plays are informed
by a distrust of open statement, a sense that the reality of character
and situation reveals itself gradually, that the characters themselves come upon it unawares, that it is this revelation which
marks the play's culminating force. The superiority of *Friendship in
Fashion* (1678) to *The Orphan* (1680), a much more celebrated work
for at least a hundred years after its first performance, is the
context of social behaviour given by Otway's burrowing into the
Etheregean genre. One might quote the remark of an actress
celebrated in the role of the 'orphan', Monimia, Elizabeth Inchbald, writing some time after the play had lost its popularity.

> It is uncivil to say to a whole Dramatic Personae, that 'they are all guilty of speaking falsehood'; and yet, excepting old Acasto, and his young daughter Serina, this may be said to every personage in the tragedy.[1]

and, one might add, in the comedy too. *The Orphan* is best seen in the light of Goodvile's ''ook to her, keep her as secret as thou would'st a Murder, had'st thou committed one';[2] as a whodunnit. The plot has a kind of non-serious tension that overrides identification with the character, and thus, in taking us past the red-herring of Chamount's incestuous fixation on Monimia to the truth of Castalio's on Polydore, it states many of Otway's main concerns without having to justify them. Like a thriller (which it is) it exhibits a control that is really a failure of sympathy. The richness of *Friendship in Fashion* lies in the tension between the characters and plot structure of wit comedy, seen as social roles and social game-playing, and the strong underlying sense of the emotional seriousness of relationship. It is perhaps neurotically strong; in his tragedies Otway exploits neurosis, with great skill, in the comedies he contains it. If one hesitates to call *Friendship in Fashion* a greater play than *Venice Preserved* (1682) – a play with the force of hysteria as well as its extravagance – it is because the comedy can seem over-wrought, too dense in detail, too elliptical in its expressions of feeling. This may be just a way of saying that it is harder to read. But the relationship between the continuously exciting surface and the cumulative neurotic plot rhythm of *Venice Preserved* has a kind of lucidity unique in Otway's work, and its continuous stage history is deserved as well as understandable. One has to bear in mind with *Friendship in Fashion* the nature of the genre he is working in, and thus the kind of reaction he shows against it, before the play opens itself out for inspection.

Otway's three comedies can all be characterized as reactions against the conventions of Etheregean comedy, implanting within the form the nodes of a criticism of it far more radical than Shadwell's. Of the characters in *Friendship in Fashion* it is Lady Squeamish and her attendant fools who represent the world of modish comedy – 'I am asham'd' she announces at the end of Act I, 'that anyone should pretend to write a Comedy, that does not know the nicer rules of the Court, and all the Intrigues and Gallantries that pass . . .'.[3] Caper's dancing and Saunter's snatches of pastoral song, including 'When Phyllis watcht her harmless sheep' from Etherege's *Comical Revenge*[4] evoke a kind of comedy very much of the Mall. They sum up the familiar ethos of the fashionable world, its attempt to transform itself to pastoral ease and dignity.

Friendship in Fashion opens on the Mall. Its extravagant use of pastoral style plotting aligns it to the comedies of mode. All the various strands of the play interweave in the 'Night-garden' scene[5] culminating in two interrupted trysts, in two of the familiar pastoral frame-ups. But Otway subtly differentiates them. When Lady Squeamish confronts Goodvile, she serves to defuse his attempt at intrigue. Squeamish exists on a permanent self-induced high. She is incapable of retaining any emotion but pleasure, and for Otway this is the most severe delinquency, as his characters experience all serious emotions cumulatively. Trivialized by her participation, his plot collapses and tips us into the darker waters of counterplot that encircle his wife. When he crazily mistakes Mrs Goodvile for his mistress he gives her the advantage in a fiercer emotional combat than merely fashionable comedy could even touch on. The play invents a plot rhythm of inexorable entrapment that was to characterize all Otway's subsequent work. Goodvile takes his marriage lightly – 'he is only confined by it that will be so'[6] – and sees friendship as a social convenience overridden by pleasure.

'A Friend is a thing I love to eat and drink and laugh withall; nay more, I would on good occasion lose my life for my Friend; but not my pleasure.'[7]

But by the end we see him committed to both, indeed defined by them as a social being, and Goodvile is above all else a social being. Only Lady Squeamish is exempt from Otway's primary concept of relationship in action; that, once entered into it redefines personality and is thus in a real sense irrevocable. The move from the Mall to the night-garden is a shift into privacy as decisive for Otway and his successors as it is for the characters in the play.

Goodvile takes upon himself the social organization of the piece, the last four acts of which take place at his house. The toasts drunk in act II are a formal recognition of scope.

'My Dear, you and I are to be no Man and Wife for this day, but to be as indifferent, and take as little notice of one another, as we may chance to do seven years hence; but at Night – '[8]

But Mrs Goodvile's approach to Truman has already placed this in an ironic light, and it is he who answers Goodvile's 'each man to his post the word' with 'Love and Wine'. The military metaphor continues to overhang the action; battle has been declared. The song they listen to as they drink provides a further context;

> Each day we grow older . . .
> The joys of Love with our Youth slide away . . .[9]

It is a play about settling down. 'This is the first year of our Marriage!'[10] Mrs Goodvile exclaims in the middle of her marvellous tirade in act IV. Her husband has avoided the reality of marriage for that year – at the end of the play a more stable basis of marital power is established.

Goodvile's house is an escape from the decorum of the mode, as the easy hospitable drinking of the early scenes shows in the light of Lady Squeamish's disapproval. It is a behind-the-scenes view of the gallant's life. But as the party disintegrates and Truman and Valentine become aware of their host's design – to marry Truman to his mistress, and replace her with Valentine's betrothed – it becomes an arena of those intensely personal emotions whose evocation in Restoration comedy was Otway's great and vastly influential achievement. Malagene's activities spell out the deceptions of fashionable friendship, and his mime is brilliantly cryptic comment on other characters' role-playing –

> 'I can act *Punchinello*, *Scaramuchio*, *Harlequin*, Prince *Prettyman*, or anything. I can act the rumbling of a Wheelbarrow . . . I can act a Fly in a Honeypot . . .'[11]

> 'This Consort of Fools' Mrs Goodvile realizes 'shall be the Chorus to my Farce.'[12]

In Goodvile's name there seems to be a suggestion of moral ambiguity quite unsupported by redeeming personal characteristics. Perhaps it really speaks of social complacency. Vile (Ville) suggests urbanity, and Good a debasement of the word in a society that invest too much in social ease and day-to-day enjoyments. Otway appears to be saying that this amoral and unserious way of life incurs deception as its desert, as it leaves no defense against it. As the play proceeds further into drunkenness, disorder and night (all literal as well as metaphoric) Goodvile is the more deeply entrapped by the urge to outplot his friends and rivals. He becomes a fly in the honeypot of his own lush privacy.

The turning-point of the play is set in his garden. Like so many such scenes it turns against the garden's owner. Mrs Goodvile rushes away from her assignation with Truman, only to be taken by her husband for his mistress, Victoria. The intrigue has slipped from everyone's grasp; it has acquired a treacherous life of its own.

Unlike the Lady Squeamish/Camilla/Goodvile imbroglio I mentioned earlier, this second plot-node evokes a complex and serious response. In effect we can see the incident from two opposing viewpoints; Truman's (sympathetic because wronged) and Goodvile's, sympathetic because powerful, both personally and structurally (all the more so as his power is on the point of collapse). Truman's glee at this turn of events has a streak of meanness in it that abruptly balances out the awfulness of his adversary. He is positively excited, even aroused by Mrs Goodvile's discomfiture of her husband – 'Delicate Dissimulation! How I do love her'. In the terms of the gallant comedy that appeals to Lady Squeamish, his 'I never really Lov'd or Liv'd till now'[13] might be the outcome of a Shakespearean love-test; in the terms of Otway's own psychological astringency it stands as an alarming insight into the petty cruelties of sexuality (of the kind literature conventionally ascribes to perverts and women).

Goodvile, unmasked, pretends to retire to the country. Even if the Goodviles had not treated the convention so mockingly in their cruelly parodic parting, it has become apparent that the townhouse and garden have a claustrophobically intense presence that cancels out the familiar evocation of country realities. Now the balance of wit comedy has been irrevocably disturbed. Goodvile cannot but return to town.

One can I think accept the truth of the letter he produces against his wife. It is typical of Otway's style to create an emphasis with this sort of weak ending; a speech with a resonant close is bound to be a delusive exercise in high style. Mrs Goodvile is a mistress of this. Like Camilla she is in control of all her masks (Otway's women are judged on how they use their capabilities of deceit).

'If *Goodvil* goes out of Town this morning, let me know of it that I may wait on you and tell you the rest of my Heart, for you do not know how much I love you yet, *Truman*.'[14]

It is a matter of rhythm – the final 'yet' seems to me to clinch it, not only as an important projection into Truman's future as her 'cavalier servente', but as a dying fall. Her reaction seems to protest too much in its familiar sabre-rattling rhetorical rhythms –

> 'Death and Destruction: it was all my own Contrivance, madded with your jealousy, I sought all ways to vex you.'[15]

She counters with Victoria's letter; her initial plan to find allies has succeeded better than she expected. And yet one cannot speak of the marriage breaking down. When she exits on

> '. . . oh that I could dissemble longer with you, that I might to your Torment perswade you still all your Jealousies were just, and I as Infamous as you are cruel.'[16]

we meet the same stylistic problem. Otway's characters go to pieces (and there is a similar tendency in his plays) into noise and movement and fragments of high style. The most painful moment of Goodvile's collapse is when he yells to Caper, '. . . dance and divert me; Dance sirrah, do you hear?'[17] Mrs Goodvile gathers similar chaos around her for the last act, when she has at last gained control of the house.

> 'Now, once more let me invoke all the Arts of affectation, all the Revenge, the counterfeit Passions, pretended Love, pretended Jealousie, pretended Rage, and in sum the very Genius of my Sex to my assistance.'[18]

These parodistic invocations are a measure of Mrs Goodvile's absorption in her battle with her husband; there is something monomaniacal about her hysterically fomented disorder. It is impossible to see her going off with Truman as blithely as a Mrs Easy does with a Lovechange;[19] indeed she has no name of her own; what we see in the last scene is a marriage cemented. Mrs Goodvile burns herself out; away from Goodvile she would have no more substance than Lady Squeamish. Goodvile's response has real pain in it, and it is here that the truth of the relationship would seem to lie –

> 'Get thee in then and talk to me no more, there's something in thy Face will make a Fool of me . . . *Truman*, if thou has enjoyed

her, I beg thee keep it close, and if it be possible let us yet be friends.'[20]

The picking up of pieces, the putting back on of masks is ironically his mistress Victoria's doing. Mistaken identity carries over into verbal irony. When she asks Goodvile, apparently of his wife

'But do you believe Sir that you can utterly abandon all sense of your past Love and Tenderness for a Woman who has been so Dear to you? . . .'

and he replies, '"I will sooner return to my Vomit"',[21] she surely refers to herself, though Goodvile misses the implication. On the strength of this she starts to reconstruct a basis of reality, ironically aware of the roles she is adopting –

'I'le . . . like a true Mrs betray his Counsels to her, That she like a true Wife may spight of his Teeth deceive him quite, And so I have the pleasure of seeing him a seal'd stigmatiz'd fond believing Cuckold: 'Twill at least be some ease to me.'[22]

When at the very end of the play Goodvile turns to Truman and Valentine again, he is reaching out for a social reality; the reduction of friendship to mere social convenience is a kind of reaffirmation of it. However battered and abused it may be, it is the essential mask Goodvile needs to face the world. Though Truman and Valentine remain politely obdurate, one can see in the rather appalling hypocrisy of Goodvile's remarks to the newly married couple that he is just managing to right himself –

'*Valentine!* look to her, keep her as secret as thou woud'st a murder, had'st thou committed one: trust her not with thy dearest Friend. She has Beauty enough to corrupt him . . . .'[23]

In a way, this is a relief. The play's journey into the dark of the Night-garden has been a disturbing one, and even compromised daylight is welcome.

Friendship in Fashion is, above all, a masterpiece of plotting. It is conceived as an intricate web of roles in relationship, spun out of the conventions of 'modish' comedy with a breathtaking finesse. *The Soldier's Fortune,* (1680) Otway's next comedy, breaks the bounds of wit comedy altogether. It is dedicated, not to a court personage, but to his printer, a gesture similar to Wycherley's dedication of *The Plain Dealer* to the bawd Lady B., if characteristically drier in wit. With this play Otway completes *The Plain Dealer's* reorientation of Restoration comedy from public image to private need.

The title is a pun, in that while the play describes the soldiers' fortune (their lot), it follows their search for money, marketing the only available commodity, themselves. The pun attacks the whole basis of the comedy of coping with life, in which 'fortune' provides; Otway cynically observes this to be a euphemism for money. In *The Atheist* the characters are able to indulge us in the legitimate pleasure of watching the comfortably-off enjoying their comforts – part of the attractiveness of this kind of play after all – Beaugard is able to say 'this comes by the Dominion Chance has over us',[24] as his uncle's legacy has secured him from seeing 'chance' as 'fortune', as a provider of necessities. *The Soldier's Fortune* is a view of wit comedy from below. It exploits the madness of a prevalent kind of farce, while systematically destroying its ability to comfort and reassure, it uses high style as a kind of understatement, an understatement of real dangers and real nastiness. Otway uses an escapist form to point out that for some there is no escape. The play's force is basically satirical; it says that life is not as comedy conventionally describes it.

Like *Friendship in Fashion*, the play opens on the Mall, the setting for the first two acts. Otway populates it with satirical grotesques, Jumble's whores, and bullies. Sir Jolly is the master of ceremonies, not only of the play's intrigues, but of the mythology of the Mall; Beaugard and Courtine greet him antiphonally at the start of Act II –

Court: Sir Jolly is the glory of the Age . . .
Beau : He's the delight of the young, and wonder of the old . .
Court: He deserves a statue in Gold, at the charge of the Kingdom.[25]

The public service Sir Jolly performs is a reduction to scurrility of the service provided by the institution of the parks. He is an equivalent monument to London under the Restoration. The animal imagery he invokes, and grotesquely embodies on his first entrance – he 'squeaks like a Cat, and tickles Beaugard's Legs'[26] – is similarly reductive, and his drooling voyeurism is monstrously funny in its pre-empting of the audience's own role. When Beaugard (selling himself) meets Lady Dunce (or Clarinda – unlike Mrs Goodvile, she has a Christian name) who has been 'sold' in marriage, the situation has pain in it that Sir Jumble's presence distances from poignancy –

> Lady D: Methinks this Face should not so much be alter'd, as
> to be nothing like what once I thought it, the object of
> your Pleasure and subject of your Praises . . .
> Sir Jolly: . . . oh law! there's Eyes! there's your Eyes! I must
> pinch him by the Calf of the Legg.[27]

Clarinda's position is a monstrous one, revealed in her uneasy flippancy with Sylvia, (one of Otway's expositions by concealment). She pretends to find Sir Davy of use, and to make as light as possible of the marriage –

> 'My Parents indeed made me say something to him after a Priest
> once, but my heart went not along with my tongue, I minded
> not what it was . . .'.[28]

and yet her frustrated thoughts of Beaugard erupt in a horrific apprehension of what it is like 'to lye by the Image of Death a whole night'.[29] Another source of her disgust is touched on lightly by Lady Dunce; his

> 'other divertissments that take him off from my injoyment; which
> make him so loathsome no Woman but must hate him . . . '

'His private divertissments', Sylvia answers, with the echoing of delicate query 'I am a stranger to',[30] but Lady Dunce energetically changes the subject. Her hints and feints speak of real frustration, that becomes explosively overt when she addresses him in Act III as 'Sir Sodom',[31] and when he tries to steer her to bed later that night with 'you are a Boy, a very Boy, and I love you the better for't'.[32] Otway attempts to bring a real sense of physical defilement to the loveless marriage; it is the darkest Restoration comedy ever becomes.

Otway scarcely requires a teasing out of undercurrents; at points of crisis or excitement his characters reveal their private hang-ups with an awful unconsciousness. Lady Dunce's revenge on her husband is cruelly apt. His delivery of the letters pushes him even further into the trap of his own obsessions. Sir Davy is the funniest of deluded cuckolds because the most cruelly observed – the humour is in the psychic chaos of a progressively more disordered mind; '"Sirrah you are a whore . . ."' he raves at Courtine,

> 'an errant Bitch-Whore, I'll use you like a Whore, I'll kiss you, you Jade, I'll Ravish you, you Buttuck, I am a Justice of the Peace, Sirrah, and that's worse.'[33]

It is a measure of the hardness of the play that we can feel this justified by his treatment of Clarinda. There is a political point in this – Sir Davy's citation of law, and hints of Whig affiliation identify him as a typical citizen-butt of the early eighties; this seems to me to be a stalking horse for Otway's psychological interests, but it does balance Sir Jolly as a representative of Court, or at least 'Mall' values – his often stated opposition to marriage, for example. They are the two poles of the play, active and passive; as in *Friendship in Fashion* we see the progress of the play as the cumulative discomfiture of one man. It is important to Otway as a political point to show Sir Davy capable of murder (which he does, I think, plausibly), if only to justify Royalist paranoias. It is here that the tragic parody comes into its own. There is no really adequate language for the irrational fears and gratuitous cruelty below the surface of comically mundane lives; parody that exists only for the length of single speeches or actions is parody that never becomes comfortably predictable. The high style appeals to the part of the mind that says 'this isn't happening' and so isolates the kind of horror one cannot take seriously. Parallel with this in the last act is the physicality insisted on by farce. Beaugard's progress from table to bed to bathroom reduces him to a bulky object. It re-enacts Clarinda's earlier image of Sir Davy's mortality – her marriage has killed love; she attempts to bring Beaugard's back to life. He is an obstacle in the house that entraps her. Their scene in bed is a brief awakening, and there is a poignancy in the glibness of her

> ' – how could you think of wasting but a night in the rank surfeiting arms of this foul feeding Monster? this rotten trunck of a Man, that lays claim to you?'

'The perswasion of Friends and the Authority of Parents.'[34] It has a shrugging, wearied tone, perhaps a formula she has often repeated, or had repeated to her. The moment is brief, and shattered by Jolly's disturbing reminder of his and our voyeurism –

'So, so, who says I see anything now? I see nothing not I, I don't see, I don't see, I don't look, not so much as look not I.'[35]

Their liaison acquires its tinge of romanticism only by a kind of negative association, and then in the shadow of mortality –' . . . A Pox of *Anthony* and *Cleopatra*, they are dead and rotten long ago; come, come, time's but short, time's but short . . .'.[36]

Silvia's trick on Courtine has a similar connotation, in turning him into a 'stragling Monkey hung by the Loins'.[37] She belongs with a familiar kind of English comic heroine, who 'never say one of your Sex in my life make love, but he lookt so like an Ass all the while that I blusht for him'.[38] 'Enchantment' runs as a theme through their relationship, as an image of irrational compulsion. They play with the idea disingenuously. We know that Courtine wants her money and that she accepts the bargain as an avoidance of a sexual or even personal relationship. In the contract scene (Vi) Courtine uses pastoral imagery in a sexual sense –

' . . . I had rather my Ox should graze in a field of my own, than live hide-bound upon the common, or run the hazzard of being Pounded every day for trespasses'.

It is she reacting against the bull image, who chooses to offer herself coldly as a property –

' . . .' tis a great pity so good a husband-man as you should want a farm to cultivate'.[39]

The Atheist (1683) continues the story of this couple. We need to see how the railing self-appointed 'plaindealer' Courtine will react to the prosperity his marriage buys, and how the sexually unaware Sylvia responds to the complex situations of a marriage that is at the same time her first sexual experience and in itself a non-sexual bond. We need to see Beaugard's good humour operating without financial trammels. But the style of the second half of *The Soldier's*

Fortune differs radically from that of the first. The play is a discussion of libertine themes in the Shadwell/Betterton mould, a semi-operatic extravaganza. It is an alternative view of the same subject – an alternative attack, that is, on the conventions of wit comedy.

The eponymous Daredevil is a survivor of Rochester's world of Lucretian hedonism:

> Methinks the Image of it is like a Laune
> In a rich flowr'y Vale, its Measure long,
> Beauteous its Prospect, and at the End
> A Shady peaceful Glade; where when the pleasant Race is over,
> We glide away, and are at rest forever.[40]

It is from this that the witty widow Porcia plans to trick Daredevil (philosophically) and Beaugard (sexually, by admitting he is faithful to one woman). And yet the glamorous phenomena of Porcia's house could scarcely be said to disprove Atheism. She can merely tease her victim, who plays at Rochester no more convincingly than Old Beaugard plays Bishop Burnet. He is, as we know from the beginning, a faux-atheist. He serves to expose some anomalies in the Christians' outlook, but slips quite happily in and out of his disguise in the final scene of his 'unmasking'. He takes neither belief nor unbelief quite seriously; even when he thinks he's dying he can enjoy an absurdity of style –

> Beau: Are you really . . . the Godly Implement you appear to be, for the scowring of foul Conscienses?
> Dare: Ha! Ha! Ha! Godly Implement! It has almost made me laugh . . .[41]

Perhaps he would have died a philosopher's death after all.

The real trouble with the play is less the widow's house of illusions – implausible, admittedly, but not irredeemable by showy staging – than the insubstantiality of Porcia herself. We do not see her unmasked until Act IV, and unmasked she is denatured. She is the apogee of all Otway's women of disguise, perhaps to be identified with the 'Queen of Fancy'[42] in the *Epistle to R.D.* or the Muse in *The Complaint*. She is also, of course, Elizabeth Barry, famous for the deceits of her private life as well as for her skill as an actress (indeed as *the* actress, after she played Monimia), whom Otway loved with a self-destructive hopelessness. The problem becomes insoluble even, one suspects, by strong production, when Otway tries to compensate for Porcia's essentially chimerical nature with the Theodoret/Gratian imbroglio, as an attempt to define her by relationship. She remains most vigorous as a tone of voice, especially in her alliance with Sylvia. When Courtine first meets her, he calls her 'A Widow . . . downright Bawdy Widow'; 'What would your Cream-pot in the Country give for that title, think you?'[43] she retorts.

Even in the middle of a collapsing Spanish/Operatic sub-plot Sylvia remains very much herself. Her attack on Theodoret is a neat, and for her, typical, blow at his virility, with the vinegary over-emphasis of her defensive outspokenness –

'If any thing in the World would make me follow a Camp, it would be a very strong fancy I have that I should never see you in one, Sir'[44]

This tone of voice is a welcome reminder of the sensitivity of Otway's style to any fully imagined character. I suspect Sylvia's assignation with a boy who turns out to be the mischievous Lucrece is the sketch of a long delayed sexual awakening, ironically by another woman. Lucrece's drag scene may mock the social role-playing of the male characters, but, again, out of disguise she has no reality; there is no linking motivation for what she does. In Otway's last, perhaps strictly unfinished, play, the women's flair for deceit has subsumed their whole being. Only Sylvia remains herself. Her final breakdown is genuinely disturbing

'I'll bear't no longer; *Bedlam! Bedlam! Bedlam!* (Courtine *sings and dances a jig)*'[45]

Otway turns to theme of the indissolubility of relationship, for the last time. Like Mrs Goodvile, she exits in a rage, like Goodvile Courtine sees that this strengthens rather than breaks the bond. It is Beaugard who can say, contentedly,' " I am beginning to settle my Family" '.[46]

Otway's early death concentrated his achievement. Had he written as much as Shadwell, Crowne or Behn, the circumstances of a professional dramatist's career may have compromised an intensely personal voice. As it is the two major comedies can be seen to have influenced every dramatist that came after simply by demonstrating just how much Restoration comedy could do. Otway intervenes in the careers of the other dramatists in this book; he discovers a potential of emotional seriousness that lays a foundation for the comedy of the nineties. That seriousness flows back from his plays into contemporary attempts to explain the mystery of his death. The gruesomely ironic tale so disliked by Johnson, of the starving author choked by the first crust in days,[47] is matched by a tale of heroic friendship, a cold caught in a rescue attempt. The romantic friendship of Pierre and Jaffeir (in *Venice Preserv'd*) was to remain a point of reference for European culture up to the nineteenth century. A modern rediscovery of a great playwright is more likely to start at his harsher comic perspective on the same ideas. The plays have an emotional power to justify attempts to relocate their mood in the author's life and death; and whatever the immediate cause, his premature death in poverty is as sure a sign as the misfortunes of Shadwell, Crowne and Lee that the Restoration theatre did not do well by its best writers.

6 Aphra Behn

Drama is a matter of seeing and being seen. Like painting, theatre posits a subject viewer and an object seen. Like painting, it gives the artist the power to organize his perceptions into 'sights' and to impose them on the second viewer, the audience. It is this power which our culture traditionally reserves for men. Our drama contains few enough roles that could be called female equivalents to Hamlet or Lear; but it is as hard to cite a female Prospero, a theatrical image of woman as artist, as it is to find representations of a female God.

The Restoration theatre, newly feminized by the employment of actresses, produced at least two notable women dramatists, Aphra Behn and, later, Susanna Centlivre, and a great many more who wrote one or two plays usually tragedies, often based on translations from the French. The subsequent rarity of women playwrights is not, I think, to be explained simply in terms of purely external social constraints. Mock scientific explanations on the other hand are nicely parodied by the Duchess of Newcastle, herself a playwright –

> . . . it has seemed hitherto [i.e. in women *not* writing] as if Nature had Compounded Men's Brains with more of the Sharp Atomes, which make the Hot and Dry Element, and Women's with more of the Round Atomes, which Figure makes the Cold and Moist Element.[1]

Those social constraints perhaps operate most decisively not on access to drama, but on definitions of what drama *is*, what its proper language is, what its conventions of representation are, and thus what is allowed as the presentation of sexual difference and social relations. Restoration women dramatists can be seen to attempt to *redefine* this language.

The Duchess of Newcastle wrote copiously in all available forms, and though her plays were never performed, they were, like the rest of her work, handsomely printed, and contributed to her general reputation of eccentricity. The Newcastles had a close marriage, an amicable liaison of oddities which, like that of the Fanshawes or the Temples reminds one of the most attractive of the fashions that Charles I and Henrietta Maria set their court. But Margaret's writings did not follow her husband's lead stylistically; she could not be called a daughter of Ben, as her radical variation on the *Magnetick Lady* theme will illustrate.

In *The Convent of Pleasures* (in *Plays Never before Printed*, 1668) the recently widowed Lady Happy attracts the usual crew of potential suitors, but at the end of Act I turns the formula round; she has decided to use her money to endow a retreat for women, like a convent or a women's college, but fun.

> Women, where Fortune, Nature, and the gods are joined to make them happy, were mad to live with Men, who make the Female sex their slaves. . . . My cloister shall not be a Cloister of restraint but a place for freedom, not to vex the Senses but to please them.[2]

She elaborates the fantasy in innocently sybaritic terms in a two–page speech in IIii. The play then takes place within the 'convent', its stasis broken by two inset sections. The second, which resolves the play, is a pastoral dream sequence, the first is a feminist drama put on by the ladies for a visiting Princess. Its recital of the wrongs of women is terse enough to allow me to quote several scenes.

> II Enter Two mean Women
> 1: I will go, and pull my Husband out of the Ale-house, or I'le break their Lattice-windows down.
> 2: Come I'le go and help; for my Husband is there too; but we shall be both beaten by them.
> 1: I care not; for I will not suffer him to be drunk and I and my Children starve; I had better be dead.
> III Enter a Lady and her maid.
> Lady: Oh I am sick!
> Maid: You are breeding a Child, Madam.
> Lady: I have not one minutes time of health.
> IV Enter Two Ladies
> 1: Why weep you, Madam?

2: Have I not cause to weep when my Husband hath play'd all his Estate away at Dice and Cards, even to the Clothes on his back?[3]

In scene V, the Lady's child is born dead. The only man in the play turns up in the last scene and asks a lady to marry him. She refuses. The epilogue points a clear moral:

Marriage is a Curse we find,
Especially to Women kind;
From the Cobler's Wife we see.
To Ladies, they unhappie be.[4]

The princess has reservations about the play. Happy falls in love with her, and dreams a long pastoral sequence in which they appear as shepherd and shepherdess. This dissolves into the discovery that the princess is of course a prince in disguise, and Happy marries him.

The epilogue to the play as a whole presents it not only as a chamber drama, but as a solitary fancy, a world of tiny figures existing around the author's candlelight and pen.

Noble Spectators by this Candle-light,
I know not what to say, but bid, good Night;
I dare not beg Applause, our Poetes then
Will be enrag'd, and kill me with her Pen;
For she is careless, and void of fear;
If you dislike her Play, she doth not care.[5]

The tendency to diminution is common not only to her early fairy poems – admired in a vivid if rather condescending essay by Virginia Woolf[6] – but to other experiments in dramatic form. In *Phantasms Masque*:

The Scene is Poetry
The Stage is the Brain whereon it's Acted.
First is Presented a Dumb Shew, as a Young Lady in a Ship swimming over the Scene in Various Weather.[7]

Her girlishness, her apologies – the 1662 volume of plays is prefaced by ten apologetic epistles each anxious about a different deviance from poetic rules, ending with an apology for apologies – irritate in a way that would justify the tone of Woolf's essay as a nervous reaction to the idea of the woman writer as freak. But the crude integrity and unembarrassed humour of her work rejects easy solutions to the problems of a woman writing plays. Her poetry dramatizes the search for a specifically female diction, as in the series exclusively written through kitchen metaphor.[8] Her other plays are not as interesting as *The Convent of Pleasure*, but in its deliberate dislocation of conventional form, its use of pastoral and fantasy elements, and, above all in its realization that a playwright determined to discuss female experience must radically overhaul conventional theater language, that play makes a useful introduction to the stylistic concerns of the much more accomplished professional writer, Aphra Behn.

For Behn the pastoral is a retreat to permitted pleasures, a golden age after Tasso's model rather than Guarini's.[9] Tasso's is the more exotic; unlike Guarini he presents a self-contained world patently not this. It is in such a world that the Lady Happy finds a fulfilment ruled out by the argument of the surrounding play. Pastoral in its more static forms comes to be internalized as an aspect of the consciousness of female characters. Lady Happy (and what better name for the vehicle of this kind of pastoral?) antedates the darker use of this convention by Rochester, Lee and Wycherley;[10] she has more in common perhaps with its eighteenth century addicts, the girls in Steele's plays,[11] or the ineffably girlish Lady Wishfort. Pastoral is almost always 'feminine'; the simple marking out of territories performed most diagrammatically in *The Way of the World* is interestingly subverted in Behn's case by her use of extravagantly mixed, exotic forms.

Behn's plays are only part of an output whose distinctness of voice and personal definition of concerns is matched to an experimental profusion of literary genres. Pastoral, wit, and intrigue inform plays, poems and novels alike. They provide the medium of an exploration of social and sexual identity. She is often engaged in an ironic exploitation of the conventions of the genre she adopts, a shrewd subversion of its implied valuations. This externality of approach seems to me to leave the poems a little below the best of the novels and plays in quality, fascinating as they are as a woman poet's analytical reconstructions of the Rochesterian mode. Two brilliant late short novels, *Oronooko* (1688) and *The History of the Nun* (1696), and a cycle of comedies represent a vast uneven oeuvre at its best.

Women are relatively autonomous in the intrigue play. They have at least an equal, perhaps a superior, ability to determine plot. This is in itself a legacy from the courtly pastoral tradition. Shepherdesses, after all, do much the same work as shepherds, and lead a life no more defined by domesticity. This gives the courtly shepherdess an equality of emphasis which the mock pastoral forms exploit more boldly. Both pastoral and intrigue allow Behn to question conventional literary representations of sexual relationship and identity. Formal experiment is at the basis of this, as an analysis of her most famous lyric will demonstrate –

Love in Fantastique Triumph satt,
Whilst Bleeding Hearts a round him flow'd,
For whom Fresh paines he did Create,
And strange Tyranick power he show'd;
From thy Bright Eyes he took his fire,
Which round about, in sport he hurl'd;
But 'twas from mine he took desire,
Enough to undo the Amorous World.

From me he took his sighs and tears,
From thee his Pride and Crueltie;
From me his Languishments and Feares,
And every Killing Dart from thee;
Thus thou and I, the God have arm'd,
And sett him up a Deity;
But my poor Heart alone is harm'd,
Whilst thine the Victor is, and free.[12]

In many of the poems the gender of the speaker is ambiguous. This may be the result of social constraints commercially reinforced, but it is articulated by the best poems into a restatement of the dramatic identities internal to neo-Petrarchan conventions and the narrative they imply. According to these conventions 'Bright Eyes' would be female, 'desire' male. 'Sighs', 'tears', 'Languishments and Feares' continue a male identification of the speaker, but the last two lines suddenly reverse it. 'My poor heart' is conventionally feminine, in presenting itself as vulnerable – 'harm'd' is the diction more of domestic pathos than heroic combat. 'Victor' is masculine, in simple grammatical terms, and 'free' enlarges the suggestion of a libertine sphere of action, unavailable of course to a Petrarchan mistress. Read back the poem can be seen to reattribute the identifications implied by its conventional diction. 'Fire' 'sport' 'hurl'd' and 'Killing Dart' suggest a 'heroic' male sexual object, desired by a female speaker unable to see her passion as anything but aggressively negative, liable to 'undo the Amorous World'. The poem undoes the amorous world's security of sexual role-play. Its ultimately irresolvable identifications reorder the poem around an oppressive male principle. Love, tyrannically, unquestionably male, is armed with the spoils of a fractured and inadequate sexuality.

Behn's flexibility within an essentially concrete but never statically pictorial theatre-language builds similarly on the conventions of Restoration drama. In her tragi-comedy *The Young King* (1679), for example, Cleomena and Semiris make a discovery while out hunting, and Behn's presentation of the incident marks a stylistic discovery of her own.

> Semiris looks about, finds the Cap and Feathers
> Sem: See, Madam, what I've found
> Cleo: 'Tis a fine Plume, and well adorn'd,
> And must belong to no uncommon Man;
> – And look, Semiris, where its Owner lies –
> – Ha! he sleeps, tread softly lest you wake him;
> – Oh Gods! who's this with so divine a Shape?
> Sem: His Shape is very well.
> Cleo: Gently remove the Hair from off his Face
> Semiris puts back his hair.
> And see if that will answer to the rest . . . .

The idea of sex-reversal is pointed up by Cleomena's Amazonian dress.[13] But that is less interesting than what the scene does formally. The male character is object, the female subject; in other words, it is she who presents, defines and evaluates him. The contrast with other Restoration drama is obvious. Behn tends to replace the male group, as the starting point and expository mechanism of the play, with a group of women who perform the same function.[14] Characters who 'see' and 'present' are hinges of the play's relationship to its audience. To systematically use female characters in this way is to feminize quite radically the conventional language of drama.

Later in the century Susanna Centlivre pursues the same stylistic means to a different end. For Centlivre it is a moral process, not, as for Behn, an erotic one. In one of her best plays, *The Gamester* (1705), the hero Valere is described before we see him by the heroine's maid. 'He handsome!' she says to his Valet 'Behold his Picture just as he'll appear this Morning, with Arms across, downcast Eyes, no powder in his Perriwig a Steinkirk tuck'd in to hide the Dirt, Sword-knot untied, no Gloves, and Hands and Face as dirty as a Tinker. This is the very Figure of your beautiful Master.'[15] This deflates in advance Valere's smug description of himself;

Lovewell: Is he a Gentleman?
Valere: Yes, Faith.
Lovewell: And handsome?
Valere: The Ladies think so.[16]

In *The Busy Body* (1709), Centlivre imitates the scene in Jonson's *The Devil is an Ass*, where the lover buys time from his mistress's husband for an interview with her. But Miranda through her asides to the audience, treats it as an opportunity to see rather than to be seen, and prolongs and mocks the interview by confusing her lover with meaningless signs. I shall return to Centlivre in a later chapter.[17] The scene I quoted from *The Young King* is typical of Behn in its use of a material object, a prop. Behn seems to be saying through her delicate and rather erotic use of the hat and plume, that there are ways of assessing things, and people in their other role, as things, that are acceptable, and humane. The element of sexual reversal is thus just part of a statement of the sensuality of the actual. Behn's most famous work, the short novel *Oronooko* (1688) is placed in the real, as events known only to the authoress, so that it becomes a kind of dramatic monologue. Two thirds of the way through the novel she meets the hero, and comes to participate in some of his adventures. But we have heard the distanced, unreal tale of his life in Africa in the frame of the vivid and concrete evocation of Aphra's life in Surinam; we can only see it as it is filtered through the mind of a story teller vigorously involved in her own ideas and concerns. There are two characters in the novel; Oronooko, object, and Aphra, subject, and explorer. 'His misfortune', she writes of her hero, 'was, to fall in an obscure world, that afforded only a female pen to celebrate his fame.'[18] But this means he is doubly his creator's object; as a slave, and as the slave of her fiction; he has no appeal out to reality the way the Aphra character has, we can only know him through her. The traveller's tale, for that is what *Oronooko* is, grants the story teller a privileged role, as the only qualified interpreter of his own fiction. It is a risky role for that reason. By evoking the real as a hostage for her fiction, Behn has made her own 'real' life irretrievably obscure.[19] Aphra becomes as exotic as Oronooko. The traveller tells his story by arranging and interpreting objects, Behn catalogues her souvenirs of the Caribbean, and presents them attractively to us. People themselves gleam with enticing vividness. Oronooko is like polish'd jet, the Indians are 'the colour of new brick, but smooth soft and sleek'.[20] Though she cannot produce material objects in a novel, she can commandeer them from the stage. Her readers are directed to the theatre for their evidence:

> we trade for feathers, which they order into all shapes, make themselves little short habits of 'em, and glorious wreaths for their heads, necks, arms and legs, whose tinctures are unconceivable. I had a set of these presented to me and I gave 'em to the King's Theatre, and it was the dress of *The Indian Queen*.[21]

The feathers, to borrow a term from E. R. Dodds, become an 'apport', the verifying gift the dream leaves behind it.[22]

One should be careful not to confuse the exotic and the pastoral. Pastoral has to have something familiar about it. The forest of Arden is more like home than Duke Frederick's court. The seacoast of Bohemia forfeits the hard-edged reality of the foreign in its nonappearance on the map. The exotic can be made to function like the pastoral, only by acquiring a suspect familiarity. In *Oronooko*, the hero's African experience is pieced together from his conversations with Aphra, and eked out, one suspects, by material from heroic tragedy and tragicomic intrigue. Both this and her interpretation of the Indians' way of life in Surinam come to mirror, fragmentarily and by opposites, ideas of Restoration London. The familiar thesis implied by a pastoral convention makes the fiction in which it is used at once familiar, and questionable. The 'golden age' ideas Behn applies to the Indians, and to some aspects of African customs, bring the philosophical springs of Oronooko's behaviour closer to us. He is in fact not so much a 'Noble Savage' as a Native Wit. As a prince of a trading nation he has ample contact with foreign ideas, and has formed his own opinion on, among other things, the execution of Charles I. His love-making and his bravery are both ascribed by Behn to his superior wit; the charming scene in which he accompanies her, her brother, and her women ('a maid of good Courage') on an expedition to converse with the Indians, is a tribute to the 'wit' of all concerned.[23] Wit is a poised willingness to explore, a self possession that regulates one's behaviour to others. Surinam, as Behn presents it, is a lost paradise of wit, whose dissolution she chronicles. A land of natural luxury, of precariously achieved though very real co-existence, is ruined by greed and dishonour and then lost to the Dutch. It is the most vivid and elegant of all the little worlds that mirror the Restoration's myth of itself.

Behn's most famous play, *The Rover* (1677), deals in a lighter vein with similar ideas. It tells the story of a group of 'Banished Cavaliers', led by Willmore, the Rover of the title, through the hazards and delights of neapolitan carnival, itself an exotic image of pleasure in a land where they order these things so much better than at home. 'I like their sober grave way', says Willmore with typical brashness "tis a kind of legal authorized fornication, where the men are not chid for't, nor the women despised, as amongst our dull English.'[24] Masking and disguise serve to generalize the women's experience in the same way that a ballerina's masked identity makes her part of an inclusive symbol. Behn's play is Etheregean in its delicate expansion of the possibilities of the masked woman as protagonist. Her plotting is always kinetic, within scenes and in progress from one scene to the next. The otherness of both the female and the exotic is animated and multiplied by this means, and Willmore's wit pitted against both. In *The Rover* the masked ladies impose their own meaning on the play, a fluently externalized game of identities whose insights are swift and poignant. The courtesan Angelica Bianca is to be auctioned, and pictures of her are displayed on her balcony. Willmore climbs up and snatches one, a violation of her presentation of self, that foreshadows, by initiating, the disorder of her feelings for him. When summoned to her presence he refuses to play any of the courtship games she knows. 'Had I given him all my youth has earned from sin', she tells her attendant,

I had not lost a thought nor sigh upon't.
But I have given him my eternal rest,
My whole repose, my future joys, my heart!
My virgin heart, Moretta! Oh, 'tis gone![25]

The loss of emotional virginity is the larger and more painful event. *The Rover* is a set of carnival variations on a theme deeply serious to Behn, the disparity of a woman's public and private selves. By the end of the play, as always in her work, the women achieve a wise and controlling presence. When Willmore is refused permission to marry Hellena, one of his friends exclaims, ''tis true, he's a rover of Fortune, yet a prince aboard his little wooden world',[26] a witty enclosure and diminishment of the cavalier's sphere of action. He is finally presented to Hellena as in a box.

The Rover is in its context an old-fashioned piece – its interest in a pre-Restoration moment links it to a cycle of plays of the 1660s. But it is old-fashioned also in its determined lightness. If Otway's, Crowne's and even, on occasion, Shadwell's plays can be called anti-wit comedies, Behn's could be labelled, 'post-wit'. Wit in other words is an important positive in her work, and Etheregean comedy is a major stylistic influence. But her investment in a personal dramatic language organises 'wit' in new ways.

Her next comedy (1678) *Sir Patient Fancy* was her most influential. It is an ambitious intrigue comedy set in London in which she opposes herself stylistically to her male rivals in general, and to Shadwell in particular. Shadwell at this point in his career is in a neo-classical phase. Behn rightly diagnoses morally corrective Jonsonian comedy as more anti-feminist in its assumption than Etheregean comedy, and the cause of wit comedy comes to be subsumed in the cause of the woman writer. In her preface to *The Dutch Lover* she becomes wit comedies' only theorist; or at least, the mouthpiece of its refusal to theorize. The play was produced a little after *Epsom Wells*, and so her dispraise of Jonson and reforming comedy can again be set against Shadwell. In recent comedy ' . . . even those persons that were meant to be the ingenious Censors of the Play, have either prov'd the most debauch'd, or most unwittie people in the Company; nor is this error very lamentable, since as I take it Comedie was never meant, either for a converting or a conforming Ordinance'. 'In short' she goes on, 'I think a play the best Divertisement that wise men have; but I do also think them nothing so who do discourse so formally about the rules of it, as if 'twere the grand affair of human life'.[27] The answer to the Jonsonists lies not in some alternative theory, but in scouting theory all together. Wit attained through rules is no wit at all.

The challenge of Behn's epilogue to *Sir Patient Fancy* is thus made not only on behalf of women writers, but on behalf of a traditional unlaboured concept of wit.

> Your way of Writing's out of fashion grown.
> Method, and Rule – you only understand;
> Pursue that way of Fooling, and be damn'd.
> Your learned Cant of Action, Time and Place,
> Must all give way to the unlabour'd Farce.
> To all the Men of Wit we will subscribe;
> But for your half Wits, you unthinking Tribe,
> We'll let you see, whate'er besides we do,
> How artfully we copy some of you;
> And if you're drawn to th'Life pray tell me then
> Why Women should not write as well as Men.[28]

Shadwell's *True Widow*, performed a few months later than *Sir Patient Fancy*, takes up Behn's challenge by parodying her style of comedy in a play within the play. They are engaged in a controversy on the nature of comedy. *Sir Patient Fancy* is densely plotted – it is basically a house party comedy, worked out in the overlapping intrigues of two households. One consists of Sir Patient, his wife, and her lover, the other of the bluestocking Lady Knowell, her nieces and *their* lovers. It is, of all her plays, the most concerned with the restrictions on women in day to day life. Typically, she focuses this on a prop, a watch, given to one of the nieces by her country suitor. The girl's brother uses it to demonstrate to the assembled company how her time will be accounted for point by point; it is 'a kind of hieroglyphic that will instruct you how a Married Woman of your Quality ought to live'.[29] However satirically this account of the life of a lady of Fashion is phrased – its point is to try and frighten the suitor off – the watch makes concrete for us a central theme of the play; that a woman's time is divided and mapped out for her. The women's sense of space is, similarly, minutely circumscribed. Lady Fancy, talking to her lover, complains that Sir Patient 'scarce gives me time to write to thee, he waits on me from room to room, hands me in the Garden, shoulders me in the balcony, nay, does the office of my Women, dresses and undresses me, and does so smirk at his handy-work . . .'.[30] Sir Patient's disagreeable intimacy is generalized through Behn's sense of stage space; there are always too many characters on stage for any one to speak freely or do what they want.

At first the conversational style of *Sir Patient Fancy* is free of double entendre, or even 'imagery'. But Lady Fancy must acquire the control of a suggestive language to help her through the encroachments, the interruptions and sheer lack of privacy that the play posits around her. Her intrigue spills over into double entendre; 'Sir, you may come at night, and something I will do by that time shall certainly give you that access you wish for.'[31] The idea of 'access' or 'admittance' proliferates suggestively throughout the rest of the play. It moves out into the garden at night; the 'garden door' becomes the focus of each woman's attempt to resolve the tensions multiplied in the more restricting environment of the house itself.

Outside in 'The Night Garden', the play acquires an emotional amplitude, generated by a mistaken identity plot. One of the girls' lovers, Lodwick, is summoned to Lady Fancy's bed in mistake for her own gallant; the gallant alarms the niece with his confident demands. Lodwick won't sleep with his Isabella – he even suspects he's impotent – and is vastly relieved, and no longer impotent, when he finds out who his seductress really is. Behn's ever expansive evocation of the sensual, blurs as night does, the distinction between persons, between indoors and out. The mistakes of the night have liberated eroticism into a hazy generality of feeling. As in all Behn's plays the characters are joined in a complicated and unschematic mesh of relationship, to be knitted even more closely by the ever evolving, even random interplay of which the plot consists. Her systematic disarrangement of a received dramatic language dislodges plot nodes and conventions only to find a new validity in them. The dominant comic character in *Sir Patient Fancy* is the bluestocking, Lady Knowell, satirically portrayed by her nieces as a woman whose own intellectual attainments conceal from her the general position of her sex; attainments she uses mainly to seduce young men. The first male to enter the play is Lucretia's lover Leander, begging rescue from Lady Knowell's overwhelming attentions. The male characters are on the run from then on: after Sir Credulous has come on the scene they are involved in a series of parody courtship scenes, impelled by choice or trickery to make themselves ridiculous in order to avoid acceptance. Behn transfers the mistaken identity plot conventional of wit comedy from female characters to male – thus incidentally deflecting also the visual attention it focuses. This aspect of the play is a

joke on the rather prim young couples, to whom, albeit accidentally, the older women teach some important lessons. Lady Knowell
has come to generate a comic warmth that complements Lady
Fancy's spinning of intrigue. At the end of the play she gives
Leander back to Lucretia – the girls had misjudged her; as one may
have guessed, the strings of the plot were in her hands all along.

> Be not amaz'd at this turn. Rotat omne Fatum – But no more –
> keep still that mask of Love we first put on. . . . Lucretia,
> wipe your Eyes and prepare for *Hymen*, the Hour draws near.
> *Thallesio, Thallesio* as the Romans cry'd[32]

Triumph confuses her grasp on languages. Scatty, generous and
finally efficient, she is an answer in witty self-caricature to Behn's
professional anxieties, a comic muse of deranged classicism.

There is a second watch in the play; it belongs to Lady Fancy's
lover. Its alarm goes off at the climax of the night's intrigues, a
summons to eclaircissement and the truths of the daytime world. It
is, of course, a borrowing from Middleton's *Mad World*.[33] Most of
Behn's output is exotic not only in subject matter, but in its use of
mixed tragi-comic or operatic forms. Plays like *The Dutch Lover*
(1673), *Abdelazar* (1676) or *The Widow Ranter* (1689), though
widely different in setting and style, are all variations on themes of
nature, legality and pleasure, all freely and busily plotted, and all a
combination of foreign settings with an extravagant mixing of
styles determinedly 'foreign' in itself. The stylistically irregular,
like the exotic, exempts itself from a kind of competitive attention
to which Behn, as a woman, feels herself particularly vulnerable.

> Plays have no great room for that which is men's great advan-
> tage over women, that is, Learning; We all well know that the
> immortal Shakespeare (who was not guilty of much more of this
> than often falls to woman's share) have better pleased the world
> than Jonsons. . . . Then for their musty rules of Unity and God
> knows what besides, if they meant anything, they are enough
> intelligible and as practicable by a woman . . .[34]

When she wrote London comedy, she dealt largely in adaptations
of Jacobean plays, commissioned by Thomas Betterton, the actor-
manager, and sometimes ascribed to him. This interest in City
comedy returns to theatrical currency a form of plotting more
realistically weighted than French style farce or Fletcherian court

plays, but neither classically shaped nor corrective in intent. The characteristics Behn and Middleton share – the plausible invention of a moment to moment psychological naturalism, the wise reservation of judgement – are perhaps temperamental affinities that lead one to the other, rather than any stylistic debt. The two major London comedies, *The City Heiress* (1682), and *Sir Patient Fancy* (1678), both take from *A Mad World, My Masters*. *Sir Patient Fancy*, the only major play of hers that is not an adaptation, retrieves the chiming watch, but *The City Heiress* imitates the plot; or rather, transplants aspects of it to a carefully established contemporary setting. It belongs to a cycle of plays about the political events of the eighties of which the most important were written by Behn, Otway and Crowne.

Behn's London comedies have more in common with Crowne than with any of her other contemporaries. His characteristic evocation of a political perspective on the events of his plays feeds less schematically into her concern to give the events of her infrequent London plays a resonantly actual context; to record its hard-edged oddity, the 'otherness' of a particular moment in time. Between them, these two writers manage to make overt in a short cycle of plays the social tensions that other Restoration comedy refers to with an elegant obliqueness. The most explicitly political are Behn's *The Roundheads* (1681) and a play of Crowne's to some extent imitative of it, *City Politicks*. Both use the sexual intrigues of wit comedy to make satirical points against the growing power of the Whigs.

Behn's play adapts Tatham's *The Rump* (1660), layering onto it the intrigues of the Roundhead women, newly come to power, and intoxicated by it.

> Mad call'st thou her? 'tis her ill-acted Greatness, thou mistak'st; thou art not us'd to the Pageantry of these Women yet; they all run thus mad; 'tis Greatness in 'em.[35]

One may jib at the presentation of Cromwell's widow as a kind of cross between Mrs Loveit and the deposed Queen Margaret; the play seems to be the work of one innocent of any historical sense. Like *The Rover*, the play revives the subject matter of the comedies of Restoration of the sixties and early seventies, but it adapts a casual wit comedy tone, a naturalistic assessment of its characters' aims and actions. Behn treats the women's uncertainty of social status, their attempt at self-realization within it, with a sympathy that aligns them to her other heroines. Their opposition to the cavaliers (or 'heroics' as they call them) is worked out as an attempt to enclose and possess.

Behn is the least intellectual of Royalists. She presents the issues decoratively, as part of a personal fantasy that impinges on the political fantasy of the Stuarts at some unexpected points. At the climactic point of its farcical structure, *The Roundheads* bears traces of the masque form.

The Rump disport themselves (itself?) as a kind of ante-masque;

> When they have flung Cushions thus a while to the Musick time, they beat each other from the Table, one by one, and fall into a godly Dance; after a while, *Wariston* rises, and dances ridiculously a while amongst them; then to the Time of the Tune, they take out the rest, as at the Cushion-Dance, or in that nature. *Wariston* being the last taken in, leads the rest.[36]

'What', sniffs Lady Lambert 'at their Oliverian Frolicks?'[37] She is revealed in a masque-like discovery –

> Flat scene draws off, discovers Lady Lambert on a Couch, with *Lovely*, tying a rich Diamond Bracelet about his Arm; a Table behind with Lights, on which a Velvet Cushion, with a Crown and Scepter cover'd.

When she holds up the crown, Lovely, a cavalier, kneels to the 'sacred Relicks of my King'.[38]

Behn attempts to pull the sexual and political intrigue together –

> Kings are depos'd and Commonwelths are rul'd;
> By Jilting all the Universe is fool'd.[39]

But her play is most interesting as a would-be realistic study of women liberated with dangerous, exhilarating suddenness under pressure of social upheaval. Behn's best play, *The City Heiress*, makes the links between public and private events more freely and precisely.

The City Heiress is an anti-Whig play, with a prologue by Otway. It opens as a comedy of dissension, rather in Crowne's manner, with Sir Timothy Treatall, the Whig Alderman, casting off Wilding, his rakish Tory nephew. In Crowne's work, families and households tend to image the state in little; Behn's political theme creates a perspective on the unresolvable dissension of her characters' private lives.

Wilding is attached to three women, Charlot, the heiress of the title, Diana, a cousin to Middleton's courtesan Frank, whose name Behn inadvertently gives her at one point,[40] and the worldly Lady Galliard. But this Lady herself is divided between the attentions of two lovers; she cannot choose between the desirable, untrustworthy Wilding, and the quieter, attentive Sir Charles. Unlike *The Rover* or *Sir Patient Fancy*, the play starts in a masculine world, but then more subtly subverts and complicates it. The rake, at first apparently wronged, comes to be seen as an unglamourized wrongdoer in the down to earth terms of the play; terms that count the cost, both human and financial. 'I have been to often flatter'd with the hopes of your marrying a rich Wife', Diana complains, 'and then I was to have a Settlement; but instead of that, things go backward with me, my Coach is vanish'd, my servants dwindled into one necessary Woman and a Boy, which to save Charges is too small for any Service; my twenty Guineas a week into forty shillings; a hopeful Reformation'.[41] Wilding's libertinism is not simply more down at heel than, say, Dorimant's, in its romantic nihilism it forfeits that greater Wit's control. In its spiralling anarchy it is a part of the social chaos of which Wilding seeks to oppose himself;

> Let Politician's plot, let Rogues go on
> In the old beaten Path of Forty-one;
> Let City Knaves delight in Mutiny,
> The Rabble bow to old Presbytery;
> Let petty States be to confusion hurl'd,
> Give me but Woman, I'll despise the World.[42]

The play reaches its climax at Sir Timothy's 'treat', a perversion of pleasure to his own political ends that echoes the distorted amusements of *The Roundheads*, this time in a kind of parody of those big social occasions that organize wit comedy and its world. But by this point in the play Wilding has been displaced from its centre by Lady Galliard.

She effects this at the beginning of the second act, controlling her lover's movements through an apparently casual appearance on her balcony – 'this city-Garden where we walk to take the fresh Air of the Sea-coal Smoak'[43] – and organizing her feelings for them as she prepares for Sir Timothy's banquet at that other image for female self-presentation, her mirror. Behn allows her to inhabit the stage space, to disrupt and redirect the progress of the play with a comic freedom no female character had ever been granted before. She, not Wilding, is the play's Dorimant, as the unaffected casualness of her reception of poor Charles makes clear.

Lady Gall.	Give me that Essence-bottle.
Charles.	But for a Recompence of all my Suffrings
Lady Gall.	Sprinkle my Handkerchief with Tuberose.
Charles.	I beg a Favour you'd afford a stranger.
Lady Gall.	Sooner, perhaps. What Jewel's that?[44]

Wilfully relaxed, like Dorimant, she steers the play on the path of her own vagaries. Like Dorimant, the only excuse for her actions is that they are her own.

In the acquisitive atmosphere of the city feast, people and things are interchangeably evaluable. The cast embroil themselves in a chaos of mercenary plotting, whose outcome they cannot confidently predict. Diana comes disguised as an heiress; Charlot, the real heiress, comes as a Scots girl. Slowly and despondently, Lady Galliard's Charles gets very drunk indeed.

Charles's difficulties with the lady are exacerbated by his difficulties with his uncle, the old Tory, Sir Anthony, whose running commentary on his nephew's attempts contrasts them unfavourably with the lurid delights offered her by Wilding –

The stealths of Love, the midnight kind Admittance
The gloomy Bed, the soft breath'd murmuring Passion;
Ah, who can guess at Joys thus match'd by parcels?
The difficulty makes us always wishing,
Whilst on thy part, Fear makes still some resistance;
And every Blessing seems a kind of Rape.

'A Divine Fellow that'; says Sir Anthony, 'just of my Religion'. Charles's courtship, on the other hand, '. . . begins like a Fore' man o'th'shop to his Master's Daughter'.[45] Behn seems to be working out her own feelings for the rake-hero. As in *Sir Patient Fancy*, the lady accidentally acquires two men in one night, but *The City Heiress* is a less schematic play; Behn wants to implant her concerns in as full a realization as possible of a mundane social world. Charles breaks into Lady Galliard's bedroom just after her assignation with Wilding – 'your willing Rape is all the Fashion, Charles',[46] his uncle had pointed out. But he makes his own sweetly personal resolution of social pressures. Instead of the kind of ambiguous rape/seduction that was to become a cliche of those dramatists of the nineties who imitate and so often devalue Behn's eroticism, Charles indulges in an incompetent, vague striptease. Lady Galliard dithers embarrassedly about, but then agree off-handedly to marry him.

At the end of the play Charlot claims Wilding in no uncertain terms –

I have thee, and I'll die thus grasping thee;
Thou art my own, no power shall take thee from me.[47]

For Lady Galliard, the last act is less conclusive. The logic of the play, its schizoid statement of male sexuality, dictates that her feelings remain irresolvable. Behn expresses them in a graceful wordlessness:

Sighing and looking on Wilding, giving Sir Charles her Hand.[48] Behn's political interests are inseparable from the aesthetic choices she made. *The Rover* could be seen as anachronistic, either ahead of its time or behind it; its revival of the myth of the cavaliers, its link of Charles's reinstatement to an unambiguously celebrated ethos of pleasure and wit, stands suggestively between the comedies of Restoration and the revival of Stuart iconography that follows on Charles's decision to rule without parliament. As the dedication and commendatory verses to her 'Poems upon Several Occasions' point out, the timing of this volume (1683) coincides with apparent Royal victory on the issue of the Exclusion crisis. Its celebratory use of the imagery and conventions of the golden age thus link it to the operatic experiments of the end of the King's reign. Indeed, Maureen Duffy has made an attractive if unargued attribution to Behn of the Libretto of Blow's *Venus and Adonis* (1681).[49] But a poem like *Our Cabal* in which she lists and describes her friends under pastoral pseudonyms is a tribute to her personal investment in a mock-pastoral concept of a society of wit. As the political reference of the title shows, her sense of her relationship to larger issues is to some extent a joke on disparities of scale. The link between private and public is in her own wit. Verses by Cooper pay tribute to her in a grandiose mythological imagery, both Christian and Pagan:

> The *Queen* of Beauty and the *God* of Wars
> Imbracing lie in thy due temper'd Verse,
> *Venus* her sweetness and the force of *Mars*.

> Thus thy luxuriat Muse her pleasure takes,
> As *God* of old in *Eden*'s blissful walks;
> The Beauties of her new Creation view'd,
> Full of content She sees that it is *good*.[50]

There, if you like, is the female God I talked about earlier. But the classical imagery is significant in making a masque-like public statement out of a point of style. Behn's muse luxuriates in the last glow of the Stuart myth. She is its unofficial laureate.

7 Marriage and the Comedy of the 1690s – Dryden's *Amphitryon* and Crowne's *The Married Beau*

The court ethos I have discussed as the product of the last two reigns was irrelevant to the next. The terms on which William and Mary acceded to the throne created a less dazzling image of monarchy, an image that their individual personalities did everything to confirm. Neither was interested in the stage, and Mary in particular was concerned to reform the moral climate in a way that may well have eventually killed off comedy as Charles II had known it.[1] That it not only survived into the reign of her sister Anne, but produced as many masterpieces in a dozen years as it had before testifies to a brief independence of fashion. It had become an established literary form, to be taken up confidently by a new generation of dramatists after so many of the old had died, gone into exile or simply stopped regular production.

There is nonetheless a sense in which this survival can be described as 'artificial'. I have described in earlier chapters the social and historical forces which inform the genre – which the genre thus expresses. A decision to imitate earlier models lies at the root of recent dissatisfaction with 'Restoration comedy' as a term; there shouldn't *be* Restoration comedies written so long after the Restoration itself, and in such different social circumstances. In Chapters 8 to 10 I shall describe what I call an 'Etheregean revival' – a conscious decision by writers, actors and theatre managers of the nineties to revive the style and concerns of the 'wits', principally by imitating Restoration comedy as Etherege had left it. It is in this very process that Etheregean comedy becomes visible as a distinct form. In the same process it comes to seem 'artificial'. It gels as a coherent artifice, imitable, but open to development only by contradictions or reversals, witty in themselves, but, by the socially attentive standards of the first Restoration comedies, also gratuitous. There is an interesting disjuncture between the values of the new court and the values of the comedy – the second phase or 'revival' produces richer or more complex individual plays but is, for the same reason, sharply constricted in scope.

In this chapter I want to preface my discussion of the comedy of the nineties by looking at two major verse plays by survivors of the Carolean court, John Crowne and John Dryden. *The Married Beau* (1694) and *Amphitryon* (1690) explore the major new concern of the comedy of the 1690s – marriage. They build around it a complex layering of social and historical allusion, marking both its potential as a model of other more public social bonds, and its actual importance as a sign of historical change.

As Dryden makes clear in his dedication, *Amphitryon* was written at the low point of his political fortunes. He was not prepared to support William and Mary, nor was he a romantic royalist like Aphra Behn, or Otway.[2] The political tone of the play is disillusioned. It opposes an absolute monarch, the baroque Jove, against a conventional marriage, a marriage not of individuals in love, but of representative players of social roles; an ideal couple. In terms of the royal myths I have traced elsewhere, Jove is Charles in his desires and James in his arbitrariness; and the public image of William and Mary lacked a sharp individuality to make them unlike Amphitryon and Alcmena; they too were projected as an ideal couple. Burnet sums it up his *Essay on the Memory of the Late Queen* (1695)

> Both seemed to have one soul, they looked like the different faculties of the same mind. Each of them having peculiar Talents, they divided between them the different parts of *Government.* . . . While *He* went abroad with the Sword in *His* Hand, She stayed at home with the Scepter in *Hers.* . . . *he* was to Conquer Enemies, and *She* was to gain Friends. *He,* as the Guardian of Christendom, was to diffuse himself to all, while *She* contracted her care, chiefly to the concerns of Religion and Vertue. While *He* had more business, and *She* more leisure, *She* prepared and suggested, what *He* executed. In all this, there was so close, but so entire an Union, that it was not possible to know how much was proper to any one; or if ever they differed in a Thought from one another . . .[3]

This was the ideal of marriage the new court held up for the 1690s. An awareness of historical change informs the play. It takes place, the epilogue assures us, in a world lost; not well lost, or lost by conquest as Dryden's other lost worlds had been, but simply decayed, dwindled for lack of intrinsic strength –

> At last, when He and all his Priests grew old,
> The ladies grew in their devotion cold;
> And, that false worship wou'd no longer hold[4]

He ends by looking forward to a return of paganism. The forecast is vague as to whether Jove's paganism is meant or the materialist/royalist world it stands for; but it remains indicative of the play's attempt to take stock of the whole post-Commonwealth period. Philosophically and politically it is Dryden's most ambitious play.

It is dramatically ambitious also; though not, of course, in an attempt at originality. *Amphitryon* is in many ways *the* classic farce, and Dryden pays due homage to Moliere and Plautus in his dedication.[5] It would be interesting to be able to number Dryden's play as Giraudoux did his *Amphitryon 38*. Perhaps Dryden's choice of plot can be seen in the light of his consistent rejection of comedy as a worthwhile genre. To use a classic plot is at once to demonstrate the sameness of comedies, and to make a kind of reparation; there is even a hint of humility in this return to beginnings. Dryden's *Amphitryon* is an attempt to prove the classic dignity of low comedy. It is an attempt at a masterpiece in the strict sense of a working through of an apprenticeship, and its ambition is that of a virtuoso's manipulation of apparently exhausted matter.

The songs and masques in *Amphitryon* were by Henry Purcell, his first major stage work after *Dido and Aeneas*. *Amphitryon* is a comedy with an operatic denouement – a generic hybrid informed by political self-awareness.

I have discussed Dryden's use of music elsewhere;[6] here it will suffice to show how his concept of comedy necessitates that use. Primarily it is a question of the scale on which the human characters are conceived. Alcmena and Amphitryon have no resilience. Jupiter himself is without wit or self-awareness, without that melancholy consciousness of lack which can make baroque non-human characters so haunting. Jupiter does not *need* Alcmena; he is simply on the rebound from Juno. His sense of her is impersonal

– 'ripen'd Peaches have not half the flavour . . . '.[7] one cannot feel that, tasty though she is, Alcmena has any more than twice their value in her seducer's eyes. And yet it is disturbing that the true Amphitryon, when he arrives, is even less attractive. The beating of the slave is a conventional scene, but the slave in this case has been introduced and made sympathetic some time before the master appears, and thus one cannot take it as part of a double act as one can in Shakespeare's *The Comedy of Errors*; furthermore by this point (IIIi) we are well aware that the play does not exist in a farce world, that power and subjection are more than just the mainsprings of a series of jokes. If the world of the play is a joke, then so is the universe whose order centres on Jupiter. Mercury uses a familiar agnostic objection to make this point. Jupiter claims that his actions will be justified by the conception of Hercules:

'Ay . . . and our Father made all those Monsters for *Hercules* to Conquer, and contriv'd all those Vices on purpose for him to reform too, there's the Jeast on't.'[8]

Not a profound point in itself, but it deflates Jupiter, or at least limits him; his arbitrariness is self-will, and that will committed to create by the need to justify previous creations. This universe is a 'Jeast' to Dryden, but the scale of the joke diffuses its funniness. The smaller irrationalities and cruelties of life under this system mirror the larger. Sosia's shrewish wife Bromia stands in for Juno; the profane, in echoing the sacred, takes on the harshness of the cosmic joke. More pervasively, Dryden negates the sense of orderly chaos that makes farce basically comfortable. Amphitryon is diminished in our eyes not only by his place in a world picture, but simply because we know that Sosia is right, and, more crucially, why he is right. Shakespear's Antipholi are tricked by chance, behind which a beneficent providence is finally perceived. Amphitryon is duped by a systematic cruelty, reasoned but not justified. Perhaps unfairly, the colder light falls on his conduct too. Amphitryon's dour belligerence is an aspect of his consciously manly, masterful role. He allows no space for reflection when the imbroglio tightens around him – either Alcmena is faithless, or she is mad. He lack trust in her, even a willingness to trust, that might alert him to the inherent improbability of her apparent conduct. He doesn't ask himself why she should reveal it herself, and so clumsily. It is a cruel exposure of their peerlessly ordinary, impersonally correct marriage, that it allows no leeway for attention to each other's individuality.

Jupiter drops a slow fuse of libertinism into this marriage; 'the being happy is not half the Joy/The manner of the happiness is all!'[9] Alcmena cannot understand the distinction he seeks to make between Amphitryon-as-husband and Amphitryon-as-lover. A more usually alert Restoration heroine would, but Alcmena suppresses the idea, and the consequences of her inability to cope with it are the more devastating. At the end of the play the real Amphitryon rejects her; when asked to distinguish between the real and the false she chooses not her husband but Jupiter, and for qualities which she could only have thought Amphitryon's by a self-deluding projection of her desire.

> Thy Words, thy Thoughts, thy soul is all *Amphitryon*
> Th' Impostour has thy Features, not thy Mind.[10]

Jupiter's specious rhetoric is firmly put down by Dryden through Mercury, and though he and his audience may be aware of its conventional libertinism, the constrictingly proper Alcmena is not. It is this, in fact, that has won her over; 'unconsenting Innocence is lost . . .'.[11] because it artlessly reveals itself, but cannot see through the disguises of others.

Alcmena has a vein of sensibility in common with the other Dryden heroines. She creates a rich imaginative world, doomed to perish at the touch of the real. She is truly in love with Amphitryon, as he, one feels, is not with her; but that again is conventional. But her love takes the form of imaginative projection;

> . . . wou'd I were there,
> And he were here: so might we change our Fates;
> That he might grieve for me, and I might die for him![12]

But if they did that they'd still be apart. Jupiter is a lover who satisfies her imaginatively; she herself is inspired to pretend the cosmic disorder he has actually effected –

> . . . you and I will draw our Curtain close
> Extinguish Day-light, and put out the Sun.[13]

The end of the long night disabuses her; dawn brings an unwelcome reality. Dryden's heroines inhabit a long beneficent night whose end diminishes them. Like the blind Emmeline, the true Alcmena lives in the dark. One can pity Amphitryon at the end of the play, but the couple's silence – they might well 'know not how to take it'[14] (Mercury again) – is the logical outcome. Wordlessness has its own dramatic force, and Dryden is the greater dramatist for his ability to use it.

As in all the darker comedies of the period, the alternative ideal can only exist in a parenthesis to the tight philosophically consistent world of the play; a hazily projected pastoral fantasy. Dryden compounds this effect by his use of the operatic conventions he had developed towards the end of Charles's reign. Music is always inhuman in his work. Here Mercury conjures it up to amuse the mercenary Phaedra. Thus the moral is stated in a context that renders it satirical; just as the Olympus/court identification focuses the satire in the retrospective political terms I discussed earlier. The medium and the message are ironically aligned within this dramatic context.

> We give, and give, and give, and give,
>   Till we can give no more;
> But what to day will take away
>   To morrow will restore.

The consumers' pastoral of the Restoration court is neatly summed up in Mercury's closing couplet –

> Our Iron age is grown an Age of Gold;
> 'Tis who bids most, for All Men wou'd be sold.[15]

Earlier Phaedra had scorned Jupiter's music, but claimed 'I cou'd dance all day, to the Musick of *chink, chink.*'[16] Dryden extends his disillusion with politics to the media those politics bred. He expands the political context of the play by making Amphitryon a victorious crusher of rebellion; what rebellion is left tactfully in doubt. Dryden's satire conceives of the whole period as 'all of a piece throughout'. It is in this focusing of ambiguities that the operatic scene is structurally important; it compresses events and expands meanings in a way unavailable to Dryden's comedy alone. The play represents the pinnacle of both genres in his work, but the comic vision sours the operatic. Dryden is never unaware of the chink of money that underlies the music. It must have been some amusement to him that lavishness sweetened the satire to such an extent that this sharp anti-feminine scene was the most liked by the feminine part of the audience.[17] The typing of sexual roles must be the most difficult target to satirize unequivocally; real life embodies these fantasies so much more adroitly.

Only Sosia could accept what happened, with a peasant equanimity fuelled by amateur philosophizing and sane, radical grumbling. In his way he represents Mercury humanized, making up in warmth what he lacks in asperity. There may well be a lot of Dryden's most agreeable comic character in the author of *King Arthur* and *Tyrannic Love*, a lumpen mischief-maker, whom Dryden finally recognizes when disabused of his trust in more grandiose schemes of order. Sosia may well be the real Dryden, the obdurate personality awash in philosophies and politics that ultimately seem as futile, if as dazzling, as the cruel joke world of doubles and disembodied selves.

Crowne's position after the Revolution was more precarious than Dryden's, his response to events more personally felt. Charles's death lost him his court connection. The sequence of dedications to his last plays are a uniquely full expression of the plight of the professional writer in times so uncertain that reputations simply disappear; fuelled as this is in Crowne's case by his sense of himself as a public writer, deserving public attention.

> How many Kings and Queens have I had the honour to divertise? and how fruitless has been all my Labours? a maker of Legs, nay a maker of Fires at Court has made himself a better Fortune, then Men much my superiors in Poetry could do, by all the noble Fire of their writings. . . . I have had a talent for begging, following and waiting. . . . my chief, if not sole attendance, has been upon the fantastical princes of my own begetting, the offsprings of my own muse, and my rewards have been accordingly fantastical and imaginary.

There is a degree of self awareness in this that is oddly moving. The theatre might well complain, that 'No ray from court shines on us, that we live . . . like people without the *Sun*'.[18] But Crowne articulates something more personal, an absorption in a unique imaginary world, where Charles, the Wits, and the accession crisis were shadowed but also transformed. His closeness to Charles was an accident of imaginative contingency; his plays may mimic outside events, but they enclose them in a way that allows no easy access. This dedication marks a step down in self-esteem from the angry retrospect of that to *The English Friar*, but it is the step into a claustrophobic privacy of feeling that liberates one of the greatest of all Restoration plays.

The Married Beau is crucially a play of the nineties. Under William and Mary, marriage becomes the central model of society's image of itself. It is not just an aspect of the uneasy relationship of individuals to community, as it is in even those Carolean comedies that discuss it most fully – as it is most *markedly* in those comedies that discuss it fully. It bears a weight of complex ideology, setting up a whole series of valuations to contradict those of the inherited comic form.

The shift of interest to a stable society of married couples effects a mutation in the concerns of Restoration comedy. Gallantry solidifies uneasily into the domestic. The process produces a rash of anxious narcissists, indeed, as we shall see with Cibber, an anxious sub-genre, the comedy of narcissism. When marriage is the dominant fact of a society, even the unmarried are defined by their relationship to the possibilities. The gallant becomes a narcissist as he has now no aim but self regard. In these plays gallantry is furtive, though not yet quite clandestine, an undertow to society, not its current. One turns to the cultivation of self regard when one loses the regard of others. This has become the libertine's dilemma.

In these plays friendship itself is subtly different in function. The tighter order of respectable life has displaced those loose groups of gentlemen drinkers, the tiny social chaos propelled by Etheregean comedy into a provisional order of its own. Friends in the comedies of the nineties are always a kind of mirror image; that is, they are always chosen, and thus express aspects of each other's character that the plays go on to explore. Social groupings become much smaller in scope; the system of friendships and pairings no longer opens out into a broader society that the society of the play implies. Marriage, friendship, the household; these are the borderlines of a narrower territory.

The Married Beau contains its large concerns within the context of domesticity by as it were, squaring it. There are four main

characters; the married couple, the Lovelys, and their friends, Polidor
and Camilla. They are echoed again by the four comic characters of
the sub-plot (Mrs Lovelys' maid and sister, and their lovers), and
apart from two servants – manservant and maidservant, the last
almost mute pair – these are all the characters of the play. After the
first act, in front of St Paul's, Covent Garden, the action takes
place in one night at the Lovely's townhouse. The main medium
is verse. Crowne transmutes the materials of Restoration comedy
into a private late chamber piece, an octet on themes of death
and loneliness.

In *The Married Beau*, Polidor is Lovely's mirror; Lovely is Polidor's butt. Their long initial dialogue reveals another aspect of the
change in the gallants' relationship. The comedy of the nineties
tends to set a 'platonic' gallant against an earthy one, where the
earlier comedy allowed both aims to coexist in one character to an
often volatile effect. But this simplification is the basis of Crowne's
startling analysis of the ideas I have outlined. Crowne locates the
flaw in Lovely's one entire and perfect chrysolite.

Lovely.   I have, whene're I please, my wife's soft arms,
            And rosy melting lips; but theres a part
            I seek much more; What Part dost think it is?
Polidor.   Oh! Fie upon thee! What a question's that?
            What part of her! What part should you seek most?
Lovely.   Her soul! her soul! I'd be admired by her.
            Oh, sir! to be admir'd by a fine woman,
            Surpasses infinitely, infinitely,
            All the delights her body can bestow . . .
            . . . thousands I'd give my wife thought this of me,
            And thousands more that I cou'd know she thought
            it.
Polidor.   Ay there's the difficulty; I have heard
            Of tubes that let the eye into the moon,
            But of no instrument to find out thought.[19]

But Lovely has invented just such an instrument; Polidor must
make love to Mrs Lovely. Lovely is an Othello his own Iago, a
rational Leontes ahead of even presumed adultery. He needs to
precipitate unfaithfulness in order to unravel the implications of an
apparently perfect marriage.

He is also a Faust. 'Say but he's handsome' Polidor had earlier

informed us 'and one may have his soul.'[20] One last element must
be added to an account of the play's centrality to its period, its use
of religious ideas and imagery. I have discussed briefly in Chapter
1 on *The Man of Mode* what I take to be an ambivalent relationship
between the religious and the material in the Baroque aesthetic to
which aspects of Restoration comedy seem to me to be aligned.[21]
One is not easily separable from the other, so cannot be said to
constitute the other's meaning; meaning flows from each to the
other in a richly ambiguous process of realization. For Collier this
constituted a blasphemy. It was in fact merely behind the tenor of
the times, as is obvious in the vagueness of the playwrights'
attempts to defend themselves – the style survived, but any rationale had been forgotten. Crowne's setting of his first act outside St
Pauls, the Inigo Jones church in Covent Garden, signals the implications of his play. The church is a dominant pesence; it is 'full of
beauty',[22] of the women characters it releases half way through the
act into Lovely's plot. The association of ideas can be paralleled in
the opening of his *The Destruction of Jerusalem* plays and so can the
imaginative precision of Crowne's architectural sense. The collapsing urban splendours of Jerusalem are internalized by the
verse as the end not just of a city but of a world view. The
topography of *The Married Beau* serves to generalize its action by
exact placing, as elegantly diagrammatic as the octet of couples.
And its resonance in increasingly sombre verse breeds a thickening
sense of wider collapse.

When Polidor makes his first attempt on Mrs Lovely, her response is to dismiss him, and to ask Camilla to the house to keep
her company. But Camilla's reaction is more serious than her
friend had evidently anticipated.

> I thought the lost perfection of mankind
> Was in that man restor'd; and I have griev'd
> Lost Eden too was not reviv'd for him,
> And a new *Eve*, more ex'lent than the first,
> Created for him . . . and he fool'd me,
> To think that *Eve* and *Eden* was in me . . .[23]

She has lost her illusion of an oasis of unfallen nature, as Diana, in
Calisto, lost hers. The audience has already seen her assessing the
pros and cons of her relationship to Polidor in a duologue of
apparently impersonal gravity. It is characteristic of Crowne to

treat her imperfect aspiration to virtue with a sympathy that in no way precludes humour. Her charm is an honesty about herself, an unaffected percipience that contrasts her with the flurry of concern for self and self-image that aligns Mrs Lovely – 'a witty beautiful coquette that loves to be courted and admired: but aims at no more . . . proud, and has great value for honour'[24] – with heroines otherwise as different as Lady Cockwood and Southerne's Mrs Friendall.

Camilla's disillusion is a disillusion with self; but it implies a disillusion with the values by which 'The only Covent Garden Saint'[25] had tried to live.

> Mrs L. I did not think you'd ha'been thus concerned.
> I thought your pious heart had been in Heaven
> Camil. Oh! Pshaw, Our Hearts are seldom such high Fliers;
> Tis well if they can fly above Commodes.
> I ne're could get my Heart above this town
> Now wou'd I were in my cold quiet Grave

Crowne exploits the limited resource of Restoration comedy blank verse in a way that places his characters' voices with critical precision; one might note the way the first speech of Camilla's that I quoted allows the characteristic failure of such verse to carry a rhythmic energy to the end of the lines to create revealingly weak, even whining, emphases on 'me'. But the exchange between the two women that ends act two discovers a telling image to enlarge the whole experience of the play. 'Why truly that is not quite out of *London*' Mrs Lovely observes

> For I believe you'd have a London Grave,
> And there y'are in old *London* under Ground;
> In a dark silent Suburb o'th'city.[26]

Crowne's vision of the dark silent suburb, into which, after all, so much of the Restoration had now gone, opens up a territory new to fashionable comedy. The play is increasingly death-haunted. Its double quartet enclose a sense of something more frightening than the 'Destruction of London'; its entrapment in an infinity of reflections.

Mrs Lovely is protected from Polidor initially by the incursions of her household. His attempts to budge her from her determined stasis on stage are lightly farcical to begin with; unwilling at first to play Lovely's game, he is enticed into it by his pleasure in Mrs Lovely's deft avoidance. Women, to Polidor, are a delightful kind of automaton; 'Let 'em go right, I never mind the springs'.[27] The seduction scenes are funny, but chilled by the sense that Polidor's skills are entirely impersonal. His adversary is equally inhuman; not so much Mrs Lovely herself, as the structure of rules and prohibitions for which her household stands. His eventual success is due to his witty turning against itself of the language of honour and religion that has for her no reference outside itself; when this is internalized he can animate the house itself to collude in its mistress's undoing.

> See yonder gentle yielding bed invites;
> The curtains wave to us, the air seems sensible
> Of hastening bliss, and dances round the room.[28]

Mrs Lovely's loss of self is as we shall see, preliminary to her remaking it. But the household exacts its revenge; her maid uses the discovery to blackmail her into an eerie reversal of roles. Camilla finds them out also, and enforces a desperately faked repentance. And then Lovely returns. Appearances by this time are hastily smoothed over. Camilla's anger demands that she take her part in the quartet 'to rattle this false Polidor';[29] and the master of the house binds his guests together in a suggestive complicity;

> . . . He's Kin to both of us:
> That is to say, he is of our Proud Strain,
> And has, like us, exquisite sense of Honour.[30]

They are the adepts of an elite and dangerous game.

Later in the evening Polidor takes advantage of Lovely's temporary absence to renew his attentions to Mrs Lovely. She refuses him in an image which suggestively echoes her scene with Camilla. She too can see an escape only in death:

Mrs L. No, we will never be this close again.
         Except in death; one grave may lodge us both.
         I shall desire to sleep with thee in dust.
Polid. Then I shall be a scurvy bed-fellow
Mrs L. Till then I am resolv'd to part with thee
                      (She goes from him)

Polid.   And can you do it?

Mrs L.   You will part with me,
         When you have sated your ill-appetite;
         Perhaps before; shou'd a disease drink up
         This little beauty, you wou'd vanish too.

Polid.   It may be so. But prethee, let me have
         Thy Body, till thy beautious face departs.

Mrs L.   No; I've given up my fort, but I will march
         Honourably away, with arms and flying colours.
         And so, sweet *Polidor*, farewell for ever.[31]

But she is not allowed a dignified exit. Lovely comes in with the
present he had intended for Camilla; ('The Lady gone, before she
has her puppy? W'ave swom down far in night') and paints for
Polidor the ensuing scene of marital bliss –

> My wife and I will be exceeding wanton
> I'll have ten tapers burning o're my pillow
> To give us both full sight of all our features[32]

Polidor breaks the illusion by confessing everything.

It seems at first pure pique; but when Lovely threatens to
murder his wife, Polidor's real anger breaks out in a sense of his
own degradation. It is that lushly uxorious fantasy that destroys
his urbanity. It has become obvious that Lovely's plot was narcissistic in itself; what he really wanted to do was to watch himself.
And faced with this Lovely too breaks down:

> Oh Sir you thought I'de ha'been ridden patiently,
> I will y'ave rid one half of me, my wife;
> Now pray sir, mount the other half, mount me.
> Who's there? Get Polidor his boots and spurs,
> A bridle he needs none; I ha' one in my mouth –[33]

The narcissist is surprised by his reflection into a fixation on other
aspects of himself than beauty, and so Crowne collapses the two
last corners of the square.

Polidor decides to 'piece up the wrack'[34] by staging another
scene with Mrs Lovely spied on this time by her husband. She
plays it in a heightened 'theatrical' style that veers on to dangerous
ironies, and Crowne ends it with the direction 'She goes out in a

great rage – and Polidor shrugs, taking her words as they are meant, in a double sense.'[35] This seems to me to underestimate the difficulties, Mrs Lovely is now completely trapped in deceits that render her more enigmatic than simple innuendo. She and her husband have become the puppets of a marriage blandly false to their real selves.

Camilla's final acceptance of Polidor is strengthened as well as qualified by the way that the worst of each has been exposed to the other. The comic characters also enter in pairs, the men no less damaged in self esteem than the serious couples whose intrigue they echoed. But the phrasing of Polidor's appeal to Camilla is serious in a way that takes one back once more to *Calisto* –

Cruel young Beauty, you are to this Town,
Like a cold Spring; how many tender Plants
Does your Severity suppress and kill?[36]

It compresses the idea of the town into a pastoral image that tenderly contradicts the intimations of mortality from which the play has emerged. It is Crowne's triumph that we do not feel his seriousness misplaced.

Polidor had earlier described his affair with Mrs Lovely as the 'church beneath the church/As Faith was under Paul's'.[37] Crowne succeeds in finding in the style of the nineties a medium for his own interests that leads one's attention back through the dark silent suburb in a restrospect, not only of his work, but of the society it chronicled. Its audience were uneasy at scenes like that of Mrs Lovely's repentance;[38] predictably so, as the plot allows no easy moral placings, no simple interpretation of any event. Crowne adopts the concerns of his period but, characteristically reorders them into ambiguities more personal to himself. *The Married Beau* is the church beneath the church of the moral comedy of the nineties.

8 The Etheregean Revival – Southerne, Cibber and Vanbrugh

I have already described the late seventeenth-century revival of Restoration comedy as 'artificial'. In doing so I deliberately evoke Charles Lamb's famous nineteenth century perspective on '. . . the Artificial Comedy of the Last Century'.[1] For Lamb, 'Artificial' would seem to mean 'of the theatre'; a comedy that insists on its 'theatrical' provenance and its consequent distance from 'the real' as affirmed elsewhere; a comedy to some extent privileged by this distance, protected from moral or political inquisition. Later critics have of course been right to push beyond this formulation. And yet, reductive though it is, it can pinpoint be used to a kind of theatricality which distinguishes the comedy of the end of the century from the earlier forms it imitated. 'The Playhouse' according to Tom Brown in 1700 'is an enchanted island, where nothing appears in reality what it is nor what it should be'.[2] The unedifying picture he goes on to paint, of the sordid contrast between theatre and reality, could not perhaps have been apparent twenty or thirty years earlier. An obvious discontinuity of social and theatrical life produces a drama informed by a new awareness of the isolating tendency of theatre to create its own place in its own imagined world; an awareness forced on it by sudden shifts in court taste and social morality.

The three dramatists whose work I discuss in this chapter – Thomas Southerne, John Vanbrugh and Colley Cibber – all work, as I shall demonstrate, from a conception of wit comedy, derived from Etherege, specifically from *She Would if She Could*, which all three imitate. They are also linked to each other professionally. Southerne became the arbiter of the comedy of the decade; Cibber, Vanbrugh and Congreve owe much to his active encouragement, as well as to that distillation of a 'pure'[3] conversational style noted by his contemporaries. Cibber's plays are in themselves less inter-esting from a literary point of view but his career is vastly more significant theatrically. A star actor, centrally implicated in the development of comic styles, he offers an important perspective on the mutation of wit comedy into what is often (I think unhelpfully) called the 'sentimental' mode. Vanbrugh's first play to be staged, *The Relapse* (1696), was an ironic sequel to Cibber's first, *Love's Last Shift* (1696). All three then, work from within the same nexus of theatrical activity; all three promote an 'Etheregean revival'.

One can I think demonstrate that this results in two types of comedy. The more fruitful was a crystallization of the Etheregean form into a set of fixed roles and convention, the material of an aesthetic perfectionism. One can see this in Vanbrugh, and, supremely, Congreve. Southerne's *The Wives Excuse* (1691) evinces the same tendency in its conscious imitation of Etherege, and in that teasing out of familiar subtleties, so reminiscent of the gibe at Henry James, that he chewed more than he had bitten off. His *The Maid's Last Prayer* (1693) delves deeper into the available conven-tions; it's an attempt at a consciously 'masculine' style of comic writing, full of echoes of *The Plain Dealer*. But *The Maid's Last Prayer* is also a kind of failure, in a way that points to the eventual vogue of a second type of comedy, more closely associated with Cibber. Cibber's understanding of wit comedy was more limited than Southerne's but his sense of public taste was infinitely more acute. Wycherleyan satire could not be so simply revived as Southerne assumed; *The Maid's Last Prayer* seems to me to collapse from within. What we are left with is a blend of exploitative theatricality and private feeling of a kind which, as I will show in the second half of the chapter, was Cibber's widely influential legacy to commercial theatre.

THOMAS SOUTHERNE

Southerne's interests and attitudes seem typical of the nineties. Nonetheless, they existed in his work from the beginning. His career had two phases, the first at the end of Charles II's reign, broken by an unsuccessful attempt to make a career in the army. This tells one a certain amount about him; in attitude he was a through professional, 'born' according to Pope, 'to raise/The price of prologues and of plays',[4] whose stable and carefully-managed career suggests that in this, as in much else, Aphra Behn was his mentrice. Southerne was seldom ambitious above the demands of commerce. 'I have given you a little taste of Comedy with it . . .' he writes in the dedication of *The Fatal Marriage*, (1694) his dreary perversion of Behn's splendid *The History of the Nun*,

> . . . not from my own Opinion, but the present Humour of the Town; I never contend that, because I think every reasonable Man will, and ought to govern in the pleasures he pays for.[5]

Southerne clearly valued himself the more for a thorough professionalism.

Like other professional dramatists, Southerne played off ideas of behaviour received from the Wits against evaluations of his own. For Southerne the very concepts of 'theatre' and 'acting' suggested a more critical way of dramatizing the social manoeuvres of manners and 'intrigue'. This is most evident in the last and best of his Carolean plays *The Disappointment or The Mother in Fashion* (1684). The 'fashion' tag links it to a whole series of post Etherege comedies of mode, but its setting on the corrupt fringes of a European court, and its opposition of a court libertine to a married couple mark it out as a companion piece to Lee's *Princess of Cleves*. In some degree it answers Lee's play. The marriage survives the libertine's assault – the corruption stems from misunderstanding in that the 'mother' of the title is actually a step-mother, an ex-bawd reverting to type, and the cast mistress is not a termagent but a lady of wit and decision. The play only half works. Already one can see how much more feeling Southerne has for marriage than for conventional libertinage. The characters in the marriage plot are distanced from concepts and manners themselves almost outdated. 'These are the mouldy Morals of the dead'[6] exclaims Alphonso in surprise when his friend tries, with a conventional defence of inconstancy, to prepare him for news of his wife's apparent infidelity. There too perhaps Southerne answers Lee's praise of the dead Rochester. The possibility of unfaithfulness seems so distant to Alphonso that he is able to imagine it only in terms of the contemporary stage –

> The common, ridden Cuckold of the Town;
> Stag'd to the crowd on publick Theatres,
> Nay, balleted about the streets in rhime . . .[7]

In fact, the mistress has, in the familiar manner, impersonated the wife (she mops up other of Alberto's attempted seductions in the same way) and all is well. This whole plot detaches itself as 'theatrical', as a series of games dictated by social convention but played by the characters against their will. Husband and wife arrange a trap for the libertine. A pastoral song by Etherege, no less, sets the mood for an idyllic encounter.

> Alberto. So the kind *Nymph*, dissolving as she lay,
> Expecting sigh'd and chid the *Shepherds* stay;
> When panting to the Joy, he flew, to prove
> The Immortality of Life and Love.
> Erminia. I must, but know not how to Act this Part[8]

Erminia's self-consciousness is Southerne's own. He remains unable to integrate his own interests with the late Carolean style. Domesticity is Southerne's subject. He is fascinated by the intimate deceits of close relationship. It is not then entirely surprising that the first play to discuss marriage in the light of the new monarchy should be his.

The Spartan Dame antedates the accession of William and Mary by about a year. Leonidas, the unpopular king of Sparta, is driven out and supplanted by his daughter Celona and her ambitious husband Cleombrotus. The play exploits Celona's plight in a way at once typical of Southerne and specific in language and detail to the contemporary crisis. Though Southerne claimed to have written the play 'without any View, but upon the Subject, which I took from . . . Plutarch'[9] it could not be produced until 1719. (Even then some sections were cut down to telegraphically terse outbursts of emotion.) Without the political reference Southerne's characters have no substance, for he can establish no other claim on the audience's interest.

His method of characterization was to remain to some degree referential. Even in his best plays very few characters evince an imaginative pressure that informs what they say or do. They exist as they impinge on a web of surmise and opinion spun by their fellows. For this reason his tragedies fall below his comedies in standard to a degree unique in an important dramatist. He needs the close social context of Etheregean comedy, its sense of constantly apprehended realities, and it is by his example that the form revives.

In *The Wives Excuse* Southerne does for the society of the 1690s what Etherege did in *The Man of Mode* for the seventies – he crystallizes aspects of everyday life into a series of genre scenes. From the brilliantly managed exposition of the footmen at dice while their masters attend the music meeting, through the concert, the masquerade, the card-party, and tea alfresco, Southerne traces a complex of social relationships through apparently casual encounters and groupings. In this as in Etherege the park has a central place. Seeds sown at the play's opening emerge gradually in the second act as the various characters organise themselves at breakfast the next day, and finally develop into a complex intrigue as they gather again in St James's Park.

Park and garden offer two contrasted images in this play, of public and private identity, and correspond to the plot and sub-plot respectively. The intrigue that gives the play its momentum (if not its title) is the attempt of the 'she-wit' Mrs Witwoud to procure her friend Sightly for Wilding, a rake. At first she means this as a bribe to win back her young cousin from him in time for an honourable marriage – though marriage is not a state she regards very highly – but her motivation becomes more complex. Only in disguise can she join properly in the game of flirtation. She tests this when she comes masked to Wilding's room, but his ardour collapses with embarrassed abruptness when she reveals her identity. At the very end of the play she risks impersonation again, and disguised as Sightly, is discovered in disarray with Friendall, an unmasking that brings the two plots together and to an end.

Sightly herself is reserved almost to the point of emotional paralysis. She fascinates Wellvile as an enigma to be pursued and scrutinized; he is the platonic lover from whom Witwoud hopes to lure her. Wellvile's long speech in the park is in some ways at the centre of the play; he has caught a hint of Sightly's involvement in the intrigue –

> I'll think no more on't, 'tis impossible; what's impossible? nothing's impossible to a Woman: we judge but on the outside of that Sex; and know not what they can, nor what they do, more than they please to shew us . . .

The enigma of 'woman' looms large in Southerne's work. For him, as well as for Wellville, it is a labyrinth of fascinating, dangerous subtleties –

She is open in her carriage, easie, clear of those arts that have
made Lust a Trade – Perhaps that openness may be design – 'Tis
easie to raise doubts – And still she may be – I won't think she
can – till I know more:[10]

All the characters criss-cross in the park, scrutinizing each other
and erecting defensive disguises for themselves; it is a theatre of
the self, of perilous improvisations and trickeries. Wellvile is himself a poet, as it emerges when Friendall interrupts his anxious
soliloquy. Southerne, of course, has nothing but contempt for the
gentleman amateur, Friendall's characteristic pose, but he allows
Wellvile to take a hint from *The Devil is an Ass* and turn the artifice
of *The Wives Excuse* inside out. The play Friendall has offered to
contribute a scene to is indeed called *The Wives Excuse or Cuckolds
make themselves*. Wellvile elaborates on this in a way that puts him
at the centre of the real play, as Southerne's baffled representative.
The plots of the characters and the plot of the author merge
indivisibly when the play moves into the park.

Friendall's garden is a more controlled environment, in whose
privacy both plots come to their emotional climax. The scene
where Sightly rejects Witwoud is in some ways the most passionate in Southerne's *oevre*. She rejects Wellvile too, eventually; her
confrontation with a world of calculated masculine deceit has bred
a caution that seems excessively stifling, though as one can see
from *The Maids Last Prayer* it is part of the logic of Southerne's
version of male–female relationships that the woman should be
repellingly self-sufficient. An altogether stronger sense of vulnerability and betrayal underlies her parting with Witwoud, especially
that final shot –

. . . what's past shall be a Secret for both our sakes; but I'm
resolv'd never more to come into your power; so farewell, and
find a better Friend than I have been.[11]

Sightly's sense that it is she who has been a false friend is on the
face of it illogical. But it throws a retrospective light on the strength
of her bond with Witwoud and reveals it to be an ambiguously
shared identity, an unconscious complicity. Both these characters
are constructed entirely out of the familiar materials of intrigue
comedy; yet their subtlety and strength is uniquely Southerne's.
At his best he approaches Henry James' gift for allusive and

dangerously playful dialogue, and has a similar sense of personal game-playing as an outcrop of a peculiarly rich and stable social organism – a sense to which the footmen's scene and their subsequent presence in the early acts helps to contribute.

It is from this sense of newly established social stability that the marriage plot gains its resonance. Mrs Friendall is a brilliant player of intimate games, as her static scene in Act II illustrates. She plays off in turn her husband, her lover and her brother with matchless aplomb, but the real manoeuvres are interior –

> I don't know that he is a Coward; but having these reasons to suspect him, I thought this was my best way to hinder him from discovering himself. For if he had betrayed that baseness to me, I shou'd despise him; and can I love the Man I most despise?[12]

Her final rejection of her husband has a marvellous judicial gravity, and a moving eloquence –

> This hard Condition of a Woman's fate, I've often weigh'd, therefore resolv'd to bear; And I have born; O! what have I not born? But patience tires with such oppressing wrongs, when they come home, to triumph over me . . .[13]

The strength of this final scene, the judgement on a final unmasking, is a resonance that goes beyond specific circumstance. The language of Mrs Friendall's great speech is impersonally judicious. She becomes representative of issues she does not fully articulate. After all, on a personal level, what has she borne? Friendall is a wine-bore, an unsuccessful philanderer and not gentleman enough to fight a duel, but he is not a monster like Sir John Brute or Goodvile, and marriages have withstood larger shocks than that of his drunken indiscretions in masquerade. There is a pathos in Friendall of which Southerne seems unaware. Like most male writers attempting a 'feminist' viewpoint, Southerne drastically cuts down his men to allow his women the benefit of the comparison. Mrs Friendall's rejection of her unattractive lover lacks a psychological intensity. She arms herself with a teatray as symbol of her wifely role and exits with a wispily ironic '. . . Are not you for Tea?'[14] And yet Southerne skirts sentimental inconcsequence. Both this and that last scene have a genuine power. Marriage is a real issue in the society the play depicts. It is indeed an image of larger questions:

. . . in a marry'd State, as in the publick, we tie ourselves up, indeed; but to be protected . . .; for few will obey but for the Benefit they receive from the Government –[15]

Lovemore enters here and cuts off Mrs Friendall's train of thought; it is tacitly re-assumed in that final scene. The acceptable price of social stability is at issue here. Southerne may no longer explicitly question the post-revolutionary settlement, but through the Friendalls he is able to weigh a peaceful compromise against the familiar demands of Restoration comedy for individual equity, and implicitly to find it wanting.

In *The Maids Last Prayer* satirical intention is more explicit. Southerne's model here is Wycherley's *Plain Dealer*.[16] The play follows the adventures of the 'splenetick' Granger and his contrastingly blithe friend Gayman in a society of grasping and infinitely mendacious married women and their gullible, social ambitious husbands. But Southerne's revival of the mode is only intermittently successful. Granger's plain-dealing is a compulsive rhetroic empty of personal meaning and random in its aim. Each scene in which we see him simply defines his voice in relation to a new object. There is no real connection between the sexual malice of the first scene and the prim back-biting at Lady Susan's. The first scene in St. James's Park is the setting of a satirical topos, owing something perhaps to Rochester's *Timon*.[17] Who is Granger? Is he a Manly, a Petulant, or the-author-as-satirist? One could only say he were all three if all three functioned in one scene. As it is he retains a centreless versatility of dissent.

Southerne's great weakness is his inability to project male character sympathetically. Paradoxically, this reveals a troubling vein of misogyny behind his identification with female protagonists. Gayman and Granger are motivated in their sexual intrigues by revenge and dislike. Maria, who might seem another Harriet in the light of her fondness for 'play'[18] emerges as completely null as her namesake in *The School for Scandal*. The focus of the play is not the woman Gayman eventually marries but she whom he so successfully seeks to degrade and abuse. The outcome of his pursuit of Lady Malapert goes beyond sexual satire into offensively misogynist male fantasy. Sex with Gayman is so wonderful that this highly expensive court whore offers him his money back. Their love-making is completely depersonalized by her ignorance of his identity. He makes no emotional contact with her, and has the satisfaction of knowing that it was he of whom she fantasized in the anonymous encounter. At the end of the play Gayman publicly announces his engagement to Maria, while giving the bawd Wishwell the means to blackmail Lady Malapert into her power. One might argue, as in Granger's case, that the emptiness of means and the nastiness of ends place Gayman with a satirical aptness. And yet this emptiness and nastiness is allowed to dominate the play. It is not that there is simply no positive. It is that the structure of the play instates Gayman and Granger as positives, and there is very little in the writing from which to infer a criticism of them. Gayman's very lack of personality lets him stand as a representative male. Indeed Maria (another characterless norm) is used to establish the two men's worth in a way that destroys their potential as either satirists or objects of satire. Gayman's 'respectful impudence' and Granger's 'Breeding' and 'Honour'[19] aligns them to the society of the play, where Wycherley took care to isolate Manly and Freeman from that of *The Plain Dealer*. It gives them a respected niche within it in which they can neither be attacked nor usefully attack. They are, as we shall see, much more like Cibber's toothlessly impudent players of sub-erotic games.

The play's method is of 'broken music', thwarted plots, games disrupted and cheated upon. Trickit finally defeats Granger's attempt on her by passing his note of assignation on to her aunt. When the ageing Susan takes her place at Rosamund's pond, Granger recognizes her but pretends to believe it is another woman in disguise – Lady Susan would not thus stoop to conquer. It is a funny and ingenious variation on a familiar device, but it furthers Southerne's tendency to seal his female characters off, as if on a different plane from the male. Trickit dismisses Granger in an even more pointed display of self-sufficiency than Sightly's. In doing so she has of course 'cheated' in the pastoral/theatrical game; 'Disappointment' is the method of Southerne's comedy. The lasting relationship of the play, the true intimacy, is between Trickit and Garnish. At the end of the play Garnish, after Trickit has dismissed him ignominiously for his jealousy in the Rosamund's pond scene, learns his lesson and is, perhaps even more ignominiously, summoned back. No other character in the play ever learns of it. Southerne's equivalents to Wycherley's Vernish and Olivia have, very privately, triumphed. *The Maids Last Prayer* is marked by a disillusion with the medium which is at least partly an awareness of failure. The social occasions in this play – the raffle, the gambling, the India house – are private and unrepresentative.

One has the sense of being whirled along in an eccentrically unlikable clique. Southerne's attempts to embody a sense of social vacuity and sexual failure in this 'broken music' of artfully disrupted structure is sabotaged ultimately by a flaccidity of dialogue and construction within scenes. But its comparative failure is more significant generically than technically. The society Southerne describes in the play is shaped by a kind of awareness different from that of the Etherege plays it imitates. The Etheregean form isolates economic and social realities within the vacuum of leisured society. Southerne's failure to cut away the facade as *The Plain Dealer* had stripped off the mask of its own age has resulted in a play that lays the blame for the state of society on a group of sexually vulnerable individually inconsequent women. We never find out why the women in *The Maids Last Prayer* want money, or why the men want place. The Etheregean form cannot tell us these things. Southerne has pushed it beyond its limits, and created, perhaps intentionally exposed, a jarring dissonance of form and context.

CIBBER AND VANBURGH

The main external impulse to the development of a style of comedy that one might usefully call 'Cibberian' – 'sentimental' seems unhelpfully unspecific – came from the split into two companies that followed the actors' rebellion against Rich's management of the United Company. One, based in Lincoln's Inn Fields and lead by Betterton, was composed chiefly of the older actors; the other, at Drury Lane, consisted of inexperienced actors, of performers whose skills dictated a bias towards farce, or, especially after the Verbruggens defected from Betterton, to the frothier kind of social comedy.[20] In the fierce competition that followed, each company determinedly staked out a style of their own. Betterton's were 'classical' and conservative, as much in the work of their greatest writer, Congreve, as in revivals of heroic tragedies and Shakespeare. Rich's were 'modern' in their gaudier farcical style and showy eroticism, as well as in their commitment to reformed manners and an up-to-date propriety. This contradiction informs what one thinks of as 'sentimental' or Cibberian plays. In applying the methods of Restoration comedy to concepts antithetic to it, the new style produced a comedy paradoxically more immoral than what had gone before. It embodies an idea of sexuality at once unreal and inhumane.

Of the three plays I shall go on to discuss in this chapter, Vanbrugh's *Provok'd Wife* (1697) is the most traditional, a careful imitation and updating of *She Would if She Could* written for Betterton's company. *The Relapse* both extends and criticizes Cibber's concerns; it is conceived as a vehicle for his 'Novelty Fashion' character. If Vanbrugh was the author of *The Relapse*, Cibber was auteur. Betterton, on the other hand, gave his dramatist access to a reservoir of skills. He was not a 'personality' of the kind that Cibber insistently, even irritatingly, created for himself. Betterton's years of experience gave him a totemic stature in the rebel company, a token of their ancestral links to wit comedy and the heroic plays. But his professionalism is detached from any easily identifiable psychological base. Betterton was a great actor by virtue of almost impersonal skills; Cibber made himself a star in the modern sense, an amalgam of performance and self publicity.

Formal change and fashionable change can be observed together in that matrix of Restoration wit comedy, its social map – the parks, as I have argued throughout this book, are the central locale of intrigue comedy. The royalist–pastoral associations that defined their place in an ethos of 'Restoration' inevitably waned under a monarchy no longer Stuart, and no longer living in St James's. Kensington palace had no place in fashionable mythology, ironic or otherwise. Society had not forsaken St James's or the Mall. But when comedy returns there with *The Wives Excuse* it is evident that the park's tone is now taken as much from the theatre as from the court.

The neo-Etheregean plays after all, are separated from their model by thirty years of social change. The park, as Cibber or Gildon sees it, is a place for seeing and being seen;

> . . . the Mall is pav'd with lac'd shoes; . . . the air is perfumed with the Rosy breath of so many Fine ladies; . . . from one end to the other the Sight is entertain'd with nothing but beauty, and the whole Prospect looks like an Opera.[21]

It is no longer the territory of any clique, or the privileged locale of a certain kind of behaviour. It has become instead a kind of theatre.

In the case of the park, the social reasons for this are easily deducible – the court was no longer at St James's. But one can also see this shift in meaning in terms of garden aesthetics, of the way a park or garden was 'read'. For Flecknoe, in the early years of the Restoration, the double meaning of 'plot' had a precise relevance; plays could be said to be made like gardens because gardens could be read like plays; as formal patterns given meaning and variety by the presence of people on them, by movements co-erced and ordered in a system of walks and vantage points. The people inhabiting the garden would be part of a group whose cohesion the garden would express; it is, in a very real sense, their play-ground. This underlies the theatrical use of gardens, up to Shadwell and Otway. A garden aesthetic to parallel the Etheregean approach to 'plot' emerges in theory – Sir William Temple's 'Sharawagi', derived from traveller's reports of the gardens of China, is just such a collusion of art and nature, such an introduction of apparently random elements to an artfully disputed patterning, as marks the implied aesthetic of wit comedy. But by the time it emerged into practice, it had undergone a metamorphosis into the 'jardin anglais' of the early eighteenth century.[22] The garden of the late seventeenth century is a modification of the earlier emblematic style into a 'readable' garden; but its meaning is imposed by organized allusion, not by its social use, by looking, not by participation. The Gimcracks' garden, or the Goodviles' are still 'plot' gardens; kinds of grid on which things happen. In *The Wives Excuse*, the Friendalls' garden is for seeing and being seen in, and landscaped to that purpose – 'we'll Drink our Tea upon the Mount, and be the Envy of the Neighbourhood.[23] Theatricality has become the keynote of the society depicted in the plays. This is not surprising, given that such society is to some extent a construct required by comic styles and forms increasingly distant from the circumstances of their initial development. When Narcissa, in Cibber's *Love's Last Shift* speaks of the 'true pleasure of the Park' she means the pleasure it affords as the comedy of real life; it is a theatre for amateurs of satire, and the action if held up as she and her friends point out passing actors, including, rather nostalgically,

> Mrs Holdout, one that is proud of being the original of fashionable Fornication, and values herself mightily for being one of the first Mistresses that ever kept her coach publickly in England . . .[24]

Cibber's reference to the world of the early Restoration also serves to measure his distance from it.

Cibber launched a career as a star actor by writing into *Love's Last Shift* the role of Sir Novelty Fashion, to be raised to the peerage as Lord Foppington by Vanbrugh; a career that stamped Cibber's image indelibly on this last phase of Restoration comedy. He is the filter through which we see the acting of Restoration plays, not only in his accounts of his contemporaries but, I would suggest, in the floridly stylized acting that passes for Restoration style with many actors today. Congreve's and Vanbrugh's plays act much better than Etherege's or Wycherley's simply because the acting style perfected by Cibber and admired by him in others has passed into theatrical tradition.[25] Foppington, or even Tattle (a non-Cibber role) demand a kind of 'overplaying' that wrecks the balance of the play if applied to Sir Fopling or Sparkish. The same thing, *mutatis mutandis*, goes for other kinds of typed roles. Cibber as an actor is a more powerful presence than Cibber as writer. Both inform the work of a greater dramatist.

In *Love's Last Shift* Cibber makes the most overt of several attempts to link himself back to the tradition of Restoration comedy in a characteristically back-firing speech of Sir Novelty's.

In Vindication of all well-dress'd Gentlemen, I intend to write a Play, where my chiefest character shall be a *downright English Booby*, that affects to be a Beau, without either Genius or foreign Education, and to call it in Imitation of another famous Comedy, *He Wou'd if he Cou'd.*[26]

The sententious Elder Worthy sums him up as 'A Thing that affects mightily to ridicule himself, only to give others a kind of Necessity of praising him'.[27] One could suspect Cibber here of unconscious self-revelation, were self-consciousness not the key-note of both the role and the man. Where Etherege achieves insouciance, Cibber only attains precocity. He attempts to amuse by surprising, by breaking decorum, but the effects are simple and isolated. One never feels as one does with Dorimant, or even Lady Cockwood, that the inability to be contained by propriety is some-how a measure of personal completeness, and complexity. Cibber's characters approach each other in little impulses of violence, on all levels, from the conversational ambition to be coyly outra-geous, to that of a plot that conceives of sexuality almost wholly in terms of rape or quasi-rape. Both can be illustrated by a speech from the end of Act I – (the speaker is Young Worthy, who reappears in *The Relapse*, to Narcissa, who does not);

> I'gad, I find nothing but down-right Impudence will do with her [Aside]. . . .Just laid within the bridal Bed; our Friends retir'd; the Curtains close drawn around us; no light but Caelia's Eyes; No Noise but her soft trembling Words, and broken Sighs, that plead in vain for Mercy. And now at rickling Tear steals down her glowing cheek, which tells the happy Lover at length she yields; yet vows she's rather die. But still submits to the unexperienc'd Joy [Embracing her][28]

Novelty is an extreme case of a general infection. One could characterize the play as a comedy of impudence.

Novelty assimilates the rest of the play. The garden setting, and the echo (indeed the Echo) that Narcissa provides for him, in a kind of competition of self-regard,[29] serve to generalize his condition; it swamps all the other characters and thus blurs the distinctions Etherege makes so sharply. He appropriates even the park-scene, and its stock impersonation. Flareit, his cast mistress, impersonates Narcissa. The characters of the 'high' plot stray in and out of the park in a way that enacts their participation in Novelty's world. Amanda inverts Flareit's impersonation of respectability – in a plot hatched and instigated there – by impersonating easy virtue. In this role she has a courtesan's necessary self-awareness; even her pleasure can be taken only in reflection –

> Does my Face invite you Sir? May I, from what you see of me, propose a Pleasure to my self in pleasing you?[30]

Neither disguise needs psychological or philosophical justification; it is enough that they are theatrical. Cibber's view of life is supremely well-adapted to the limits of his dramatic mode. All his characters are on the same narcissistic/theatrical wavelength. Loveless' conversion is more satisfying than that of any of Cibber's later attempts at this simplest of formal conclusions, in its consistency with his sub-Etheregean concept of life-as-theatre; it can be extended to express the most intimate moral truths, though at the extortionate expense of reducing the characters to their own puppets. Loveless, as Worthy suggests in Act I, has had motives for

rakishness no more permanent than Sir Novelty's motives for
dress – ''twas more an Affectation of being fashionably Vicious'.[31]
Not even vice is real. Thus Cibber is able to convey Loveless's
change by the simplest possible means – 'Enter *Loveless* in new
Clothes'[32] – and to convey the stasis preceding change of heart in
the immortal stage-direction – 'Stands in a fix'd posture'.[33] Every
important shift of feeling in this scene is conveyed in pantomime,
though none with the blissfully silly panache of the Act IV bedroom scene –

> Stand off [cries Amanda] distant as the Globes of Heaven and
> Earth, that like a falling Star I may shoot with greater Force into
> your Arms, and think it Heaven to lie expiring there – RUNS
> INTO HIS ARMS.[34]

This is true camp, executed, like everything else in the play, with
one eye on the mirror.

Cibber seems gradually to be converting the characters of his
high plot into the puppet-aristocrats of *The Comical Revenge* or *The
Mulberry Garden* a process Vanbrugh compounds in *The Relapse* by
going back into verse. Vanbrugh does not criticize Cibber's shallowness, for it is this that fascinates him. He enlarges the context of
the play, making sharper distinctions between the separate worlds
of its characters and manipulates the theme of roles and role-
playing, with a conscious, rather than a weakly self-conscious,
bravado. A crucial transformation of material occurs in scenes
played by Cibber with Mrs Kent. In both plays there is a mock duel
to point up Novelty's cowardice – in Cibber's Mrs Kent plays
Flareit, but in Vanbrugh she plays his brother, Young Fashion.[35]
The point made is subtly modified. Whereas Cibber seems to be
suggesting, by one of the mirror images he uses to relate Novelty
to the rest of the cast that Flareit and he are two kinds of old
whore, Vanbrugh, characteristically more generous, allows Foppington's unwillingness to fight to become a kind of *hauteur* entirely fitting to his recent ennoblement, and suggests, through the
device of travesty, that Fashion's dash and heroism are themselves
a kind of affectation – just another role.

If this allows Fashion to exist only as a surface, one could with
some justice say the same of the play, or at least, of its mode of
characterization. The superiority from which one can infer a criticism of Cibber is ultimately that of skill, not of insight. It is for this

reason that *The Relapse* is more fairly seen as sequel than parody. Vanbrugh takes seriously Cibber's assumptions of sexual role-playing and self-regard. Detached from the demands of Cibber's personality they provide the apparatus for a more ambitious discussion.

Where the cast of *Love's Last Shift* seemed all too consistent with each other, too much of a piece, *The Relapse* fragments into as many separate worlds as there are characters. Vanbrugh has a gift for creating not only individuals but whole lives in a single line. (One thinks of the constable in *The Provok'd Wife* who responds to Sir John Brute's invitation to go whoring with a dignified 'No thank you Sir, my Wife's enough to satisfy any reasonable Man.'[36]) In the unfinished *The Journey to London* the characters tend to expand so luxuriantly that by the time he breaks off in Act IV there is still very little indication of what the piece as a whole is moving to. But it is precisely this which allows him to break down Cibber's tight, shallow little world into workable units, without disturbing or guying the original conception. *The Relapse* is the first evidence of his gift for transposition and adaption which was to be exploited later in his translations, and indeed in his architecture. Vanbrugh's major modification is to revive the distinction, basic to *The Man of Mode* as to so many of the comedies, between the mores of the town and those of the visiting country girl – here, Amanda. Foppington does not merely represent the town – though this is how Loveless sees him on their first encounter in the play – by virtue of Vanbrugh's marvellously deft management of the first few scenes, he comes to embody it. The first scene shows Loveless leaving the country, the second Fashion arriving in London, and in the third the life of the town is established for us by Foppington's leave in which 'Shoemaker . . . Taylor . . . Hosier . . . . Semstress and Barber' conspire in a voluptuous orgy of narcissism – 'let my people dispose the Glasses so, that I may see myself before and behind; for I love to see myself all round . . . '[37] - by the end of which he is become a monster of artifice within which 'nothing should be seen but his eyes'. Vanbrugh's characters hold the stage with the solidity of objects. It is impossible to imagine this baroque monument ever succumbing to the indignity of a fall, as he does in II.i of Cibber's play; it would amount to demolition. Removal to the country cannot lessen his urbanity. Pinioned and baited – a traditional fate for monster-heroes – he shows an imperturbability which, like true stoicism, has nothing to do with lack of either feeling or wit. Like all great comic characters he takes a lifestyle to its heroic limit. Foppington simply is the town.

But One could not really call the retreat where we first see Amanda and Loveless 'the country'. Vanbrugh gives no scene direction – we are in a blank verse limbo of noble sentiments. The bonelessness of the writing enables it to act as a sort of cocoon. Loveless's first speech is dangerously self-contradictory; if 'Heaven is seated in our minds' there would really seem to be no need of the 'Little soft retreat'.[38] Vanbrugh exploits our vagueness about what happens when the curtain first goes up by being thus vague himself. The scene detaches itself as somehow prior to the real play, in which Loveless's delusions of humility are to be destroyed. Besides making the listener uneasy by its tendency to cloy, the verse also blurs distinctions between the characters' voices, in a way that never happens when Vanbrugh writes prose. Their relationship is itself messily narcissistic, they talk in flaccid echo forms, where the sharpness with which Vanbrugh usually writes marital disputes is weakly sugared with sentiment.

Whether by accident or design, the very first lines of this play echo the very last lines of Dryden's *State of Innocence*.

For outward Eden lost find Paradise within[39]

Loveless's thoughts later in the scene take a teleological direction –

The largest Boons that Heaven thinks fit to grant
To Things it has decreed shall crawl on Earth,
Are in the Gift of Women form'd like you.
Perhaps, when Time shall be no more,
When the aspiring Soul shall take its flight,
And drop this ponderous lump of Clay behind it,
It may have appetites we know not of,
And pleasures as refin'd as its desires . . .[40]

It was not simply an interest in marriage that made Milton's paradise a major point of pastoral reference for the dramatists of the nineties. The reform of manners encouraged by Mary became a largely female preoccupation. An attempt to impose a particular kind of behaviour may well lead one to ask whether it is 'natural', and if not what is? Milton derives his conception of Eve's innate narcissism from Tasso's *Amyntas*. By placing it in so unchallengeable a context of innocence, he seems to be correcting Tasso's equation of it with corruption:

> I have heard
> That nymphs and shepherdesses formerly
> Were not thus knowing, . . .
> . . . The world, methinks, grows old,
> And growing old, grows sad.[41]

But the characterization of Eve seems instead to challenge the rest of the poem. Milton does not manage to coerce his readers into his own assumptions of woman's nature. *Paradise Lost* can seem as full of comic ambiguities in Eden as it notoriously is of tragic ambiguities in Hell. Vanbrugh, in both his major plays, exploits these ironies to broaden out a discussion of sexual roles and social self-awareness essentially derived from Cibber. This first scene is, in this light, a parody of that where Adam tries to persuade Eve not to go pruning alone. It is a parody in that Eve and Adam have changed places, and this sets the tone for the play.

The question of shifting sexual identity, externalized in the casting of young Fashion, runs as a slightly disturbing undertone to the high-plot scenes of *ménage-à-quatre*. Berinthia is self-mockingly aware of her expected role as a woman at the beginning of her first duologue with Amanda, when she speaks of the 'Modern Philosopher (whose Works, tho' a Woman, I have read)'[42] and yet once Amanda tells her of Worthy's advances, her tone takes a conventionally masculine intransigence, using typically masculine arguments to persuade Amanda to adultery. Then she dissolves it with the coy 'Don't I talk madly? . . . Yet I'm very innocent'. Berinthia resolves the question of femininity into a paradox. She decides to marry so 'That I never May . . . I'm a Woman, and form my resolutions accordingly . . .'. Invertedly, in other words, like a mirror image. To be a woman, as Berinthia conceives of it, is to live in a paradox, which she resolves (as do all four eventually) by denying moral responsibility, in conceiving of her actions as enforced. Her solution to Amanda's problem, of how to respond to Worthy, is to suggest she think of it in terms of rape.[43]

In Vanbrugh's garden scene (III.ii) the reason for her sudden intrasigence is revealed; she is Worthy's ex-mistress. It is typical of her that she thus feels herself to be his creature, encouraging

Amanda even before he asks her to. Typical also of Vanbrugh's clear light on Cibber's sexual ethos is the disparity between the motive Worthy suggests and the compulsion she owns to herself. He is narcissistically impudent, vain in a way he projects on to her –

> Now am I almost in Love with you again. Nay, I don't know but I might be quite so, had I made one short Campaign with *Amanda*. Therefore, if you find 'twoud tickle your Vanity, to bring me down once more to your Lure, e'en help me quickly to dispatch her business, that I may have nothing else to do, but to apply myself to yours.[44]

In this endangered Eden roles are again reversed; behind Berinthia's self-consciously feminine pretence it is she who tempts, and Loveless, naive and self-deluding, who is tempted.

There is something self-defeating in the determined triviality of the seducers. They tend toward the condition of predatory abstractions, and while Berinthia is clearly a good acting part, Worthy's chances are consistently pre-empted – his first entrance by Foppington, his second by Berinthia, and throughout the rest of the play, by Amanda herself. If Vanbrugh extends Cibber's notion of role playing to the whole business of sexual identity – and at one point Worthy and Berinthia use the expression 'Males and Females'[45] almost as one might say cops-and-robbers – in creating his pair of sexless seducers he switches the source of real sexual tension to the conventional Amanda and Loveless. It is Amanda whose endangered virtue provides the firmest imaginative focus. The irony by which it is she and not Loveless who breaks the cloying twosome with which the play opens is strong in its insight into the motivation of both putative adulteries. They are generated by the otherwise imperceptible failure of the marriage, and thus the play contains Berinthia's shallowness, and the curiously nebulous quality in Worthy. Vanbrugh convincingly internalizes Amanda's feelings. He enlarges on a hint of Cibber's to make her persistent shrugging off of praise into a kind of nervous tic of insecurity. Her reactions on seeing Loveless with the masked Berinthia are sharply revealing. Vanbrugh does not need to enlarge on the disguise motif, as we are now prepared to see Amanda's collapse come from within. 'Perhaps' she wonders '. . .

sixteen has greater charms for him.' Is it likely that, even masked, Berinthia could pass for sixteen? More alarming is Amanda's exclamation to the maid –

> What do'st stand troubling me with the Visits of a parcel of impertinent Women; when they are well seam'd with the Small Pox, they won't be so fond of shewing their faces – There are more cocquets about this town.[46]

The intrigue of *Love's Last Shift* turned wholly on Amanda's having been made unrecognisable by smallpox. Unlike other country heroines she has not the integrity to withstand the town's confusion of reality and image. Her firmness is undermined by that very self-consciousness which Cibber allows her to exploit in the cause of virtue.

Vanbrugh might profitably have vilified Amanda, as Fielding does Richardson's Pamela, for her willingness to prostitute herself for virtue. One recognises Vanbrugh's Amanda in details of Cibber's, yet this crucial fact of plot is never alluded to. Perhaps silence is the more tactful criticism. And yet, exciting and consistent as Amanda's last scene is with its almost *Clarissa*-like polarity of angel–victim and devil–rapist, and its sense of a rejection that nonetheless inevitably traps both characters, one is left with a sense both of undeveloped potential, and of imbalance between the members of the quartet in which Amanda silently takes her place for the last scene. The sense of unease surrounding the foursome in which no one member is entirely aware of the actions or motives of the others is at least partly the unease of uncertain writing. Vanbrugh allows the point to be resolved by sheer theatricality, as the four come at the end to represent the town in the way that Foppington did at the beginning. The sub-plot arrives swiftly at the point to which the main plot has moved barely perceptively. Hoyden's introduction to the pleasures of the town enacts the point made by Hymen in the concluding masque –

> But I have not pretended, for many Years past,
> By marrying of People to make them grow chast.[47]

In this society marriage is a girl's introduction to the development of her sexuality, and not its outcome. When Worthy claims

The Coarser Appetite of Nature's gone, and 'tis methinks the food of Angels I require.[48]

he picks up a system of images of progressively refined appetites which helps to unify the several strands of the play. Like the characters who take *The Journey to London* in a coach laden with food, the country characters in *The Relapse* are obsessed with eating. Their scenes become a romance of primitive life, of a sort of golden age, much more convincing than the posturing of the town Adams and Eves. Collier was surely right in seeing Sir Tunbelly as a creature of fairytale;[49] the vigour with which Vanbrugh treats them, instead of mocking romance, bloats it almost to the stature of epic. The 'desert beyond High Park' is as thickly populated with monsters as a mediaeval map. It is in a sense a childhood world, in which the images of sexuality surrounding Hoyden, in being conveyed through food metaphors, become strictly presexual, part of a world devoted ravenously to oral gratification only. Hoyden herself is imaged as an egg,[50] as radical an image of innocence as one could get. The hinterland beyond London is the hinterland of the London characters' psychology, the reality of appetite that exists beyond the conscious 'manliness' and 'womanliness' of Worthy and Berinthia, beyond the marriage Loveless ironically affirms as his last utterance. It is as if Vanbrugh is reaching beyond the psychology implied by the fall myth to something more primitive still.

The Provok'd Wife, the play Vanbrugh wrote for Betterton's company, builds on *The Relapse* in only a rather limited technical sense. There is no real development of concerns particular to the author. Vanbrugh's lack of a personal investment in his creations in no way diminishes the skill and energy with which he constructs them; but of all the writers of Restoration comedy he seems least concerned to extend the form, or subvert it, by exploring a personal voice. *The Provok'd Wife* reorders essentially the same material as *The Relapse*, into a play that elegantly accommodates itself to its performers. Of the two, *The Provok'd Wife* is vastly more traditional in form. One could date an outline of the plot almost anywhere between *She Would if She Could* and the Licensing act. *The Provok'd Wife* is in fact the fullest and most intelligent of all imitations of the Etherege. Southerne's stylistic debt – that 'purity' of conversational style admired by Dryden[51] is the more profound, while Cibber's links of Etherege are really just a referential pointing up of similarities of content. Vanbrugh transposes elements of both on to the ground plan of the earlier play. He tightens Etherege's deceptively improvisational looseness of structure, unifying both halves of the plot by, literally, marrying them. Lady Brute makes up one of the quartet of lovers, while Sir John pursues an increasingly violent helter skelter through the night-life of the town. The interfering 'other' woman is distanced, and, as we shall see, trivialized, in the figure of Lady Fancifull, an affected woman of fashion.

These departures accommodate Etherege's plot to the themes of the times. Marriage displaces the 'rambling ladies' in the play's structure, as it had displaced such freedom in contemporary society. The two gallants are an exclusive pair, out of touch with any wider society of gallant life, and defined against each other as a platonic/anti-platonic duality, like similar characters in *The Maids Last Prayer*, *The Old Batchelour*, or *The Married Beau*. As in that last play the pairing is echoed in other doubling patterns and used to enclose a sense of domesticity, located and made concrete by Sir John's 'great chair' and the smell of tobacco imposing his presence on the house, pervading his wife's sense of entrapment within it. Again, this focus on domesticity can be set against the strictly temporary lodgings that the Cockwoods took up, the only fixed point on the heady impermanence of their London of pleasure. The Brutes' domesticity is loomingly permanent. It is a kind of unformed threat, that the action of the play comes to define, and to challenge.

Vanbrugh can work fewer variations than Crowne on his binary patterning. He is dependent on the duologue, as his most trustworthy mode of exposition. In *The Relapse* the undermining of social trust was a poisonous inheritance from the Cibberian world. It isolated almost all the characters; the play reveals Vanbrugh's gift of conveying intimacy – particularly between members of the same sex – but only in sinister parodies, like the scenes between Amanda and Berinthia. Berinthia invests all she has in social manoeuvring; it is her lack of a personal centre that makes her invulnerable, and at the end of the play she is the only character untouched and undamaged in its insidious intrigue. She is in that sense the most refined manifestation of Vanbrugh's character drawing. He has not a firm enough imaginative grasp on his characters' inner life to allow them a casual self-revelation or any but the most extrovert, even, parodistic, soliloquy. In *The Provok'd Wife*, the dialogue is used to reveal character precisely, but in two dimensions; the play unfolds as a series of facades.

Lady Brute's agility in arguments for an affair covers a much wider ground than anything in *The Relapse*.

Well; and he promis'd to be kind to me.
But he han't kept his Word –
Why then I'm absolv'd from mine – ay, that seems clear to me.
The Argument's good between the King and the
People, why not between the Husband and the Wife? O, but that
Condition was not exprest – No matter, 'twas understood . . .[52]

An excursion into hermeneutics makes a point to be nicely taken up by Christopher Hill:

Lady Brute: . . . he is the first agressor. Not I Bell.; but you
know, we must return Good for Evil.
Lady Brute: That may be a mistake in the Translation.[53]

The lovers all argue with a daring clarity; they are cool, aware and play hazardous games with ideas. Vanbrugh sets this most brilliant and best informed of all such quartets against Sir John and his cronies, Tories of the most nihilistic kind, the kind for whom everything is reducible to the pleasures of the bottle. And yet, as we shall see, the ends of both strands of the play come to coincide, if not converge. Lady Brute may make the kind of appeal out to those larger issues, which in other plays, *The Wive's Excuse* for example, would instate the marriage plot as a microcosm. But when Belinda follows the clue of sexual politics to a query posed by contemporary feminism – 'Why then don't we get into the Intrigues of government as well as they?' – it is shelved by Lady Brute's poised reductionism in a way that foreshadows the undercutting effect of the plot; 'Because we have intrigues of our own, that make us more sport, Child. And so let us in and consider of 'em.'[54]

Femininity is embodied in Lady Fanciful, or, rather, Lady Fanciful is the construct of a self-conscious femininity. She is rococo to Foppington's baroque; fashion has hardened over her as it has over him. For them, fashion is not, as it was for Sir Fopling or Melantha, a strategy of the self-made, it is a process of accretion by which a person disappears within a thing. The doubling motif builds an idiot grandeur into her boudoir scenes; she is framed between her two maids, a sarcastic English-woman and the compliant Madamoiselle, as between two aspects of her nature. She can no more manage her masks than Mrs Loveit could, though her vacillation is the more giddily farcical. The style of her scenes is ornamentally dotty. Language and behaviour multiply into an infinity of alternatives, that makes them, eventually, quite meaningless.

When we first see her, she has received a challenge to assignation in the park. There she meets Heartfree, who tries to cut through her affectation.

Heart:	I mean to tell you, that you are the most ungrateful Woman upon Earth.
Lady Fan:	Ungrateful! To whom?
Heart:	To Nature.
Lady Fan:	Why, what has Nature done for me?
Heart:	What you have undone by Art.[55]

There are two park scenes in the play, the first set in St. James's, the second in the Spring Garden. Their structural placing is almost identical to those in *She Would if She Could*.

Where the earlier Restoration Comedy gave place meaning through topographical exactness and carefully evoked social connotations, Vanbrugh uses his parks and gardens emblematically; as space given meaning by art, most specifically by the art of literary allusion. Lady Fancifull takes into the first park scene that familiar strand of ideas I picked up in *The Relapse*, the use of Edenic imagery to focus the idea of woman as created object. Heartfree, for his part, is the anti-platonic of the two gallants. Though he claims to lack interest in women, his idea of woman-as-construct is itself a kind of erotic fantasy, as Congreve demonstrates in *Semele* (1710), where Jupiter enjoys the idyllic possibilities of an affair with his own creation. Heartfree's impulse to deconstruct is more directly sexual than his friend Constant's 'platonic' devotion. '. . . I have lov'd . . . more than e'er a Martyr did his Soul; but she is cold, my Friend, still cold as the Northern Star'.[56] However earnest his pursuit, its end would be the end of this romantic fixity, the only validity his feelings have. Vanbrugh is well aware of the brakes on his characters' emotional movement. Their philosophical awareness ends by imposing a restricting pattern. They may or may not believe what they say – their formulations are provisional, their rationales quite brittle – but it organizes their feelings nonetheless.

Their actions are regulated by a moral life entirely their own construct. At the end of one of Constant's most fluent protestations, Lady Brute exits to leave him chewing on one word.

> . . . she gave me Hope; did she not say gave me Hope? – Hope? Ay; what Hope? – Enough to make me let her go – Why that's enough in Conscience. Or no matter how 'twas spoke; Hope was the Word: it came from her, and it was said to me.[57]

After Heartfree has seen Belinda, his elegant badinage on Constant's love for Lady Brute is persistently tripped up by his unconscious substitution of Belinda's name for hers. The quartet's flair for language becomes irrelevant and collapses under an impulse of feeling. They become assimilated to the state of Lady Fancifull and Sir John.

The second park scene is diagrammatically precise in its meaning, to the point where it almost becomes balletic. Lady Brute and Belinda have made an anonymous assignation with Constant and Heartfree and gone 'meanly dressed'. Lady Fancifull, jealous of Heartfree's interest in Belinda, has dogged them there. Her language is unmeaning by now; in an earlier scene she and Lady Brute has scrambled the ceremony of leave-taking till it became a kind of fanfare to her exit. The action of the park scene has to be showy and externalized to cut against the dazzling nonsense into which the play's verbality has spun itself. It maps out Belinda and Heartfree's cautious exploration:

> '. . . Come Sir, shall we go pry into the Secrets of the Garden. Who knows what Discoveries we may make . . .'.

Lady Brute's articulate evasions reduce Constant to physical force, but 'as he is forcing her into the Arbour, *Lady Fancifull* and *Madamoiselle* bolt out upon them, and run over the stage'.

Lady Brute:	Ah; I'm lost.
Lady Fan.:	Fe fe fe fe fe
Madam.:	Fe fe fe fe fe
Const.:	Death and Furies, who are these?[58]

Lady Fancifull is a kind of malign genius of the place, a coincidental manifestation of Lady Brute's fears. The lovers retreat to Sir

John Brute's house; and there he eventually encounters them. He comes home reduced by his adventures to a comic physicality. His wife listens stoically till he too runs out of language; he falls asleep in the 'great chair';

> And what do you wear now? ha? tell me.
> What? you are modest, and can't – ?
> Why then I'll tell you, you Slut you.
> You wear – an Impudent Lewd Face –
> A Damn'd Designing Heart – and a Tail – and a Tail full of –
>   [he falls fast asleep, snoring][59]

His interruption by physical fact instates him as the moralized effigy of this part of the play, as Fancifull was at its beginning. Brute is the detritus of his wife's ambition. In the revised version of the revelling scenes, made at Garrick's suggestion, Brute had disguised himself in one of his wife's dresses and acted out a monstrous parody of her grandeur and wealth. It is a brilliant decoration of this strand of the play. He is an hermaphroditic realization of their marriage, a nasty joke on their 'one flesh'.

Rasor, the footman who has to carry Sir John off, is a late introduction, but an important one. He is Madamoiselle's lover; when they exchange gossip, they act out her narrative of the events of the Spring Garden. Like *The Married Beau*, the play continually throws up enactments of itself, repetitions and mirrorings. Lady Fancifull pulls all the strands of the play together and completes the imitation of *She Would if She Could* by throwing in the letter-device.

It's too late of course; the timing trivializes it by depriving it of any structural emphasis. It is soon demolished anyway by Rasor's regret of 'so much Sport going to be spoil'd'.[60] Again, Vanbrugh's structural flair allows him to push action into the play against our consciousness of its imminent end. Rasor stages a little improvized masque, to echo that of *The Relapse*, and to restate, finally, the theme that spans the play;

> Woman tempted me, Lust weaken'd me – and so the Devil overcame me; As fell Adam, so fell I.[61]

'Heartfree is catch'd for his extravagant failing at woman-kind', Vanbrugh wrote in his reply to Collier's attack on the 'immorality' of the play in *A Short View* 'and Constant gives himself a great deal of trouble, for a thing that is not worth his pains. In short, they are most of 'em busy about what they sh'd not be'.[62] I think this is true to Vanbrugh's sense of what's going on in his play, though it would only make it a moral piece if there was any sense of what they *should* be busy about. One might set both that remark and Sir John Brute's disillusion against Clarissa's comic anguish in *The Confederacy* – 'I always know what I lack, but I am never pleas'd with what I have. The want of a Thing is perplexing enough, but the Possession of it is intolerable.'[63] This is a *felt* paradox – unlike most of Gay's – and can be intuited behind the whole of Vanbrugh's dramatic *oevre*. His characters find possession intolerable, because they become what they possess. The plays, with an easy construction and a lovely wit, enclose the people and subtly diminish them. Like Blenheim they are splendid constructions, but one would scarcely want to live in one.

9 Congreve

Before Congreve's first play, *The Old Batchelour*, reached its final form, Dryden and Southerne had already begun to promote his work as the culmination of Restoration comedy. Not surprisingly in these circumstances, it is he who brings the self-consciousness of the theatre of the nineties to its most dazzling peak. I want to look at him in the context of the tradition the rest of this book has described; to explore the ways in which his own consciousness of it informs his plays. Congreve's consciousness is a consciousness of form, of what it implies and what it must omit. A stylistic device is always more to Congreve than the production of a particular effect. When Dryden first discovered him, he may have seen a first version of *The Old Batchelour*; but he must also have seen *Incognita*, a short novel that explores the theme of disguise through an awareness of the disguise employed in the business of story-telling.

'When I degress' Congreve explains to the reader at one point, 'I am at that time writing to please myself, when I continue the thread of the story, I write to please him; supposing him a reasonable man, I conclude him satisfied to allow me this liberty, and so I proceed.'[1] This gentleman's agreement is already rendered dubious by the use of the third person; if the reader is 'he' then who are we? At the end of his longest and most important disgression, the narrator's slightly mad aloofness breaks down into a real comic irascibility –

> I could find it in my Heart to beg the Reader's pardon for this Digression, if I thought he would be sensible of the Civility; for I promise him, I do not intend to do it again throughout the Story, though I make never so many, and though he take them never so ill. But because I began this upon a bare Supposition of his impertinence, which might be somewhat impertinent in me to suppose I do, and hope to make him amends by telling him, that

183

by the time *Leonora* was dress'd, several ladies of her acquaintance came to accompany her to the place designed for the tilting, where we will leave them drinking chocolate till 'tis time for them to go.[2]

Congreve's losing battle with the demands of narrative award it only derisory victories; he may suppress the central fact of his tale and relegate mere event to a flurry of expository speech, mock-apologetic when it is the narrator's and mock-earnest when one of the character's, but he can tell us things whose only interest is that he bothers to us tell them – 'By Computation now (which is a very remarkable circumstance) *Hippolito* entered this garden near upon the same instant, when Aurelian wandered into the Old Monestary and found his *Incognita* in distress.'[3] *Incognita* is an anti-narrative; the subtitle deprives us of the usual romantic plot dynamic, for with 'Love and Duty Reconciled' what can a novel be about? About nothing of course. The tilts, amorous encounters and duels are trivialized by their context of 'manners', the nothing of a life where ladies get dressed to drink chocolate until it's time to stop. The tale runs constantly into a kind of narrative hiatus, like Sterne's black page. The same process is at work in the events of the tale;

Coming by a Light which hung at the Corner of a Street, he join'd the torn papers and collected thus much, that his *Incognita* had written the Note, and earnestly desired him (if there were any reality in what he pretended to her) to meet her at Twelve a Clock that Night at a Convent Gate; but unluckily the Bit of Paper which should have mentioned what Convent, was broken off and lost.

Aurelian walks on 'unwittingly' after this unfortunate lesion in romantic plotting 'till at length a Silence . . . surpriz'd his attention'.[4] Congreve goes on to explain how this might be, but an attentive reader is already aware that the 'Dominions of Silence and of Night'[5] are encroaching; silence disarrays the narrative, as night deranges the events it chronicles; the flimsy characters of banal romance face, wtih a comic inexpressiveness, vast rents and gaps in their world.

Incognita is a play by negatives. It is based on what, because it is a novel, one cannot see, as plays are based on unspoken feelings,

which, because they are plays, cannot be expressed without some-
one to speak them. It is the presence in a play of real people –
actors – that is for Congreve the reason why 'all Traditions must
undisputably give place to the Drama'.[6] *Incognita* is what might
happen if there were not even an actress behind the mask of the
lady-in-disguise, the Incognita. Congreve shrugs off character
more insouciantly than he could shake off plot. Aurelian, we are
told, is the 'Type' of Fabio, and looks on his friend Hippolito as a
'second self',[7] so one character is defined by reference to another
defined by reference to another still. The only distinguishing
moment comes in the tilt scene, when Aurelian, disguised as
Hippolito sees Incognita 'and had no other way to make himself
known to her, but by saluting and bowing to her after the *Spanish*
mode'.[8] Identity, when it is defined by manners, is easily trans-
ferred. The novel articulates its range of feeling through a pair of
couples contrasted only in the circumstance of intrigue; their
dialogue in the ball scene is the high point of its parabolic course.
Had the lovers not decided to stay in disguise, 'Love' and 'Duty'
could have been reconciled from the start. All their mistakes and
adventures, the whole fabric of the book in fact, ramifies from a
simple failure to say the obvious. This, I think, is at the root of a
fiction itself at the root of Congreve's career. *Incognita* reaches
stasis in the convent garden, whose associations enforce purity on
the passion conventionally expressed there. But the song in which
Leonora expresses her feelings (to be overheard, of course, by the
hidden Hippolito) is a graceful parody of the forlorn maiden's
lament, a parody by negatives. She is

> Not by Alexis' Eyes undone,
> Nor by his Charming Faithless Tongue,
>   Or Any Practis'd Art;
> Such real Ills may hope a Cure,
> But the sad Pains which I endure
>   Proceed from fansied Smart.[9]

Incognita reaches a pause on this lyric; afterwards it can only rattle
through to the end of the intrigue.

The prologue to *The Old Batchelour* (1693) wittily disintegrates as
the actress 'dries'.

> He prays – O bless me! What shall I do now!
> Hang me if I know what he prays, or how!

And 'twas the prettiest Prologue, as he wrote it!
Well, the Deuce take me, if I han't forgot it . . .
I shall be hang'd for wanting what to say.
For my sake then – but I'm in such Confusion.
I cannot stay to hear your resolution

Runs off.[10]

She has 'forgotten' that part of the prologue most personal to its author, the part that, as well as pleading his case, would complete his comparison of the present state of the stage with the 'former days' talked of in the first lines. But the prologue is complete in its rhymes and metrically elegant. It reserves to itself whatever it had to say. It's a piquantly 'impudent' opening to a first play; and it restates aspects of *Incognita* that *The Old Batchelour* locates in a psychological awareness. Congreve's preciosity thins his sense of the unrespectable realities of sexual relationship into the fabric of a brilliant and troubling play.

The Old Batchelour is the most uncompromising of all those plays of the 1690s that centre on a pair of gallants, one 'platonic', the other anti-platonic. Unlike Crowne and Vanbrugh, for example, Congreve explores the possibilities of this conventional contrast through its logical complement in plot; the device, invented by Aphra Behn, by which one gallant consummates the intrigue began by another.[11] When the intervention is caused by accident, the upshot is unrespectable but inoffensive farce – as Edward Ravenscroft's *London Cuckolds* (1681) demonstrates, a play derivative in everything but its hilarious energy and solid good nature. Congreve turns over the possibilities of motivation; he moves towards Otway's interest in the darker springs of comic behaviour but withdraws, even more disturbingly, to suggest an impossibility of knowledge, an irrevocable disjunction of behaviour and feeling.

All Congreve's comedies begin with a short scene between the hero and a close associate, which involves an action trivial in itself but encoding something of the movement of the play. (His tragedy begins with the heroine and her attendant – tragedy was by now a feminized genre.) Bellmour meets his friend Vainlove in the street and mocks him for the letters he's carrying; business letters, apparently. His speech is a conventional, and very literary, expansion of the carpe diem topos, but Vainlove brings it, literally, down to earth.

'. . . Leave Business to Idlers, and Wisdom to Fools . . . wit, be my Faculty; and Pleasure, my Occupation; and let Father Time shake his Glass. Let low and earthy Souls grovel till they have work'd themselves six foot deep into a Grave – Business is not my Element – I rowl in a higher Orb and dwell
Vain: In Castles i' th'Air of thy own building. . . . well as high a Flyer as you are, I have a Lure may make you stoop.

(Flings a Letter.)
Bell: I marry Sir, I have a Hawks Eye at a Womans hand . . . .[12]

It's not even the letter he meant to throw down – a summons to assignation with the banker's wife, Laetitia – but a letter from a previous mistress, Silvia, previously shared as the two men mean to share Vainlove's more recent conquest. The gesture is ambiguous – is it a challenge, or the first move in a game? The other characters in a largely static first act discuss Vainlove's behaviour with a polite but edgy distaste, which Bellmour tries to deflect:

Bell: He takes as much of an Amour as he cares for, and quits it when it grows stale or unpleasant.
Sharp: An argument of very little Passion, very good Understanding, and very ill Nature.[13]

The play's lightness of tone, the flippant assumption of intimacy set by that initial group of male characters, is achieved by a constant undercutting, as much of the stylistic devices themselves as of the characters who use them. Sharper enters to interrupt Bellmour in an expository speech to the audience, 'I'm sorry to see this, Ned', he says, 'Once a man comes to his Soliloquies I give him for gone.'[14] By the time Heartwell, the play's satirist, enters we are primed to see his attitudes as an essentially defensive presentation of cliches. Satire, in Congreve's plays, is never to be understood simply in the terms it sets itself. 'Wit' is never detachable from character, never 'free', Congreve always sets careful limits to his characters' capacity to make jokes, there is always a qualifying circumstances in motive or plot, a shadow thrown by the movement of the play. Satire, too, is never to be understood in its own terms. When Belinda tells Araminta 'you play the Game and consequently can't see the Miscarriages obvious to every Stander by', [15] Araminta is easily able to turn the remark back on her. It could be extended to an observation on the play as a whole. The characters seem diminished when set beside those of the later comedies, in that none of them are allowed even the illusion of 'control'. Everyone is placed in the disadvantaged position outlined by Belinda – the play's action *is* a game, and we are the only 'safe' spectators. Heartwell is a 'pretended Woman-hater'[16]: his nervous infatuation with Silvia is to be winkled out by the play, whose ironical outcome is to make his woman-hating real. Detachment – a fantasy of emotional privilege – turns out to be just as dangerous for Vainlove.

One could summarize the plot of *The Old Batchelour* as Vainlove's attempt to fob off two past attachments, Letitia with Bellmour, and Silvia with Heartwell, the old bachelor of the title, and to come to terms with Araminta, a girl apparently willing to play the game to his rules. Congreve introduces the first female characters unconventionally late, in a scene at the end of act two that serves to focus and to challenge the cool evasive rhetoric of the men.

Araminta assents eagerly to Vainlove's 'romantic' but sexless wooing:

> If Love be the Fever which you mean; kind Heav'n avert the cure; Let me have Oil to feed that Flame and never let it be extinct, till I myself am Ashes. [17]

The cure of their 'sickly peevish Appetite'[18] (as Sharper calls it) would be, of course, its gratification, and it is this which she is anxious to avert. But Araminta has earlier touched on an idea, introduced by the more sceptical Belinda and Bellmour, that links up to the darker side of Congreve's apprehension of love. 'You are the Temples of Love' says Vainlove. 'Rather poor silly Idols of your own making', she replies, 'which, upon the least displeasure you forsake, and set up new'.[19] The second stanza of the song I quoted from *Incognita* goes on to develop a parallel idea, picking it up from that long 'degression' whose presumed rejection by the reader so irritated the teller of the tale.

> Twas fancy gave Alexis Charms,
>   Ere I beheld his Face;
> Kind Fancy (then) could fold our Arms,
>   And form a soft Embrace.

But since I've seen the real Swain,
And try'd to fancy him again,
    I'm by my Fancy taught,
Though 'tis a Bliss no Tongue can tell,
To have Alexis, yet 'tis Hell
To have him but in Thought.[20]

According to Congreve, love invents its objects. The human disparities to which this gives rise are never wholly comic.

In his brilliant libretto on the Semele story Congreve expands the theme into an ironic divertissement by introducing the pastoral change-of-identity plot, and the Guarinian plotter, in the shape of Juno/Ino. Jupiter, in a slyly blasphemous interpretation, takes on the primary aspect of the Christian God, that of creator. Semele colludes in her role as a mechanism of pleasure. 'With my frailty don't upbraid me' she disingenuously reminds her lover, 'I am Woman as you made me.' 'Frailty in thee is ornament' Jove concedes, with, it will turn out, misplaced complacency, 'In thee perfection / Giv'n to agitate the mind / and keep awake men's passions.'[21] Araminta introduces a song into her first scene in *The Old Batchelour* which, she says, '. . . comes pretty near my own opinion of Love and your Sex'.[22] On one level it fulfils the usual function of songs in Restoration plays. Distanced by their performance by an unnamed or marginal character, they focus our attention on the characters listening to them, and thus become a convention for unspoken thoughts. It is thus a reaction to the received language of passion to parallel Belinda's draconian resolution of her own doubts into her command to Bellmour that she 'would be Ador'd in Silence'.[23] The song is a warning to women to prolong courtship as long as possible –

Men will admire, adore and die,
While wishing at your Feet they lie:
But admitting their Embraces,
    Wakes 'em from the golden Dream;
Nothing's new besides our Faces,
    Every woman is the same.[24]

But its position in the play also lends it a structural weight. Its resonance is as an expression of that reductive quest for more of the same into which male libertinism has dwindled – of that 'sameness' which the women's counterplot is about to explore in its revenge.

In the next scene Silvia and Lucy, her maid, lunch the letter/ disguise plot in a variation probably suggested to Congreve by Southerne's handling of the Lady Susan intrigue in *The Maids Last Prayer*, and evidence again of his determination to rethink plot . ideas in the terms of his 'platonic' theme.[25] Lucy sends Vainlove an open avowal of love purporting to come from Araminta. The trickster characters set up another impersonation plot to involve Lucy and Silvia in 'witty' marriages, both plots crossing each other in the Park, where one starts and the other finishes. If, as Lucy claims, deceit is second nature to women, it is because the styles that bridge the vast gap of comprehension between men and women in the world of the play are themselves implicitly mendacious. All this layered on to the Behn-derived *male* change-of-identity plot suggests an aspiring virtuosity seemingly intent on exhausting the possibilities of 'impersonation' once and for all, while simultaneously demonstrating the variety of levels on which it can work.

Vainlove confronts Araminta in the Park and tries to give her the letter. She drops it to the ground in unwitting repetition of a moment from the beginning of the play that darkens on recall. He refuses to stoop for it confident that 'she will be unwilling to expose to the censure of the first finder' [26] the false signature at the bottom. That she does eventually stoop for it marks her loss of this little contest. Congreve manages Araminta's crisis with deft understatement. Belinda returns from a circuit of the park to find her gone. When Araminta reappears at the end of the play her primness seems fortified by decision, and her refusal of Vainlove's suit is inevitable.

'As love is a Deity', Vainlove says earlier in the play, 'he must be serv'd by Prayer.' 'O Gad' replies Belinda 'would you would all pray to Love then, and let us alone.'[27] It is precisely as a ploy for letting Araminta alone that Vainlove adopts a style of 'romantic' wooing. The park-scene knits up suggestively a vein of speculation that runs irregularly on the play's polite excluding surface. *The Old Batchelour* seems to suggest that the 'honourable' forms indulged in by Vainlove and Heartwell are paradoxically more indecent than Bellmour's libertinism. But it consistently deflects the possibilities of revealed motivation or confident judgement. When Vainlove at the very start of the play remarks on Bellmour's pursuit of pleas-

ure, his friend answers 'Ay What else has meaning?'[28] The characters all puzzle at meaning; at the feeling behind style, the woman
behind the mask. The gallants' double act could be seen to make
sexuality unmeaning – as marriage and courtship are rendered
unmeaning by Lucy and Silvia's disguise, and the letter-plot,
respectively. The play is a kind of teasing out of the implications of
disguise plots; there is a parallel to Southerne in the move towards
an expression of vacancy, of 'disappointment'. The song on sexual
'disappointment' that Heartwell has sung to Silvia, seems anachronistic in the 1690s; traditionally 'libertine', traditionally 'witty'. But
it inserts into the play a lyric expression of the same overriding
sense. All four women unmask simultaneously at the end of the
play, a coup that drew applause from the first-night audience.[29]
The quartet of Incognite state with a fine flourish that apprehension
of vacuity which informs both Congreve's novel and his first play.

It would be difficult (and perhaps unrewarding) to establish a
kind of ur-*Old Batchelour*; to decide which parts of the play are
juvenile Congreve and which are determined by Southerne's and
Dryden's tutelage, and the author's adaptation to theatrical conditions. '. . . had it been Acted, when it was first Written', Congreve
writes in his Epistle Dedicatory, 'more might have been said in its
behalf; Ignorance of the Town and Stage, would then have been
excuses in a young Writer, which now, almost four Years experience, will scarce allow of'.[30] On a form so dependent on an idea of
social life, it is impossible to say where ignorance of the town
might end and ignorance of the stage begin. *The Old Batchelour* is
looser in structure than anything else of Congreve's; it is also – a
predictable consequence – more lightweight, its characters less
imposing. 'Ignorance of the Town' is at the base of this in the
simplest sense. The people in the play meet each other by chance
in unnamed streets – the play makes less geographical sense than
almost any other Restoration comedy. But it is also the result of
an attempt at Southerne's 'feel' for open structure and casual
insights. Congreve demonstrates a gift for forming his play into
moments of emphasis in the congruence of apparently random
realistic detail – as in the park-scene. But his mature plays are
shaped as wholes, through the imposition of abstract, even 'gratuitous' formal principles. *The Double Dealer* (1694) is an achievement of formal grandeur, the entrance to 'mature' Congreve.

The Double Dealer brings to climax that literary self-consciousness
characteristic of the comedy of the 1690s, a self-consciousness

often simplified to the decade's equally characteristic idea of theatricality. Southerne's commendatory verses to *The Old Batchelour* carefully place Congreve as the almost inevitable outcome of the tradition of Wit comedy.

> . . . *Wicherly*, in wise Retreat
> Thought it not worth his quiet to be great.
> Loose, wandring, *Etherege*, in wild Pleasures tost,
> And foreign Int'rests, to his hopes long lost;
> Poor *Lee* and *Otway* dead! CONGREVE appears,
> The Darling, and last comfort of his Years.[31]

'His' in this case means Dryden's. Where Southerne is vague, avuncular and only sporadically cogent, Dryden, in his prologue to *The Double Dealer*, creates a 'high' counterpart to *MacFlecknoe*, a movingly serious confirmation of artistic succession. His praise implies a restrospect, precise but large in scope

> Our Age was cultivated thus at length;
> But what we gain'd in skill we lost in strength.
> Our Builders were, with want to Genius, curst:
> The second Temple was not like the first . . .[32]

The firm placing of his metaphor allows Dryden to suggest another history in little of the Restoration settlement. The 'temple' suggests St Paul's; the drift of the poem instates wit and its traditions as equally central to Restoration London. *The Double Dealer* is structurally informed by Congreve's need to validate his claim.

The Double Dealer is an exercise in classical control of a kind very similar to *Incognita's*. In both, the carefully measured space before a marriage is taken up by the overcoming of obstacles. 'I would have mirth continued this day at any rate', Mellefont argues;

> . . . tho' Patience purchase folly, and Attention be paid with noise; There are times when Sense may be unseasonable, as well as Truth. . . . I would have Noise and Impertinence keep my Lady Touchwood's head from Working; For Hell is not more busie than her Brain, nor contains more Devils than that Imaginations . . .[33]

Comedy is thus evoked from the start as a strategy to head off the possibilities of disaster. 'Plot' is identified as the source of this

disaster; 'Imaginations' are equated to 'Devils', and Lady Touchwood is identified as the unpredictable medium of both. The
'good' characters are forced to try to impose a stasis on the play by
blocking the 'bad'; the bad provide its dynamic, an inversion
which gives the play its sense of diabolic energies, but which also
renders the central pair of lovers, Mellefont and Cynthia, so
bizarrely numb. Their frozen helplessness is dream-like, or, more
accurately, nightmarish. *The Double Dealer*, uniquely in Restoration
comedy, obeys all three unities, of place, action and time. Imposition of the unities can have two basic effects – to establish a
convention for reality, by skirting the need for more blatant narrative structuring within the play, or, conversely, to achieve a sur-
reality, a dreamlike seamlessness and compression. This last effect,
as Anne Barton has pointed out,[34] dictates the tone of *The Double
Dealer*. It focuses on one time and one place with an hallucinatory
intensity heightened by our sense that such limitation is, in terms
of Restoration comedy, unconventional, odd.

Congreve's preface defends 'the Hero of the play as they are
pleas'd to call him . . .' but this label for Mellefont is carefully
evasive. Maskwell, much less ambiguously, he calls 'A Villain'.[35]
His accomplice Lady Touchwood's language is fed with the cliches
of heroic diction, a high style of low passion. But as their scene
together at the end of the first act makes clear, her partnership
with Maskwell is riskily unbalanced. The 'heroic' intensity that
traps her within the moment of feeling is in contrast to his complete detachment. It is his steady sense of time that emancipates
him from that impulse of foresight and memory, of guilt and
anticipation, that tug the other characters through a maze of
intrigue. It is an awareness, like a neo-classical dramatist's, of the
mechanics of action in time, of the effects of proportion and
disproportion:

One Minute gives Invention to Destroy,
What, to Rebuild, will a whole age Employ.[36]

Maskwell's 'unbuilding' is the building of a classical play. He exists
in the present, like theatrical illusion; he has neither future nor
past, he is enclosed in a bubble of unity of time, and the plays
ending must be his end also. His sense of time is clear in that it is
emotionally discontinuous – 'I lov'd her once' he says of Lady
Touchwood, and then, 'I must dissemble ardour and ecstacies. . . .
How easily and pleasantly is that dissembled before Fruition! Pox

on't that a Man can't drink without quenching his Thirst. . .'.[37] He
must oppose 'Fruition', it ends that 'dissimulation' which is the
only being he has. It is an impulse that links him back to Vainlove
and forward to Angelica; an isolation within individual character of
an impulse general to the Etheregean form. Congreve's plays are
shaped by an opposing impulse, *towards* a formal consummation.
The frequency of soliloquy tends to interiorize the action of the
play; Maskwell uses it to offer reflections of the other characters,
and implicitly, of the audience. He speaks of motivation as if to
place the very idea at a distance. It is a superficiality, a rationale
provided by others:

> 'Cynthia, let thy beauty gild my Crimes; and whatsoever I
> commit of Treachery or Deceit shall be imputed to me as a
> Merit . . .[38]

His own rationale is to turn the mirror to us:

> Why will Mankind be Fools, and be deciev'd?
> And why are Friends and Lovers Oaths believ'd;
> When each, who searches strictly his own mind,
> May so much Fraud and Power of Baseness find?[39]

Of all the characters in the play, Maskwell lacks individual substance. Existing as he does only within the circle of Mellefont's
immediate concerns, he could almost be seen as his dream self.

This, again, suggests a parallel to *Incognita*, the friendship of
Aurelian and Hippolito is of the same kind as that of Mellefont and
Maskwell, in the overtones of one man's patronage of another
whom he takes, unquestioningly, to be his double. As in all the
plays, though with different degrees of emphasis, the hero's marriage is preceded by the loosening of this narcissistic bond. Maskwell and Mellefont are more intricately implicated in each other's
concerns than a simple hero/villain opposition would allow. In his
preface Congreve describes Mellefont's actions in terms of psychological probability, but Maskwell is explained structurally.
They are both heroes, one passive, the other active; or they are the
halves of a hero, Maskwell the half that acts on the play, and
Mellefont the half that reacts to it. Congreve clearly invests more of
himself in the latter. 'I have the same Face, the same Words and
Accents, when I speak what I do think; and when I speak what I do

not think, the very same': says Maskwell 'and dear dissimulation is the only Art not to be known from Nature.'[40] The arts of deceit, the arts of the theatre, are concerns that Congreve and his 'villain' share; they would seem to share also an apprehension of negativity, the sense that an operation of deceit can make 'reality' un-meaning.

Cynthia closes Act III in meditation on the same problem;

> 'Tis not so hard to counterfeit Joy in the depth of Affliction as to dissemble Mirth in the company of Fools – Why should I call 'em Fools? The World thinks better of 'em; for these have Quality and Education, Wit and fine Conversation, are receiv'd and admir'd by the World – If not, they like and admire themselves – And why is not that true Wisdom, for 'tis Happiness. And for ought I know, we have mis-apply'd the Name of this while, and mistaken the thing . . .[41]

That social fiction embodied by the other couples is a disguise that seems to dislodge meaning from the most immediate emotional concepts. The interim between contract and ceremony is filled for Cynthia by a series of encounters with grotesque parodies of marriage, acted out by the Touchwoods' house-guests. The men had been introduced in Act I in a discussion of the superior wit of *not* laughing at comedy. The first laughter we hear after this is in the context of Maskwell's tricking Mellefont. The laughter of *The Double Dealer* is of a peculiar quality. Highly successful farcical situations are defused and soured by the amusement of characters with whom the audience cannot identify. Lady Froth and Brisk, for example, deceive her husband in double-entendre;

| Lady Froth: | I'll do it with him, my Lord, when you are out of the way. |
| Brisk: | [aside] That's good I'gad, that's good. Deuce take me I can hardly hold Laughing in his Face.[42] |

The cheapness of this marks the limit of our assent to the intrigue. The scene where Plyant urges Careless to help him get Lady Plyant with child drifts over depths of pathos by provoking the laughter we give to what we know is not laughable. Cynthia attempts to re-impose order on her and Mellefont's perception of the events around them;

Mell: . . . Marriage is the Game that we Hunt, and while we
          think that we only have it in our view, I don't see but
          we have it in our power.

Cyn: . . . Within reach; for example, give me your hand; why
          have you look'd through the wrong end of the Perspec-
          tive all this while; for nothing has been between us but
          our fears.[43]

But as in *The Old Batchelour*, the gesture between lovers echoes,
with the consequence of dreams, a gesture from the hero to his
friend. 'There's comfort in a hand stretch'd out', Mellefont had
said earlier to Maskwell, 'to one that's sinking, though ne'er so far
off'.[44] The marriage of Cynthia and Mellefont must be preceded by
an exorcism of the nothing that is their fears; the play is, one level,
a comedy of the unconscious, in which only the infinitely pathetic
Sir Paul can insist that he is not drowning but waving.

'Guilt is ever at a loss and confusion waits upon it' Maskwell
says to Lady Touchwood, at the beginning of the scene in her
chamber, the only scene to break the unity of place, 'When Innocence and bold Truth are always ready for expression.' Lady
Touchwood's reply touches on the underlying logic of the Etheregean form:

Not in Love, Words are the weak support of the cold Indiffer-
ence; Love has no language to be heard.[45]

Her insight has potentially tragic implications. Lady Touchwood is
an intensification of the type of an opposite extreme to that evinced
in Vanbrugh's Lady Fancyfull. Maskwell however only attains
tragedy by imitation, or, more aptly, by 'acting'. The echoes of
Shakespeare that recur through the play thicken towards its climax
as Maskwell tricks Mellefont into a parody of the closet scene from
Hamlet, one of the most famous moments of Betterton's celebrated,
and very recent, performances of the play.[46] But Maskwell *is*
Betterton; he is haunted by ghost-like reminiscences of his Shakespearean roles, tributes to the sinister vacuity of theatrical illusion.
It is for this that the play moves out of its other Hamlet-like setting,
the gallery where characters walk, soliloquize and accidentally
encounter each other. Lady Touchwood as 'plotter' has driven the
play, Maskwell as 'actor' steers it. He is able to flatter her into a
tragic hubris – ' . . . Fortune is your own, and 'tis her interest so to

be.'[47] Her fall comes in the frenzy of plotting that constitutes *his* hubris; it explodes in a flurried double version of the impersonation plot, that bursts across the path of the comic characters, as they gather slowly on stage, to return to 'respectability', from the successful upshot of their own little intrigues. The 'tragic' plot recedes in importance. Mellefont's failure to defuse it goes unremarked by Cynthia, though it was a condition of her acceptance. They marry, of course, in the end. Perhaps the plotters cannot be allowed to impose their own values in the play even to the extent of defining virtue by their opposition – they evaporate, but the play of necessity evaporates with them. The play, Congreve's funniest, presents an inverted image of the world, of a kind more familiar to us from tragedy than comedy. It is defined by Congreve with an hallucinatory precision, and a clear awareness of the closeness of hilarity and alarm.

Congreve's next play, *Love for Love* (1695), was again built around a role for Betterton, but in the context of the actor's rebellion from Rich's company and the founding of his own.

> . . . the poor Husbands of the Stage, who found
> Their Labours lost upon the ungrateful Ground,
> This last and only Remedy have prov'd;
> And hope new Fruit from ancient Stocks remov'd.[48]

The extended garden metaphor of Congreve's prologue establishes the new company's style as a 'natural' tradition, and Betterton's tending of it as careful and sensitive cultivation. In terms of the rivalry between the two companies, *Love for Love* makes a conservative, consciously traditional choice of available dramatic styles, a choice that links both play and company back to the traditions of wit comedy and stage libertinism. 'We hope there's something that may please each Taste' the prologue goes on '. . . of homely Fare we make the Feast.'[49] *Love for Love* is homely fare in a way *The Double Dealer* wasn't. It eschews abstract formal virtuosity for a different kind of literariness, a revival and reappraisal of the conventions of both 'manners' and 'humour' comedy.

The prologue goes on to make the familiar bow in Wycherley's direction, but comparison to *The Plaindealer* shows that this play's satirist, Scandal, operates from no real emotional or moral base. His is simply a more sophisticated version of the narcissim endemic to that society whose news he carries. He employs a cyclic logic that closes and diminishes the conversational essays of the other characters. 'I'm afraid *Jeremy* has Wit' he declares, 'for wherever it is, its always contriving its own Ruin. . .'.[50] The effect is essentially complacent, and easily turned against him. ('You are as inveterate against our Poets as if your Characters had lately been expos'd upon the Stage.)'[51] Scandal has an effect on the play quite opposite to that of the conventional Plaindealer. He cools it down, imposing a disengaged, a 'knowing' tone. 'To converse with *Scandal*' as Valentine realises 'is to play at *Losing Loadum*; you must lose a good Name to him, before you can win it for yourself.'[52]

The play's first scene is itself a kind of prologue; the impoverished Valentine tries to write a play, to take some of 'the Trade' from the 'wits'.[53] Wit is now no more than a trade, its method is a continual anxious transformation of contiguous life, life Congreve presents as rubbish and decay. Jeremy, Valentine's servant, expands the idea into a grand satirical–allegorical panorama. His picture of a 'worn-out Punk with Verses in her Hand, which her Vanity had preferr'd to Settlements'[54] is a warning emblem that writing can dwindle to mere words on paper, the dross that replaces substance. But settlements are words on paper too. Valentine's surname is 'Legend'. The whole play concerns itself with writing and reading, inscription and interpretation. Its literariness is initially of a nightmare kind where words must do for food, and Valentine lives on a 'Paper-Diet'.[55] The imaginary 'pictures' whch Scandal offers to show Mrs Frail, 'The satires, descriptions, characters and lampoons' seem by their placing at the end of the act to open up for us the world of the play;

> 'I can show you Pride, Folly, Affectation, Wantonness, Inconstancy, Coventousness, Dissimulation, Malice and Ignorance, all in one Piece. Then I can show you Lying, Foppery, Vanity, Cowardice, Bragging, Lechery, Impotence and Ugliness in another piece; and yet one of these is a celebrated Beauty, and t'other a profest Beau . . .'[56]

'Picturing' is the method of the play's satire. But there is a distance between the world and those for whom it arranges itself in pictures. Scandal's sustained rhetoric suggests mysterious insight and a prophetic stance, but the play undercuts a kind of knowledge that comes to seem dangerously closed and circular. The process of satire is of more interest to Congreve than its product. He uses the idea of satire as he used the idea of theatre in *The Double Dealer*, as a process analogous to the other kinds of process which form the play. In *Love for Love* these are processes of 'knowing'.

'I could heartily wish it yet shorter' Congreve claims in his preface, 'but the Number of Different Characters represented in it would have been too much crowded in less room'.[57] The play works through contrasted character. It is planned symmetrically, organized into encounters, satirical or amorous, and articulated in a systematic pairing of 'humours'. Scandal's counterpart is the beau, Tattle; 'you are light and shadow, and shew one another; he is perfectly thy reverse both in humour and understanding; and as you set up for Defamation, he is a mender of Reputations'.[58] They unfold society, as opposites in the kind of knowledge it offers. Scandal creates a personal secrecy in his revelations, Tattle creates revelation in his secrecy. Old Foresight the astrologer and Sir Sampson, the traveller, match them, to make a square around Valentine. The Restoration 'humour' is more abstract than the Jacobean. Like Shadwell's, Congreve's humours are less self-generated oddity than obsessive strategies for organizing time and awareness. Foresight imaginatively encompasses time as Sir Sampson does place, all within the cramped space of the Foresights' city house. 'The homely fare' offered by the prologue implies a withdrawal from the modish surface of a play like *The Double Dealer*, a quizzical reconsideration of solid Jacobean domesticity. '. . . if the Sun shine by Day and the Stars by Night', Sir Sampson claims, 'why, we shall know one another's Faces without the help of a Candle, and that's all the stars are good for . . .'.[59] His words touch on the play's central concerns – but when he encounters his son Valentine he is seen to read faces as the same kind of cramped and ludicrous code into which he and Foresight translate the learning they amass: 'Has he not a Rogue's face . . . he has a violent death in his face.'[60] Valentine sets himself up as a philosophical libertine; his father wants to disinherit him, but to become a bare forked animal, is, Valentine claims, impossible; 'you must deprive me of Reason, Thought, Passions, Inclinations, Affections, Appetites, Senses, and the huge Train of Attendants that you begot along with me'.[61] Appetite, for Valentine is a philosophical imperative, and this defines his role in life as sanctioned consumption. This gives him and Scandal a knockdown argument for not paying debts:

Trap: I did not value your Sack; but you cannot expect it again
          when I have drank it.
Scand: And how do you expect to have your Money again
          when a Gentleman has spent it?[62]

Congreve establishes Valentine as a libertine by means less pictur-
esque than directly dramatized promiscuity. One demand on his
purse is 'Bouncing Margery' with '. . . one of your children from
Twitnam'. Valentine's response to this rude incursion of his past
brutally deflates the romantic aloofness of his pose – 'she . . .
might have overlaid the child a fortnight ago if she had had any
forecast in her'.[63] The Libertine cuts himself off from both parents
and children. He must play that losing game on which Valentine,
at the start of the play seems set.

Even in the Dramatis Personae, Valentine and Angelica are
defined in financial terms that mesh suggestively.

Valentine: fallen under his Father's Displeasure by his expen-
          sive way of living, in love with *Angelica*.
Angelica: Niece to Foresight, of a considerable Fortune in her
          own Hands.[64]

The obstacle to an apparently inevitable resolution lies in the
willed mysteriousness of behaviour with which Angelica adver-
tizes her independence. The callous nonchalance of her behaviour
to Foresight at the start of act II sharpens, when he threatens
Valentine, into a satirical translation of the old astrologer's occult-
ism into images of a cramped misshapen sexuality. She describes
the grotesque obverse of a beauty–magic identification that tinges
her own role, and in doing so deepens her enigma; there is no way
of knowing whether her anger is at Foresight's cruelty to Valentine, or his assumption that this is of interest to her. *Love for Love*
suggests a romantic bargain – it suggests also the provisional
contract of a game. The funniest round is that between Tattle and
Prue – it is the thinnest part of the play, the most blatantly
calculated to entertain, but it is also the most transparent – one
sees through it into the links between Angelica's behaviour and
the way of the world she lives in. Prue starts from square one – she
is the blankest and most biddable of all the country girls. Her thirst
for knowledge impels Tattle to spell out the rules that have fogged
our sense of relationship in the rest of the play:

All well-bred Persons lie – Besides, you are a Woman; you must never speak what you Think; Your words must contradict your Thoughts; but your Actions may contradict your words.[65]

Prue reverses those norms of courtship that Angelica protracts to a hazy extreme; she's so willing that it becomes a formality, a decency almost, extended only by Tattle's wit. Angelica presents herself to Valentine as almost wholly passive –

Val: Well, you'll come to a Resolution.
Ang: I can't. Resolution must come to me, or I shall never have one.[66]

Reserve, even immobility, may be the only way to remain uncompromised in a social world whose poles are Scandal and Tattle, a world in which Valentine invests to the extent that he can know '. . . no effectual difference between continued Affectation and Reality'.[67] This scene between the four of them, the first in the play to bring Valentine and Angelica together, builds into an impromptu tribunal, but it resolves nothing. It decorates the fact of Angelica's reserve without explaining it. Her mystery is deepened further in her lie to Sir Sampson – a lie that the audience cannot at this point see through –

'. . . if ever I cou'd have lik'd anything in him, it should have been his Estate. . . . But since that's gone, the Baits gone off, and the naked Hook appears'[68]

It posits the alarming possibility of a reading of the play in which financial realities are more 'real' than other kinds – a logical extension of a motive we might almost conventionally impute to Valentine. This little exchange is literally and metaphorically central to Congreve's structure. Stressed by our doubts about it, it becomes the climax of both the play's unknowability, and Angelica's.

Valentine attempts to resolve his personal and financial uncertainty by pretending to go mad. Angelica is the first to arrive at his lodging; Scandal engages her in a game of dissimulation, and loses; it recalls the rather unnervingly spirited Angelica of her first scene, and in a favourite card metaphor, echoes the title of the play; '. . . If I don't play Trick for Trick, may I never taste the Pleasure of Revenge.'[69] Scandal is out-manoeuvred by Mrs Foresight when she flatly denies the assignation we saw her make with him at the end of the last act. His exclamations – 'You make me mad. You are not serious' – have more than an accidental irony. Mrs Foresight makes him mad by rendering what he knows meaningless; her fortune-hunting sister Mrs Frail seems 'mad' to her former target, Ben; opportunism and deceit scramble and make meaningless her words and behaviour when she changes tack to the re-instated Valentine. His hero's 'madness' allows Congreve another eccentric variant on the impersonation plot; no mask is needed to delude a madman into thinking that Mrs Frail is Angelica. At first he ornaments the plot with the pastoral fantasy of a madman's imagination –

> Endymion and the Moon shall meet us on Mount *Latmos*, and we'll be Marry'd in the dead of Night.[70]

But then he decides to externalize, mockingly, a hypocritical purity in the 'nun' and 'friar' disguise. As a madman Valentine gains privileged access to 'vision'. He has finally become both a 'wit' and a satirist. But Scandal's experience might have warned him that madmen forfeit a claim to meaning. Valentine has evaded the need to complete the document disinheriting him in Ben's favour; but he has pushed further off the possibilities of being known or truly knowing. Angelica has a scene with Tattle to parallel that with Scandal – to demonstrate her mastery of them. Then she challenges Valentine.

> Do you know me, *Valentine*?
> O, very well.
> Who am I?
> You're a Woman – One to whom Heav'n gave Beauty when it grafted Roses on a Briar. You are the reflection of Heav'n in a Pond, and he that leaps at you is sunk. You are all, white, a sheet of lovely spotless Paper, when you first are Born; but you are to be scrawled and blotted by every Gooses Quill . . .[71]

Valentine insists on woman as something to be 'read', not as something that writes, as something written on. He presumes that disguise can be sloughed off and reality – a reality that *he* defines – simply acknowledged. He pulls in our sense of the play's structure

to establish his claim; '. . . the Comedy draws towards an end, and let us think of leaving acting and be ourselves . . .'.[72]
Angelica refuses to comply with his expectations of the end of romantic comedy. So does Jeremy, though the genre in which he plays his part is perhaps a degree lower – 'Why, you thick-skulled rascal' Valentine rages 'I tell you the farce is done, and I will be mad no longer.'[73] By beating his servant however he contradicts his own word in action, for this is the simplest kind of farce and it seems quite likely to continue. As we saw in Prue's scene, the lie is the basic unit of social currency. Women and servants are parallel in their enforced dependence on that 'Figure of speech' which according to Jeremy 'interlards the great part of my conversation'.[74] But Angelica's parting words are not a 'riddle' as Valentine presumes. Their meaning is in excess of his ability to understand –

Uncertainty and Expectation are the Joys of Life. Security is an inspid thing, and the overtaking and possessing of a Wish discovers the Folly of the Chase. Never let us know one another better; for the Pleasure of a Masquerade is done when we come to show Faces.[75]

Their resonance can only be placed by an imaginative leap out of the routine misogyny, the mechanical intrigue, of his libertine pose.

Tattle spurns Prue on their next meeting. She has Margery's sense of the permanence of her choice, and this cuts inconveniently across the one other convention of the fashionable world which Tattle now explains to her; that the span of its awareness is no longer than a day. He's off to take Valentine's place in the marriage with Mrs Frail/Angelica – Jeremy has tricked him into the plot. The disguised couple, both duped, burst onto the stage to frame a final unravelling of deceit.

Valentine offers to disinherit himself as a sign of his love for Angelica – apparently on the point of marrying Sir Sampson. The declaration means less at its face value than in the tribute it implies to her – his acceptance to her right to set the conditions of the comedy's true end. When Angelica tears the document she effects the destruction of all the other kinds of 'knowledge' that would lead the play to a different event at this climactic point. Foresight, Sir Sampson Legend, Mrs Frail and Tattle, are all diminished and defeated. Scandal steps in to offer a moral; all the tags at the end of the acts have so far been his; that at the end of act IV, though spoken by Valentine, is a quotation from his 'Satirical Friend . . . who says

> That Women are like Tricks by slight of Hand
> Which, to admire, we should not understand.[76]

It is this complicity in cynicism from which Valentine has broken, and in doing so he has rendered Angelica comprehensible. Angelica gracefully accepts Scandal's 'conversion' as the ground of her assumption to herself of the authority to close the play.

One might trace in Congreve's four comedies a development by which the male characters' strategies for organizing a libertine diversity of experience are replaced as the structuring impulse of the plays by the reserve and dissimulation involved in a woman's attempt to establish a personal reality of feeling. This happens within each play. It happens also over the sequence. Araminta and Cynthia have stubborn strengths and a reserved insight, but the action of the play goes on at some little distance from them. As was the case with *Love for Love*, it is a woman who must bring *The Way of the World* to a close and gather the characters to her for an adjudication. The tangle of events that present themselves to Lady Wishfort would bewilder a mind more consistent than hers. *The Way of the World* cuts itself off from audience complicity with a virtuosity so perverse it can seem to mimic the effects of incompetence.

Mirabell loses the card game that ends just prior to the start of the play; he wins that much larger game, whose action concertinas all the possible meanings of 'play'. His method is concealment; to use her husband's description of Mrs Fainall, he throws up his cards, but keeps 'Pam' in his 'pocket'.[77] It would seem to be Congreve's ploy too. Mirabell's 'Sir Rowland' plot is incomprehensible to the audience in act I, vague in act II and only fully spelt out in act III (by Mrs Fainall, to Foible), as it is about to be sprung. There is no surprise effect involved, nor do the concealments reveal individual character. They are a strategy for directing our attention. The play takes great risks (in its game with its audience) to decoy us with plot into confronting relationship. Its style is disturbed sequence. Language, logic and manners are carefully disordered. Everything about the play is, in Mincing's term, 'crips'.

The Way of the World seems to me to be an astonishingly graceful and economical (or 'easy') transmutation of theatrical means into literary form. Fainall, like all Betterton's Congreve roles, is developed out of the libertine tradition but at a distance dictated as much by the actor's age as by the dating of those conventions he had embodied in his roles of the late seventies and eighties.[78] They are comments on that tradition, referential characterizations of ideas *about* the libertine. Fainall is a rake trapped into marriage, who has managed nonetheless to adapt to the new style of libertine behaviour; the half-clandestine style, defined by its 'daring' relationship to society. A society that derives its rules from an idea of 'reputation' implicates its members in a series of gambles. Fainall, who would 'no more play with a Man that slights his ill Fortune than . . . make Love to a Woman who undervalu'd the Loss of her Reputation',[79] claims to take pleasure in knocking others out of the social game. As villains, Marwood (played by Elizabeth Barry) and Fainall are conceived entirely in terms of the actors' skills. When they exit at the end – after Congreve has made the point that the whole cast are now on stage – they escape from the only sphere of their being, and thus present no lasting threat, or uncomfortable loose ends. An insubstantiality, an improvised identity dictated by 'plot', is common characteristic to all Congreve's villains – and indeed those of many other dramatists, ('motivelessness' is the best dramatic means of suggesting malignancy). When Foible sees Marwood in the park-scene, moving about off-stage, she is vaguely seen, and masked. She has no more reality beyond the feints and disguises of intrigue than had Porcia, Mrs Barry's role in Otway's *The Atheist*. The method of *The Way of the World* is complex, but it is not an overflowing sense of character that complicates it. I stress this because the play can seem untheatrical; anti-theatrical, even. Theatricality – a *perverse* theatricality – seems to me not only to shape the play, but to dictate, through the reminiscence it implies, its content and function. *The Way of the World*, at once so modest and so grandiose in the promise of its title, is a summation of Restoration comedy; the comedy whose history Southerne and Dryden had so carefully recalled, and whose own 'Restoration' they looked on Congreve to effect.

Much is made in the first act of the separate society of the sexes. In act II they meet, on the neutral ground of the park. Congreve continues and elaborates the tortuous retrospect of his expository method into the reminiscence of past amours and deceits germane to its fashionable (and dramatic) function. It is this retrospect that instates the action we *see* as a kind of culmination, and invites us to puzzle over the past, for an explanation of the bewildering 'present'. The opening conversation between Marwood and Mrs Fainall builds a more blatant structure of dissembling and reversal of sense than that of the parallel opening to act I. When the men enter all four are engaged in a game of skirting dangerous admissions, and gracefully turning back. When they split up into *tête-à-têtes* our sense of things becomes clearer, but what is made clear is, paradoxically, the complexity of real and dissembled relationship. 'You are not Jealous?' Fainall asks Marwood at one point. 'Of whom?', she asks, having herself lost track.[80] The subject of these discussions is of course that central pre-occupation of the comedies of the nineties, the validity and use of kinds of social contract. Love, friendship and marriage have all become mere masks. 'The Way of the World'[81] is Fainall's phrase, originally. It attaches itself to his wife; our sense of that world's injustice, of Mirabell's smug opportunism, comes to be represented by her.

When Mirabell and Fainall quiz Witwoud as to what might be his friend Petulant's most striking conversational incompetence, Mirabell incidentally allows an insight into his own characteristic style; '. . . he speaks unseasonable Truths sometimes, because he has not Wit enough to invent an Evasion . . .'.[82] The idea of 'wit' Mirabell posits is bland and defensive, but it *is* basically decent. Congreve seems to propose a new rationale for wit, conciliatory and constructive, in obvious contrast to the personal aggression of the libertines. 'Then ought'st thou to be most asham'd of thyself when thou hast put another out of Countenance'[83] he tells Petulant, who, like Wycherley's Manly, 'makes Remarks'.[84] Mirabell is the master of a cool emotional self-defence. Mrs Fainall's 'Why did you make me marry this man?' hangs over the rest of the play. It finds no answer in his reply – 'Why do we daily commit disagreeable and dangerous actions? To save that idol reputation.'[85] The danger and the disagreeableness were hers, not his. If Millamant knows anything of her suitor's involvement with Mrs Fainall she never lets slip any reference to this or any other contingency of the plot. She alone is exempted from retrospect. In a sense, her use of style is as defensive as Mirabell's. Her inversion of cause and effect – 'a sort of Poetical Logic'[86] as Congreve called it in *The Old Batchelour* – both deflects an attention to disagreeable fact and blocks, more subtly, the treacherous strategy of romantic language that Mirabell attempts to extend to her. 'One's Cruelty is one's Power', she claims 'and when one parts with ones Cruelty, one parts with ones Power; and when one has parted with that, I fancy ones Old and Ugly.'[87] This may not make sense, but it is, as the fate of her too-susceptible Aunt goes to prove, the way of a world that may not make sense either. It is Millamant who finally and triumphantly inverts that disturbing emotional logic traced earlier in *Incognita*, *Semele* and *The Old Batchelour*.

Mir.: . . . Beauty is the Lover's Gift; 'tis he bestows your Charms.

Mill: Beauty the Lover's gift – Lord, what is a Lover, that it can give? Why one makes Lovers as fast as one pleases, and they live as long as one leases, and they die as soon as one pleases; And then if one pleases one makes more.[88]

Millamant's meditative reminiscences of scraps of Waller internalize the pastoral fictions of courtship. They clash wittily with the rustic Sir Wilful's attempts to catch that 'critical minute' of successful courtship on which the pastoral lyric is so often built.[89] Real rusticity has no bearing on the fiction whose import for Millamant is as the vehicle of a privacy of feeling. When Mirabell enters to cap her quotation, he demonstrates his right to step inside her bubble of style. Millamant's rudeness to Sir Wilful and Witwoud is sustained by the security of the knowingly loved. The 'proviso scene' is a ceremonial expansion of artifice, seamless with this mock-pastoral 'chase'. That it is not primarily a practical contract is made clear by comparison with its probable model in Sedley's *Bellamira*. The scene between Merryman and Thisbe at a similar point in the play characterizes their relationship as a shrewd respite from the more fraught contracts of mercenary or romantic relationship that the other characters seek. In the Sedley, the provisos balance out equally; in the Congreve they all relate to Millamant's privacy and to Mirabell only as he impinges on it. Merryman may be persuaded to give up ale and to diet, but we have no idea whether there will be more Mrs Fainalls. Millamant draws a veil of ignorance over her future husband's private affairs. As an ideal of marriage, the scene is limited and coy. But its force for Congreve is, in a sense, metaphoric. Their love is real without declaration; it is expressed by how much Millamant can take for granted, how much, in other words, Congreve can leave out. Mirabell has learnt to trust her silence, to respect her privacy. The common-sense contract is freighted with our sense of that image of support and assent, of yielding and trust, into which Congreve has shaped the whole play.

"'Tis true he was hearty in his Affection of Angelica' Jeremy Collier had said of Valentine, '. . . Now without question, to be in love with a fine Lady of 30,000 Pounds is a great Virtue!'[90] Love is supported by interest even more completely in *The Way of the World*. Mirabell is entirely the 'fine gentleman' whose success Collier laments. The story is built on Collier's premises; it is the story of how a gentleman-sharper wins. Its attitudes are defiantly tough. *The Way of the World* is a diamond-hard summation of the plays written before it. It is built out of a realization and excision of the sentimental or melodramatic potential of the form, by the creation of a perfect dramatic structure within which all the elements of this kind of play find a precisely apt place. There may be a sense in which Congreve is indebted to Collier. *Short View* argues, in effect, that the comedy of the period is amoral in outlook. The foundations of Collier's argument crumble easily, but his observation is clear. The main thrust of his argument is opposed to Restoration comedy's lack of respect for hierarchy;

> . . . has our stage a particular Privilege? Is their *Charter* enlarg'd, and are they on the same Foot of Freedom with the *Slaves* in the *Saturnalia*? Must all Men be handled alike? . . . I hope the Poet's don't intend to revive the Old Project of Levelling, and *vote* down the House of *Peers*.[91]

Lady Wishfort recommends the *Short View* to Marwood. But Collier's supporter is to be cruelly handled by her servants' saturnalian overthrow of rank.

Mirabell's comment on Lady Wishfort in the park-scene colours the setting autumnally, and prepares us for Millamant's immediate entrance in a curiously affecting way.

> An old Woman's Appetite is deprav'd like that of a Girl – Tis the Green Sickness of a second Childhood; and like the faint Offer of a latter Spring, serves but to usher in the Fall; and withers in an affected Bloom.[92]

Lady Wishfort registers the passage of time in the most immediate and personal way. She proves that Collier's values make splendid fuel for the fire they seek to put out. Her fear of offending against decorums makes her, like Wilde's Lady Bracknell, a muse of farce, an embodiment of the rules of the game. It is also an interest more up to date than the ideal of beauty reconstituted from her portrait. That 'sort of dyingness'[93] is a fashion of the earlier Restoration, a measurement of time lapsed more tactful than its hint of a dyingness of another kind. She is catapulted pathetically from hopes of marriage to a helplessness close to a senility. But she is at the centre of the play nonetheless. The last three acts take place in her chamber, and the fortunes of the gamesters come to rely on her flickering insights into their motives. All the other characters come to make deceitful overtures to her; Millamant embellishes her gentle dissimulation with ironical turns of style, Fainall is crudely insolent, and Mirabell treads his usual tightrope of evasive politeness. Lady Wishfort remains undeceived. The mockery of frivolous parent-figures has been a staple of these plays from Sir John Everyoung on. But when the Sir Rowland plot collapses, Lady Wishfort has, if not greatness, at least responsibility thrust upon her.

Mirabell had earlier drawn a careful line between town-society and the inconveniently rural demands of family in his reverberant remark that he would rather be Sir Wilful's relation than his acquaintance. Millamant – who wishes that one could treat acquaintance as one does old clothes – is torn by a similar duality, a loathing of both country and town.[94] The town-world would seem as preclusive of escape as it is for some in *The Man of Mode* or *The Country Wife* – and yet Mirabell benefits from being both Sir Wilful's relation *and* his acquaintance. Millamant steps out of her bubble of nonsensical fancy, into the continuing possibility of a shared life. (It is one of the few Restoration comedy marriage to envisage the production of children.) They do not join in the dance at the end of the play, and in a sense this marks them out as winners in a game for losers. The play ends with reality rediscovered, not transformed. We gain a fuller sense of Mrs Fainall's life history than we do of any other character. Witwoud runs a close second, and in both cases it is because the centre of the play has shifted to Wishfort and that spokesman of plain values, Sir Wilfull, to a reconsideration of family relationship. But the final plot twist fixes the source of Mrs Fainall's 'generosity' for us. Mirabell's protection of her interests tacitly demands her care for his. Sexual opportunism and generous sentiment are equally unrealistic bases for a woman's behaviour. Shared obligations are the way of the world.

Fainall promises Mrs Marwood retreat 'to another World'.[95] Lady Wishfort suggests that the same lady and herself should 'leave the World, and retire by our selves and be *Shepherdesses*'.[96] The ways of the world on stage are so completely realised that other worlds seem impossible – and yet that world is too heavily freighted with the past to pass convincingly into a possible future. The play is full of evocations of a concrete and vigorous life that it admits only in stylistic device – in Witwoud's similes, or Petulant's 'remarks'. Its sense of trivia can also remind it of a side of itself as dilapidated as that 'old peel'd Wall'[97] to which Lady Wishfort compared her face, or the list of items called to her mind by the most deeply felt of all her betrayals, Foible's. The random objects she remembers from Foible's stall form themselves into a soiled still-life, a vanitas;

> . . . an old gnaw'd *Mask*, Two Rows of *Pins* and a *Childs Fiddle; a Glass Necklace* with the Beads broken, and a *Quilted Night-cap* with one Ear . . .[98]

Foible's reward for her trickery is a farm. She, not her mistress, achieves a pastoral retreat.

There is another echo of Sedley, in the praise of 'Terence the most correct Writer in the World . . .' with which Congreve prefaces his play. Sedley intended a corrective prescription, but Congreve seems to identify with the Roman writer, to use him as a mask from behind which he can lay down the terms in which he himself desires to be judged.

> The Purity of his Style, the Delicacy of his Turns, and the Justness of his characters, were all of them Beauties, which the greater Part of his Audience were incapable of Tasting . . .

By this point analogy has turned by degrees into self-revelation. *Incognita* and the preface to *The Double Dealer* were informed by the same nervous hauteur in relation to their audience. In his dedications he consistently judges himself against an ideal of perfection, projected on to the dedicatee in a way that would seem to mask an anxiety more personal than the straightforward competitive virtuosity normal to seventeenth century writers working in conventional forms. 'As Terence excell'd in his Performances, so had he great Advantages to encourage his Undertakings; for he built most on the Foundations of Menander; His plots were generally modelled and his Characters ready drawn to his Hand.'[99] Congreve invents nothing, his plays are virtuosic rearrangements of received ideas. There is even a sense in which he seems to want to be the *last* Restoration writer. His comedies imply no further comedies. Alone of any major Restoration dramatist he bequeaths the form no new conventions or types. His withdrawal from writing is scarcely unique among dramatists, in any period. But the story sticks to Congreve in its consonance with an aspect of his writing; that withdrawal implied by an artifice almost morbidly conscious of itself. Of all Restoration dramatists he is the most classical; but it is a classicism of an intensely personal kind.

10 The Last Restoration Comedies – Farquhar, Centlivre and Steele

Restoration comedy was informed by facts of social life which had begun by the end of the seventeenth century to modify ahead of the form's intrinsic energy. The 'end' of Restoration comedy is simply the falling away of the contingencies that had shaped it. George Farquhar, on whom the beginning of this chapter will concentrate, can seem to be a transitional figure; it is certainly true that his work spans a distinct change in comic styles, from the 'artificial' style of the Etheregean revival, superficially fashionable, but crucially distant from real 'manners', to a realist comedy of broader social scope and robustly moral intention. But, like so much in the history of a genre, this seems a general change, not the result of any individual author's innovation. Through the chinks in a disintegrating comic ethos the playwrights begin to perceive a world elsewhere. Farquhar steps decisively into it; his last two plays look back to London comedy from a firm footing in new territory. His last play, *The Beaux Strategem* (1707), offers in addition his most elegant and lucid statement of an ideological shift equally central to the transformation of 'Restoration' comedy into a form expressive of recognisably eighteenth-century concerns; the growing importance of a concept of 'law'. I shall end my discussion of Restoration comedy as I believe the form can be said to an end – with the imposition of legality in the moral comedy of Centlivre and Steele and then, as an epilogue, the ironic recovery for pastoral of that legality in *The Beggars Opera*. The move out of London and the imposition of law are thus the two main themes of this chapter; they dismantle finally that metropolitan pastoral of fashionable life which constituted the ethos of Restoration comedy and fixed it as a form.

212

With the exception of Vanbrugh's *The Relapse*, Farquhar's is the only work of any lasting interest done for Cibber's Drury Lane company. Their tone – light, modish, daring, but rather glibly 'pure' – was evolved in reaction to the traditions of classical revival and aesthetically conservative wit comedy maintained by the rival company, headed by Betterton, Mrs Barry and Mrs Bracegirdle. Farquhar's prologue to *The Constant Couple* (1699) attacks their reputation for 'good' plays.

> Our plays are farce, because our house is cram'd
> Their plays all good; for what? - because they'r damn'd.
> . . .
> To engage the fair, all other means being lost,
> They fright the boxes, with old Shakespeare's ghost:
> . . .
> Let Shakespeare then lie still, ghosts do no good;
> The fair are better pleas'd with flesh and blood;
> What is't to them, to mind the ancient's taste? . . .[1]

The Constant Couple is very much a Drury Lane piece; but Farquhar's way with the clichés reveals an imaginative fleetness, and the kind of off-hand innocence revealed in his dedication.

> . . . Some may think (my acquaintance in town being too slender to make a party for the play) that the success must be desir'd from the pure merits of the cause. I am of another opinion; I have not been long enough in town to raise enemies against me; and the *English* are still kind to strangers . . .[2]

Its disengaged tone is a prophetic pointer to his development away from London comedy. He was, like so many of his characters, just passing through.

The central character of Farquhar's first play, *Love and a Bottle* (1698), is, like Farquhar, an Irishman confronting the London world. According to Roebuck, Ireland boasts 'Ladies and whores; colleges and playhouses; churches, and taverns, fine houses, and bawdy-houses; in short, every thing that you can boast of, but fops, poets, toads and adders.'[3] Reptiles apart, his qualifications show a certain distance from London society. Roebuck's down-at-heel rakishness is itself a dozen years behind the times; Lovewell, his London friend, tries to persuade him into the more modish game of 'honourable' courtship. The play's country character, Mockmode, comes from the University, where 'we dare not have wit . . . for fear of being counted rakes . . .'. Mockmode is anxious to keep up with the fashion, which he looks for in 'The great poets'.[4] *Love and a Bottle* draws self-consciously on those conventions of town-life and park-pastoral, which had come to be identified with the professional 'wit' of the theatre. Farquhar's poet-figure, Lyric, describes comedy in terms the author himself was to use in his *Discourse upon comedy*:

> Lyr: . . . the hero in comedy is always the poet's character.
> Love: . . . what's that?
> Lyr: . . . A compound of practical rake and speculative gentle-
>   man, who always bears off the great fortune in the play,
>   and shams the beau and squire with a whore or a chamber-
>   maid . . .[5]

And Lovewell, still in the park, goes on to do just that.

The Constant Couple introduces its three male leads in the park. Vizard launches it in fine style with some rather dashingly vicious libertinage. But this is to be ironically overlaid.

> Viz.   *pulls out a Book, reads and walks about.*
>   *Enter* Alderman Smuggler.
> Smug: Ay: there's a Pattern for the young Men o'th'times, at
>   his Meditation so early, some Book of pious Ejacu-
>   lations, I'm sure
> Viz: This Hobbes is an excellent fellow. (aside)
>   O Uncle Smuggler! to find you in this end o'th'town is a
>   miracle.
> Smug: I have seen a miracle this morning, indeed, cousin
>   Vizard.
> Viz: What was it, pray Sir?
> Smug: A man at his devotion so near the court – I'm very glad
>   boy, that you keep your sanctity untainted in this infec-
>   tious place, the very air of this Park is heathenish, and
>   every man's breath I meet scents of atheism,[6]

Farquhar's expository trick, in substituting one type figure for another, is interesting not only for what it says – that libertinism is now clandestine, and that when clandestine it becomes villainous

– but for what enables Farquhar to say it. The play deals in well worn judgemental counters; character, situations and reading matter, have unambiguous and easily apprehended meaning, and Farquhar shuffles them as fast as he can. Vizard's counterpart, the flamboyantly libertine Sir Harry Wildair, is set up by an entrance that recyles the social style of Dorimant and Fopling into an extrovert two-dimensional fluency;

> Viz: The joy of the playhouse, and the life of the Park.
> [*Enter* Sir Harry Wildair, *crosses the Stage singing, with Footmen after him.*]
> *Sir Harry Wildair* newly come from *Paris*.[7]

The false entrance allows Vizard to expatiate on the virtues of one 'entertaining to others, and easy to himself'[8] before Sir Harry returns. His words are flat incontestable exposition; Farquhar is not interested in extending Vizard's deceitfulness to his use of language, or indeed in any way that might imperil the plays brightly extrovert relation to its audience.

Wildair, Vizard and their friend Colonel Standard, are all suitors to the same woman, Lady Lurewell, a female Don Giovanni with the whole male cast in her catalogue;

> Parly, my pocket Book – let me see – Madrid, Venice, Paris, London – ay, London! they may talk what they will of the hot countries, but I find love most fruitful under this climate –

Her ambition is to be 'a second Eve to tempt, seduce, and damn the treacherous kind'.[9] But Sir Harry finds a better image for this attractively shallow femme fatale. She is his 'legerdemain mistress who, *presto, pass* and she's vanish'd, then *Hey*, and in an instant in your arms again'.[10] They come to operate as a kind of team, duping her other lovers into beatings and disguise. The action is homespun, even brutal, and its coarseness points up the uncertainty of Farquhar's social placings. One expects sophisticated humour from sophisticated characters. But Farquhar's inability to imagine a comic action to express their status is as sharply revealing of the state of London comedy as of his own real disengagement from it. The types Lurewell and Wildair represent are still theatrically attractive, but so detached from reality as to become commedia figures, a Harlequin and Columbine in high life.

Wildair's detachment becomes, if not psychologically internalized, at least assimilated to his own rationale. 'How pleasant is
resenting an injury without passion' he exclaims after blinding
Smuggler with 'Snush', ''Tis the beauty of revenge'.[11] The hint of a
careless cruelty is satanic in a way that points to the last stage
libertine, MacHeath. Wildair is already halfway to the detachment
of the outlaw. The rake, after the nineties, is rejected by the society
of the plays; but society at large retains the right to enjoy his
exploits. He is granted the privileges of an entertainer symbolic of
some aspects of those he entertains.

> . . . I make the most of life, no hour misspend,
> Pleasure's the means, and pleasure is my end.
> No spleen, no trouble shall my time destroy.
> Life's but a span; I'll every inch enjoy.[12]

As the great rake of his time, Wildair has the flashy ephemerality
of a toy.

In Lurewell's case, the disparity between the type and the use
Farquhar makes of it *is* internalized. Her motive is to revenge the
loss 'of that jewel, which preserv'd, exults our sex almost to angels;
but destroy'd, debases us below the worst of brutes, mankind'.
The narrative of her deflowering at fifteen by a stray Oxford
undergraduate at her father's country house is operatically fluid,
and punctuated by her maid's interjections, as a kind of ritornello.
'. . . resolving to divert my melancholy', she concludes,

> and make my large fortune subservient to pleasure and revenge,
> I went to travel, where in most courts of Europe I have done
> some execution; here I will play my last scene; then retire to my
> country-house, live solitary, and die a penitent.[13]

Her vamp's grand tour is an hilariously improper revenge for an
affront to propriety – motive and incident have been wrenched
apart by the demands of Cibberian comedy for a moralistic titil-
lation. The role spans a double identity of the kind conferred on
Angelica by trickery. Vizard gives Sir Harry her address, telling
him it is that of the most proper kind of bawdy house. It is a joke
on the incoherence of social manner; the innocent Angelica and the
rakish Sir Harry simply do not understand one another. When she
berates him for his lack of 'Wit and Manners' he is so astounded he

repeats the phrase over and over again. The park, where this trap was set, had introduced a series of discrete and opposed conventions of male behaviour. St James's no longer stands for any kind of social unity; Wildair has no hold on a territory that one might have predicted to be his by inheritance.

The trick aligns us to a double perspective on Angelica – we can see her as simultaneously innocent and available. It is a precise exploitation for comic effect of the double meaning Cibber's plots build around his heroines, double meanings that in his case spring from the author's double intent. For Farquhar the process is extrovert and unmoral, a stylistic game whose point is the well-rubbed familiarity of the cards. Wildair makes a move towards the alarmed Angelica:

Ang: Think not I am defenceless 'cause alone.
       Your very self is guard against your self;
       I'm sure there's something generous in your soul;
       my words shall search it out,
       and eyes shall fire it for my own defence.
Wild: [mimicking] Tall ti dum, ti dum, tall ti didi didum.
       A million to one now, but this girl is just come
       flush from reading the *Rival Queens* – I gad I'll at
       her in her own cant – *O my Statyra, O my Angry Dear,
       turn thy Eyes on me*, behold thy beau in buskins.[14]

Her exclamations are end-stopped pentameters; no early edition prints them this way, perhaps to emphasize that her attitudinizing is unconscious. Like the scenes in Newgate – to which, as the low comedy characters find to their cost, Lady Lurewell's boudoir would seem to be an antechamber – they point to Gay in both content and style; in the extent to which style *is* their content. Farquhar uses the setting for jokes on style and class. 'How severe and melancholy are Newgate reflections?' moans Clincher in a kind of parody in advance of Steele's *The Lying Lover* 'last week my father died; yesterday I turn'd beau; today I am laid by the heels, and tomorrow shall be hung by the neck . . . to hang in hemp, like the vulgar, 'tis very ungenteel . . .'.[15] Farquhar explores the *lack* of meaning of his material. *The Constant Couple* is a play of exhilarating dexterity; theatrical legerdemain.

The Comparison between the Two Stages notes *The Constant Couple*'s success with the less fashionable part of the audience; 'the middle

Gallery' and 'the footmen'. 'I believe 'tis about the pitch of their understanding;' the critic in this three-sided dialogue remarks, 'but if ever it diverted one man of tolerable sense I'll be hang'd . . .'.[16] Farquhar formalizes and distances his upper-class characters as if to make obvious the discontinuity of their life from that of the audience. The sequel, *Sir Harry Wildair* (1701) presents the fashionable world as a heap of unmeaning things, the 'Puffs, powders, patches, bibles, billet-doux' of the definitive Queen Anne pastoral, *The Rape of the Lock.* That slap-dash Circe, Lady Lurewell, is diminished into a mere woman of fashion; with the help of a French fop she cuckolds Sir Harry retrospectively by faking evidence of the apparently dead Angelica's unfaithfulness. Angelica's 'ghost' appears – to carry on the attack on Betterton's company – she has in fact been alive all the time, disguised as her 'brother' Beau Banter, a trick the cast list nicely colludes in. At the end of the play both women, and then Sir Harry, make speeches about perfect femininity. '. . . we are but babies at best', says Angelica 'and must have our play-things, our longings, our vapours, our frights, our monkeys, our china, our fashions, our washes, our patches, our waters, our tattle, and impertinence . . .'.[17] This time Farquhar *has* stooped to the Cibberian untruth, and moralized his tale.

Farquhar was the last writer to find in Restoration comedy an adequate form for his own interests. He explores a sense of the incipiently unfashionable, in a series of plays whose relation to London society becomes increasingly ambivalent. To say that Restoration comedy goes 'out of' fashion is not simply reductive; fashion is one way in which societies codify change. The plays of the beginning of the 1690s seem uncertain whether to stay in London or not; there was by now little reason to assume that London and comedy were necessarily synonymous. Southerne takes his characters to France, or the West Indies, Behn to Virginia, and Ravenscroft to Canterbury. Shadwell and Mountfort less adventurously explore Bury and Greenwich respectively.[18] In *The Lancashire Witches* Shadwell uncovers an aspect of regional gothic; but, as in later comedies, the capital dictates a norm. In Southerne's *Oronooko*, the girls have to explain to the audience why they are *not* in London. These plays transplant London comedy, they do not find forms native to the place. But Farquhar, in the banal and irreducible reality of country settings, finds the basis of a style as warm and solid as Queen Anne brick.

Country life always lies a little beyond the borders of literary convention. Burlesques, like Duffet's and Gay's find humour in the clash of the literary and the anti-literary, and can do so by translating 'high' plots into the terms either of criminal low-life, or mundane rusticity. Both are a kind of rock-bottom. *The Relapse* is informed by just such a burlesque view of country life, but it presents town and country in dialectic; they have equal validity within a stylised imaginative world. When pastoral is urbanized literature is unable to organize its perception of country life. That life is then only available to realism or burlesque (which is a joke that realism makes). Country life is thus that which is not literature. Just such a sense of the country lies behind Restoration comedy; it is the reality from which all visitants come, endlessly dull, endlessly actual. Farquhar's two greatest plays rely on essentially the same distinctions. But he dissents in an imaginative investment in those very aspects of country life which rendered it uninteresting to other dramatists.

In *The Recruiting Officer* (1706) Worthy has been foiled in his attempt to keep Melinda as his mistress by her sudden inheritance, and consequent leap in self-esteem. But in Shrewsbury there is none of that apparatus of intrigue that in London comedy could be activated against her. 'We live in such a precise, dull place', he complains to his friend captain Plume, 'that we can have no balls, no lampoons . . .'.[19] When Melinda complains of provincial life, the affectation is in itself provincial;

> . . . no air can be good above half a year; change of air I take to be the most agreeable of any variety in life.[20]

Silvia reminds her, to her embarrassment, of those simple physicalities from which the play derives a realism and a humour that are practically identical.

> . . . I remember the time when he never troubled our heads about air, but when the sharp air from the Welsh mountains made our noses drop in a cold morning at the boarding-school.[21]

The two women quarrel, and Melinda dashes off a malicious letter, the first of two that stretch an attenuated thread of intrigue across the play. The games Melinda and Worthy play are an aspect of their mock-sophistication; Plume and Silvia respect the parameters of small-town life.

Captain Plume returns to encounter the outcome of an earlier visit. His 'old friend Molly at the castle'[22] has just been delivered of a child. This echo of *Love for Love* is another delusive exposition, but this time Farquhar creates a character who out-grows his label, rather than simply tricking us with the wrong one. There's an innocent airiness in Plume more child-like than libertine. 'Suppose' he suddenly wonders, as an argument for sleeping with Silvia before marrying her, 'I marry'd a woman that wanted a leg?.'[23] Silvia's male disguise incidentally solves the problem. In the meantime, this sense of appetitive realities is focused on Rose, different from the country-girl characters of other dramatists in only the relative delicacy of her treatment. As emblem of herself she bears a basket of chickens; her sweet dimness breeds dialogue of a wonderful silliness;

Sil: . . . pray what do you expect from this captain, child?
Rose: . . . suppose that he should promise to marry me?
Sil: You should have a care, my dear. Men will promise anything beforehand.
Rose: I know that, but he promised to marry me afterwards.
Sil: Afterwards! After what?
Rose: After I had sold him my chickens.[24]

It is in these bathetic sexual jokes that our sense of Plume's rakishness drains away. When he and Silvia meet in her father's house, they breezily parody the 'soldier's return', with a mock-seriousness answered by the real gravity of his gesture, in showing her his will. He had left her everything. She counters with her knowledge of his bastard, but this only reminds us of her unsentimental generosity in looking after it. They communicate in deeds, not words or social forms; they look for a language of affection that is honest and personal, and can find it in only the most pragmatic of actions.

'War is your mistress' Balance had earlier said to Plume, in an attempt to dissuade him from Silvia, '. . . it is below a soldier to think of any other'. 'As a mistress . . .' Plume answers, '. . . But as a friend, Mr Balance?'[25] The Justice is roundly sceptical. But the incident builds towards a sense of disparity between Plume and the image he consciously, if not quite deliberately, projects. When Silvia disguises herself as a potential recruit she pushes these issues towards a resolution. If Silvia could not be his friend, 'Jack

Wilful' can. Farquhar's is the most telling Restoration use of the travesty device, in being the most Shakespearean. It is the heroine's entry into the masculine world, and the discoveries she takes from it are an enlargement of her perception not only of men, but of herself. By taking Rose to bed with her, (and turning Plume down) Silvia has not only kept Plume and the country girl apart; she dodged the opportunity of an intimacy that would reassure both partners that each was in possession of all their limbs. But Farquhar's witty avoidance is all the wittier for uncovering a truth of feeling behind Plume's concern with masculine self-image. *The Recruiting Officer* plays the teasing game of the comedy of its time, but only to lead one into a humane physicality of its own.

Of all his many reasons for objecting to Silvia's marriage, the most immediate to Balance is the probable fate of his estate.

'. . . I should have some rogue of a builder by the help of his damned magic art transform my noble oaks and elms into cornices, portals, sashes, birds, beasts, gods, and devils, to adorn some maggoty, new-fashioned bauble upon the Thames. And then you should have a dog of a gardener bring a *habeas corpus* for my for my *terra firma*, remove it to Chelsea or Twitnam, and clap it into grassplots and gravel walks'.[26]

It is an extreme of conservatism to see all change as magical – but Balance's fears translate into his own context an imaginative identification of the author's. The heathenism that Smuggler scented in St James's Park is located more precisely when, in *Sir Harry Wildair*, an anxious Colonel Standard runs into his wife's maid there. 'Never christen'd!' he exclaims after asking her about her background, 'her father a mountebank!'[27] Parley would seem to have inherited her mistresses quasi-magical powers, now that Lady Lurewell has dwindled into a wife. At the end of *Love and a Bottle*, Lyric the poet brings on his landlady Mrs Bullfinch, dressed as a parson.

Love: What, Pope Joan the second! were you the priest?
Bull: Of the poet's ordination.
Lyr: Ay, Ay, before the time of Christianity the poets were the priests.
Mock: No wonder then that all the world were heathens.[28]

Park and poet go together in the theatre of the nineties. For Farquhar they are two aspects of transforming art; a magic that is an art, not a science, and thus reducible to mere trickery, like the theatre. These are the cheapjack powers flaunted by the town. It is a rootless heathenism. The springs of Farquhar's plotting are most readily available to those of unknown parentage, and no permanent home, like 'Jack Wilful' or Plume's aide, Sergeant Kite. Kite was 'born a gypsy and bought from my mother, Cleopatra, by a certain nobleman . . . who, liking my beauty, made me his page'.[29] So, like Parley, he knows both kinds of trickery, the modish and the magical. In all Restoration comedy the town is the place where people change. Farquhar sees this transformation as magical, but unserious – they change masks only, they have no roots in the real world, within the play or in its reference out to its audience. In *The Recruiting Officer* the crux of the intrigue plot is set in the mountebank's tent. Kite's disguise as astrologer invents mock-futures for characters whose real futures are determined by the realities of country life (and thus predictable from within the play; unavailable in this case to any sequel). The device proves as useful in dealing with Melinda as with the rustic recruits. The implied equation undermines her pretensions, as acutely as it reveals a superstitiousness both provincial and girlish. Melinda's attempts to pursue an intrigue have only involved her with a frazzled grotesque like Brazen. There's little choice in Shrewsbury. Her tone of voice has a peevish sophistication; there is always something a little slipshod in her attempts to turn a fine phrase:

> And pray, was it a ring or buckle or pendants or knots, or in what shape was the almighty gold transformed that has bribed you so much in his favour?[30]

Brazen's pretensions are several degrees cruder, but in the same vein, and thus parody both hers and the mode they exist in, the mode of provincial fancy that decorates Shrewsbury's answer to park-pastoral, the 'Severn Walks'.

> Thou peerless princess of Salopian plains
> Envied by nymphs and worshipped by the swains,
> Behold how humbly does the Severn glide,
> To greet thee, princess of the Severn side.
> Madam, I'm your humble servant and all that, Madam. A fine
> river this same Severn; do you love fishing, Madam?[31]

One piece of epistolary trickery – Melinda's – is exposed in Kite's legerdemain, another – Lucy's – is begun. The maid has inherited this outworn plot as a kind of hand-me-down.

Country realities are the realities of kinship as well as of appetite. When Justice Balance goes off-stage at the end of his first scene with Plume, it is to receive a letter. It contains the news of his only son's death. In following on the news of Molly's son's birth, it implants a rhythm of mortality outside the scope of London comedy. In the country, these things happen. Balance's reaction seems gruff and, initially, callous –

> the decree is just. I was pleased with the death of my father because he left me an estate, and now I'm punished with the loss of an heir to inherit mine . . .[32]

It is important of course that Balance would have been a young man at the time of the Restoration proper, when in comedy at least his attitude to his father was commonplace. Farquhar thus marks his distance from traditional town comedy. But it is important also that balance now lives in a comic world where 'family' is presented as an actuality whose developments may well be difficult to cope with – the rationales of unacceptable and irreducible events are hard won and unsatisfying. Farquhar's realism is not afraid to evoke more than comedy can deal with. The play comes to trust family, the pattern that binds a country community together in ways that resist and finally assimilate the initial disruptiveness of the Farquharian adventurer.

Unlike Shrewsbury in *The Recruiting Officer*, Litchfield, the setting of *The Beaux Stratagem*, is defined from the start in relation to London. 'Come from London?' the innkeeper Boniface asks Archer. 'No.' 'Going to, London, mayhap?'[33] It allows Farquhar to present London selectively, through his heroes' eyes. The park is, as ever, a space for fashionable society to display itself, but Archer and Aimwell observe it from the disabused vantage of the impoverished

> Aim: . . . did you observe poor Jack Generous in the Park last week?
> Arch: Yes, with his autumnal perriwig, shading his melancholy face, his coat older than anything but its fashion, with one hand idle in his pocket, and with the other picking his

useless teeth; and tho' the Mall was crowded with company, yet was poor Jack as single and solitary as a lion in a
desert.[34]

Archer is disguised as Aimwell's footman. Aimwell considers
himself in disguise; money, and their lack of it, has dislodged the
signs of social class into a chaos, from which, as Archer reminds
him, they can remake their own positions. But if money has
reordered their world, only money can reinstate them in it, and
money imposes a sense of criminality on those who lack and desire
it, irrespective of any actual crime. '. . . 'tis still my maxim', claims
Archer, 'that there is no scandal like rags, nor any crime so
shameful as poverty'.[35]

Pastoral talks about money, but in its own code, a code that
carefully blurs the distinctions between personal and financial
fulfilment. 'I read her thousands in her looks' Aimwell says of the
country heiress Dorinda, 'she look'd like Ceres in her harvest, corn
wine and oil, milk and honey, gardens groves and purling streams
play'd on her plenteous face.'[36] Litchfield is described at the beginning of the play in the same code; it is characterized by its most
famous product, Boniface's ale '. . . smooth as oil, sweet as milk,
clear as amber, and strong as brandy'.[37] Aimwell's preciosity, his
assumption of a romance role ('. . . call me Oroondates, Cesario,
Amadis . . .')[38] is an aspect of that sense of style as deceit that
informs all Farquhar's fashionable heroes. His apprehension of
Litchfield's fruitfulness suggests a possible reconciliation of town
'fancy' and country 'reality' that allows him at the end of the play
to confess to Dorinda that he is all a 'fiction'.[39] If Wildair, or for that
matter Archer, admitted so much it would amount to self-erasure.
'Her face! her pocket you mean', scoffs Archer, 'the corn wine and
oil lies there. In short, she has ten thousand pound, that's the
English on't . . . .'.[40] There are traces in these paired heroes of the
anti-platonic/platonic distinction of the nineties.[41] But that would
effect a focus on sexual issues of little interest to Farquhar and his
public. Archer is the equivalent of the anti-platonic. He is the more
down-to-earth, his interest in food nearly breaks the disguise in his
determination to have a say in ordering dinner. But their real
difference is as kinds of performer. Aimwell, according to his
friend, 'can't counterfeit the passion without feeling it'.[42] But
Archer is the *detached* Farquharian hero, the player at feelings, calm

and fluent in his handling of the counters of social identity, ready to slip into song or banter if the situation requires it, and always reserving an actor's control. He goes on to mock the gap between actuality and rhetoric in an account of his adventures with Cherry:

> The nymph that with her twice ten hundred pounds
> With brazen engine hot, and quoif clear starch'd
> Can fire the quest in warming of the bed
> There's a touch of the sublime Milton for you, and
the subject but an innkeeper's daughter.[43]

The pose is apparently commonsensical, but the detachment it implies is that of a refusal to engage with reality, a retention of the entertainer's role. Boniface and his daughter think the 'Beaux' must be highwaymen, part of that peripatetic underworld to which they themselves belong. Cherry has fantasies of illegitimacy – to be 'misbegotten' is to be free of the imposed roles of social class, a social uncertainty that Archer plays with when he woos her. It lends them a dangerous equivalence. But the same 'freedom' makes him attractive to Dorinda's sister-in-law, Mrs Sullen. His sense of make-believe, his pliancy, and assumed triviality of manner feed into the web of intrigue that expresses her real discontent.

Mrs Sullen is herself from London, and her imaginative world is formed by a town sense of the pastoral:

> . . . not that I disapprove rural pleasures as the poets have painted them; in their landscape every Phillis has her Coridon every murmuring stream and every flowery mead gives fresh alarms to love – besides, you'll find that their couples were never married . . .[44]

She has a London sense of monetary value, too. She reserves the familiar right of town characters to educate country characters – as Archer had Cherry. Her instruction of the placid, uninformed Dorinda, has the rattling brightness of sophistication in a vacuum. But Farquhar collapses our initial expectations of intrigue. He explains the grating archness of her earlier scenes, in a speech of self-revelation, placed identically to Lady Lurewell's. Farquhar here can make the disparity between this and her normal mode work as a shock of emphasis.

Mrs Sull: . . . what law can search into the remote abyss of nature, what evidence can prove the unaccountable disaffections of wedlock? can a jury sum up the endless aversions that are rooted in our souls, or can a bench give judgement upon antipathies?

Dor: They never pretended sister, they never meddle but in cases of uncleanness.

Mrs Sull: uncleanness! O sister, casual violation is a transient injury, and may possibly be repair'd, but can radical hatreds be ever reconcil'd?[45]

Farquhar cannot dramatize 'radical hatreds' in action. But this obsessive and hopeless rhetoric, once broached, returns intermittently throughout the play.

Life in the country may have contributed to Mrs Sullen's unhappiness, but it is exile from the town that allows Farquhar to express it so fluently. Lady Lurewell's 'confession' was 'rustic' in its almost Chaucerian fabliau style. Its archaic overtones fill out other resonances in the Lady's past – it hints fleetingly at an earthier magic at the beck of my Lady Legerdemain. It also splits the narrative off from the rest of the play – any 'feeling' in *The Constant Couple* is stranded in its flimsy town-world. Mrs Sullen looks back on the town from that 'reality' always evoked in the form's inverted pastoral; its very insubstantiality puts an odd pathos in her choice. When Dorinda has accepted the apparently rich 'Lord' Aimwell's offer of marriage, she rattles off the detail of her new life with an unfeeling enthusiasm:

Lights, lights to the stairs. My Lady Aimwell's coach put forward. Stand by, make room for her Ladyship. Are not these things moving? What! Melancholy of a sudden?

Mrs Sull: Happy, happy sister: your angel has been watchful for your happiness, whilst mine has slept regardless of his charge – Long smiling years of circling joys for you, but not one hour for me [Weeps]

Dor: Come, my Dear, we'll talk of something else.[46]

Farquhar respects Mrs Sullen's unhappiness. But his own imaginative investment is in a positive myth of country life – the creation of another kind of pastoral, that solidifies towards the end of the play and displaces the mock-pastoral of intrigue. At the height of her discontent Mrs Sullen runs into a country woman waiting to see the dowager Lady Bountiful for help for her husband's sore leg. Mrs Sullen impersonates her mother-in-law and gravely advises the woman, in a minutely detailed recipe '. . . . to season it very well, then roll it up like brawn, and put it into the oven for two hours'.[47] But this revenge by proxy on her own husband coexists uncomfortably with our sense of the other lives the country holds – that of a woman who came 'seventeen long Mail to have a cure for my husband's sore leg'.[48] Lady Bountiful is not satirized in the way the modern misappropriation of the name might suggest. From the very beginning of the play she has been, as an exemplar of rural virutes, almost on a par with Boniface's ale. As a healer she complements the familiar identification of the rural and the physical. Dorinda, like Margery, had experienced first love primarily as sickness, and it is Aimwell's pretended need of Bountiful's powers that brings the lovers together. She, not Dorinda, is the comic Ceres; an embodiment of the renewal that country stability can offer, of the resistant virtues of a sense of place.

'The old family building'[49] of the Sullens undergoes a variety of comic shocks in the play's last act. Archer discovers Mrs Sullen in her bedchamber, soliloquizing about him. He silently takes up 'the posture she describes',[50] an emanation of her fantasy that frightens her in its congruence to repressed desire. When he carries her off her cries merge into those of her servants; by a coincidence of timing, the house is invaded by robbers – a metaphoric violation, a paranoid joke on doubling and transgression, to cap the gentler erotic one. But the incursion of Boniface's gang serves also to dramatize and objectify the concept of lawlessness. It presents *real* criminality, unindulged by the play, thus breaking up and isolating the fragments of that notional criminality originally posited by Archer.

Farquhar goes on to flout the structural conventions of Restoration comedy, by introducing a new character at the beginning of act V, a gentleman whose identity is not revealed to the audience till near the end of the play – he is Sir Charles Freeman, Mrs Sullen's brother and Aimwell's friend, a *deus ex machina* whose careful reasonableness re-patterns the farce but cannot quite resolve it. He encounters Sullen, the drunkenly drowsy consciousness of this disorderly rural world, and spells out the facts of marriage and legality.

Sir Charles: . . . rational creatures have minds that must be united.
Sullen: Minds.
Sir Charles: Ay, minds, Sir, don't you think that the mind takes
             place of the body?
Sullen: In some people.[51]

Charles is not *overbearingly* just – he lacks that sense of reality to which Sullen bears witness in the accidental wit of his answer. He comes into the play to represent 'law'; enforced reasonableness, and humane solutions. But the play posits a reality to which this is inadequate. The divorce ending is oddly exhilarating. It is a little improvised ceremony, another kind of 'country dance'. But only within the temporary discipline of dance, in the play-within-a-play of ceremony, can feeling and law, reality and desire be equivalent. Comedy alone is inadequate to the reconciliation. The ends of Farquhar's comedies always propose unresolved fates, characters who, like the recruits and their families, move out of comedy's scope. When the fashionable characters leave Litchfield, they go to a life that the play has rendered less real, because less fully invested in feeling and relationship. Cherry, hearing of the robbery 'wanted to have discovered the whole plot, and twenty other things . . .'[52] to 'Martin', the name she knew Archer by. She manages to send the two Beaux their strongbox; the strongbox, we know has been empty all along, but the note she sends with it is freighted unexpectedly . . .

. . . could I have met you instead of your Master tonight, I would have delivered myself into your hands with a sum that much exceeds that in your strong box, which I have sent you, with an Assurance to my dear Martin, that I shall ever be his most faithful friend till death.

'There's a billet-doux for you',[53] Archer concludes on reading this to the company. Such events cannot but have a different weight for the adventurer than for those on whose lives he impinges.

By dedicating *The Recruiting Officer* to 'All Friends round the Wrekin' Farquhar placed himself in ironical relationship to Congreve and the way of his world. It was Sir Wilful Witwoud who embarrassed his fashionable brother by reminding him of the times when he 'cou'd intreat to be remember'd . . . to your friends

round the Rekin'.[54] This gentler parallel to the ironic dedication of
The Plaindealer is expanded on in the prologue to Farquhar's next
play, *The Beaux Stratagem*, beginning as it does with a reference to
Wycherley's still-celebrated comedy, the exemplar of that tendency of Restoration dramatists to gradually broaden the scope of
their comedies towards a final ambitious criticism of money and
manners.

> When strife disturbs or sloth corrupts an age;
> Keen satire is the business of the stage.
> When the Plain-Dealer writ, he lash'd those crimes
> Which then infested most the modish times.[55]

But this turns out to be the drawing of another line of demarcation
between Farquhar's comedy and that of those 'modish times'. 'But
now. . . . There scarce is room for satire all our lays / Must be, or
songs of triumph or of praise.'[56]

The reason Farquhar gives for this points not only to a court still
further from 'Restoration' styles than that of William and Mary,
but to a crucial change in social ideology; the growing primacy of
the rule of law. 'When Anna's sceptre points the laws their
course. . . . There scarce is room for satire':[57] the imposition of law
comes to leave little room for wit and intrigue either, for it would
deprive them of the right to dictate the outcome of the play. The
end of *The Beaux Stratagem* is effected by an imposition from
outside of rational law. Sir Charles is the acceptable advance guard
of a movement to make comedy an unambiguous statement of
shared social values; to rescue comedy from wit in the name of
didacticism.

In *The Plaindealer*, or *The Way of the World*, 'law' is a means of
social interaction, an organization of the play from inside; its
beneficiaries possess skill, not rights. But 'law' in later comedies is
an appeal to regularization from outside the play itself. The terms
in which Queen Anne licensed Vanbrugh's Haymarket theatre, or
those in which Steele promoted his directorship of Drury Lane,
define actors and characters as potential deviants, in need of a
constant supervisory vigilance.[58] A policing of the content of comedy, as of society's relationship to the players, comes to be a part of
the play's design on its audience. As replies to Collier so cruelly
reveal, Restoration comedy, the victim of its own nonchalance,
had lost what little rationale it once possessed. It was still possible

to write it but not to explain why. Collier, as so often, was right in the wrong way. The *Short View* is interesting less for the epidemic of prudery it has been supposed to have caused, than for the new drama it asked for; a drama aware of its relation to a new audience, and through that to society as a whole.

The idea of 'sentimentalism' blurs the distinction between this 'moral' comedy, and the style I earlier labelled 'Cibberian'.[59] Cibber's interest is primarily – perhaps exclusively – in theatricality. This of course necessitates his adoption of any current theatrical style. In *The Careless Husband* (1704) Lord Foppington follows the court to Windsor. The end of the play finds himself serenely blessing the lovers' match; that the old monster goes soft is indeed a sign of the times. The main plot, in enclosing Sir Charles Easy's intrigues within his own household, is repellently claustrophobic even by Cibber's standards. The operation of exploitative theatricality on a softened kind of privacy of feeling is Cibber's characteristic mode, and the falling away of the tougher intrigue style finds it in full flower. But his moral concerns are simply a brake on his own imaginative prurience; they don't reshape his comic method.

One can find something closer to a new 'moral' form in the work of Susanna Centlivre. Her stylistic and structural model is Congreve; like his, her plays tend to focus on a single object – the black box, the deed of trust in his case, or, for example, in hers, the jewelled portrait passed erratically from hand to hand in *The Gamester* (1705). Her plays also tend to resolve themselves on a single 'adjudicating' female figure; as so often the imitation is to some extent corrective. *The Gamester* flaunts its relationship to *Love for Love* in naming its hero and heroine Angelica and Valere, but Centlivre's Angelica is carefully unenigmatic; she is wholly adjudicator, not reward. The plotting of her plays is always in the hands of the characters, usually the female characters, so its moral balance is determined from within. Even the maid in *The Gamester* is governed by considerations of 'desert'. Her clear sighted and morally decisive heroines – all of whom believe, with Mrs Plotwell in *The Beau's Duel* (1702), that 'Justice can never be dishonourable'[60] – drive plays shaped by the author's primary interest in relationship between men and women, her determination to derive from this a morality both practicable and just. Lady Wealthy's 'conversion' in *The Gamester* is plausible in a way those of Steele's and Cibber's characters are not, in that Centlivre has been able to show us Wealthy struggling throughout the play with her consciousness of the necessity to make moral judgements. Her affectation is thus a perversity of manner, the shedding of which is an unambiguous positive.

The debit side of Centlivre's style is a certain four-squareness in the plotting, literally so in *A Bold Stroke for a Wife* (1718) where the hero has to win over each of his mistress's four 'humorous' guardians in turn before she will grant him her hand. But all in all, she wrote more good plays than anyone between Farquhar and Wilde. Her comparative neglect can perhaps be explained by a stylistic conservatism that makes her anomalous in literary–historical terms. There is something enormously engaging in finding her recreating swingeing Restoration farce as late as *The Busy Body*. In her work the park still stands for freedom in the old Carolean way. When Isabinda swoons, it is to block access to the cupboard where her lover is hidden. She reconciles herself to her father and accepts his choice of suitor only when she learns that it is her own choice in disguise. Her behaviour is on the surface that of the 'sentimental' heroine, but its motivation always comes out of the breezy search for self-fulfilment that drives traditional farce.

This conservatism is to some degree forced on her by her interest in independent women characters. To write a 'feminist' play in the early eighteenth century was of necessity to look back. Women are relatively autonomous in the intrigue play; they have at least equal, perhaps a superior, ability to determine plot. At this point in the history of comedy this kind of plotting is overtaken by another, one that focuses on the social stability of the family unit, and thus tends to define its women characters as either wives or daughters. This change is obviously part of the same social shift as that interest in law, and its effect on comedy is similarly pervasive.

We have seen both providing Farquhar with a confirmation of his own imaginative interests. In the case of Richard Steele, the effect is more ambiguous. His play *The Lying Lover* (1703) opposes itself to the very idea of wit and intrigue; play is their medium still, and the park their play-ground, but the comedy Steele's preface hopes 'might be no improper Entertainment in a Christian Commonwealth'[61] carefully demonstrates the melodramatic consequences of frivolity and deceit. Centlivre achieves a moral style, a taut innuendo-free comedy, grounded on shrewd humane assessment of relationship. Steele's characters have no autonomous ability to form relationships. They are puppets, deployed by a moralist playing providence.

'Playing' is, in his better work, the operative term. Two at least of
his comedies are saved by their subverting charm.

Steele says of the hero of *The Lying Lover* that

> . . . he uses the Advantages of a learned Education, a ready
> Fancy, and a liberal Fortune, without the Circumspection and
> good sense which should always attend the Pleasures of a Gentle-
> man; that is to say, a reasonable Creature.[62]

Steele begins his fable for young gentlemen in St James' park,
whence young Bookwit, disguised as a soldier, sets out to conquer
'those regions of Wit and gallantry, the Park – the Playhouse . . .'.[63]
Overhearing an account of a serenade by water, he pretends to
Penelope, the lady to whom it was addressed, that the serenade was
his, thus incurring the enmity of Lovemore, her betrothed, and the
jealousy of Victoria, her friend.

He meets them again in the park at evening, decorating the setting
with a riot of pastoral fantasy that the disgruntled ladies turn against
him;

> . . . Let's go, my dear, leave him to the Woods, as you say.
> [Aside] I wish 'twas full of Bears . . .[64]

But the hazards of Romance are more immediate than that. After
apparently killing Lovemore in a duel, Bookwit ends up in Newgate,
soliloquy, and the blankest of blank verse.

The play is subtitled 'The Ladies Friendship', the point being, of
course, that there is no such thing. Steele invents type-characters and
situations to replace those he discredits. Penelope and Victoria act
out, with an icy politeness, what must be the first version of the
Gwendolyn/Cecily tea-table scene (in Wilde's *The Importance of
Being Earnest*) Penelope later 'helps' Victoria dress for an encounter
with Bookwit, maliciously setting her clothes awry, and daubing
her with powder. 'Now' she says, with some satisfaction, 'she
looks like a Spright.'[65] The effect is of one doll dressing another; its
distance from Restoration ideals of beauty is pointed up by Old
Bookwit's memories of his wife;

> . . . some young Women suffer in Shapes of their Mothers' mak-
> ing, by spare Diet, straight Lacing, and constant chiding. But 'twas
> the Work of Nature, free, unconstrain'd, healthy . . .[66]

When compared to Centlivre's women, Victoria and Penelope seem to belong to a different culture, and in a sense they do. '. . . Love is a union of minds' says Young Bookwit 'and she that engages mine must be very well able to express her own . . .'.[67] But this ideal is also out of date. Just as young Bookwit ends in tearful reconciliation to his father, so Penelope mourns Lovemore when 'dead' and accepts him thankfully when he turns out, predictably, to have been alive all along. His lie is apparently to be rewarded, not punished, despite the cruelty of its immediate effects.

The end of the play opens up Steele's frame of reference to take in, in a song, the political and royalist connotations of the park setting.

> The rolling Years, the Joys restore,
> Which happy happy *Britain* knew,
> When in a Female Age before
> Beauty the Sword of Justice drew.
>
> Nymphs, and Fauns, and Rural Powers
> Of Christal Floods, and shady Bowers
> No more shall here preside;
> The flowing Wave, and living Green
> Owe only to their present Queen
> Their Safety and their Pride.[68]

The Lying Lover begins its attack on romance in a proscriptive examination of manners and intrigue; it completes it with a Whig attempt to demystify the monarchy, to disengage it from that playful, quasi-magical imagery that linked the monarch to the capital, and through the capital to the country as a whole.

The Lying Lover was not a popular success. When Steele returned to similar idea in *The Tender Husband* (1705) he employed a much lighter touch. The park is seen through the eyes of the visiting country character, Gubbin, to have a bright child-like quality – '. . . How prettily this Park is stock'd with Soldiers, and Dear, and Ducks and Ladies.'[69] Steele's heroine is the heiress Gubbin is to marry. She and her guardian are called in the play simply 'Aunt' and 'Niece'; she lives in a fantasy world culled from romances, one of whose functions is to free her from the anonymity of family relationship, to colour and 'name' the world around her. Gubbin she casts as a wildman, and changes her own name, Bridget, for 'Partenissa'. Steele, again, has established a comic type, the

teenage girl for whom books are more real than life. It is an attempt
to diminish romance, to enclose it within the actual foreshadowed
in *The Lying Lover*, when Lettice the maid reads *Argalus and
Parthenia* in bed – '. . . I hope they'll come together again at the
end of the Book. – And marry, and have several Children'.[70] But
the play comes to collude with Bridget/Parthenissa. 'I'd change it
for another', says her other suitor, the Captain, after listening
sympathetically to her 'naming' problems . . .

> . . . I could recommend to you three very pretty Sill-
> ables – What do you think of *Clerimont*?
>
> Niece: *Clerimont*! *Clerimont*! Very well – But what right have I to
> it?[71]

For once 'romance' and 'reality' have chimed; 'Clerimont' is the
captain's real name, and on that basis she accepts him.

Her '. . . best of Savages'[72] ends up married to a character from
the plot that gives the piece its title. Clerimont Senior, the Captain's brother, has seemed to be 'tender' in encouraging his affected wife's affair with a gallant. 'He' is in fact the husband's
'wench', and, Gubbin's eventual bride. But though Mrs Clerimont
initially agrees to give up her frenchified ways and be as her
husband wishes her, when she enters for the last scene, she has
reverted to affectation. Perhaps Steele found it impossible to imagine her 'reformed'; he may wish to slough off the style of Restoration comedy, but he has no alternative conventions for drawing
character. This engagingly silly and amoral farrago is easily his best
play; interestingly, it bears his least public dedication, to his friend
Addison.

The Conscious Lovers (1722), Steele's most celebrated play, has
acquired a reputation as the acme of the sentimental drama. Its
emotional sensationalism is always at the service of its didacticism.
Steele exploits basic audience responses in order to stress or
magnify those ideas of social morality to which this of all his plays
is most unequivocally designed. It is an exposition of copy-book
behaviour, of right and wrong action in social and family situations. There is none of the easy social intercourse of the Restoration plays; the hero is scrupulously cold and insulting to his valet,
Tom. Humour, like wit and fashion has been banished below-
stairs. Occasionally this throws a light of irony on the behaviour of

the 'high' characters. 'I thought, I heard him kiss you', the puzzled Lucinda remarks to her maid. 'Why do you suffer that?' 'Why Madam', Phillis replies, 'we Vulgar take it to be a Sign of Love . . .'.[73]

She goes on to make a comparison with the signs and seals that will ratify her mistress's marriage. But Lucinda's 'sale' at Mrs Sealand's hands is criticised by the play only for the manner in which it is carried out. Steele is himself concerned to promote a social rather than a personal idea of marriage. The aristocratic Sir John Bevil and the merchant Mr Sealand discuss the contract between their children in terms that suggest a wider historical context, a context that Steele points up by setting the scene in St James Park.

Sir John: O Sir, your Servant, you are laughing at my laying any stress upon Descent – but I must tell you, Sir, I never knew anyone, but he that wanted that Advantage, turn it into ridicule.

Mr Seal: And I never knew anyone, who had many better Advantages, put that into his Account. . . I have made no Objection's to your Son's Family – 'Tis his Morals, that I doubt.

Sir John: Sir, I can't help saying, that what might injure a Citizen's Credit, may be no Stain to a Gentleman's Honour.[74]

The tone is polite, strained, circumspect; the strain is to some extent Steele's own. In seeking to conciliate two different and fundamentally opposed class moralities, without offending either, he forfeits his own integrity or independence as moralist. But the point of a need for social regeneration through an alliance of the aristocracy and the merchant classes is made almost ceremonially. It is of this that the famous tearful last scene is an emblem.

The Conscious Lovers exists in the aftermath of Restoration comedy. Its studied badness – its diagrammatic action and careful impersonality – deprives it of the energy to link itself to this or any other vigorous dramatic tradition. The concerns of the moralist are not always the dramatist's defects; in this and his other plays Steele shows a gift for evocations of day-to-day life which though not dramatic in itself, does provide his play with a context of actuality that no other aspect of them earns. But like Cibber, as a dramatist he invests imaginatively in those aspects of his subject which as moralist he condemns. A scholar pretending to be a soldier, a young heiress redeeming her situation by fantasy; these are essentially innocent creations. Disguise and play are what interest Steele in the theatre – they are certainly those aspects of it that draw from him his most delicate response. Steele's plays evince the growing identification of romance with the world of the child. They side, albeit unconsciously, with escape.

Conclusion: Newgate Pastoral – John Gay and *The Beggars Opera*

Pastoral, like comedy, shifted irrevocably in tone and meaning during the last years of the seventeenth century and the beginning of the eighteenth. The pastoral controversy, as the discussion surrounding this shift is sometimes called, could be summed up as an opposition of 'simple' pastoral to 'complex'.[1] The complex – promoted by, among others, Pope, Gay and Swift – exploits the fictiveness of pastoral; its location in impossible time and place, the artifice of its action its characters' ambiguity of social class. This kind of pastoral is at once traditional and abstract; that is, it imitates, builds on and complicates classical and Renaissance models and in so doing it exposes the formal elements of pastoral as isolable devices, flexible by virtue of their limitations, not in spite of them. Simple pastoral, of the kind that writers like Addison, Phillips and Purney developed belongs to a shift in literary taste that, as Earl Wasserman has put it 'tended to reject the aesthetics based upon authority and pre-established definitions of the *genres*, and to evolve one logically from the nature of the human mind and the sources of its enjoyment'.[2] Its main dynamic, in other words, is to depict and thus to reproduce the pleasure an urban readership may take in a limited and distanced encounter with country life and country people. Its tone tends, to use an apt term of Purney's, to 'the Soft'.[3]

If I am right in assuming that Restoration comedy is a kind of town-pastoral, then the town–eclogue is in some sense its heir. Plot and character, in the town comedies of Farquhar and Cibber, are the flimsy underpinnings of a presentation of fashionable life that threatens to break loose altogether into catalogues of objects and events, mere heaps of unmeaning things. It is a short step

237

from this to the plan of *Six Town Eclogues*, published in 1747 by
Gay, Pope and Lady Mary Wortley Montague:

> 'Monday. Roxana, or the Drawing Room': 'Tuesday. St James's
> Coffee-House. Silliander and Patch.'; 'Wednesday. The Tete a
> Tete. Dacinda'; 'Thursday. The Bassette-Table. Smilinda and
> Cardelia.' 'Friday. The Toilette. Lydia.' 'Saturday. The Small-
> Pox. Flavia.'[4]

Pope's main refinement on the eclogue form was to make it more
dramatic, in specifying and differentiating characters and setting.
This is all the dramatization required to present the essential
sameness of fashionable life. The town–eclogue, within its limited
scope and blatancy of paradox is the last really inventive literary
expression of that ironic sense of social class that informs the
courtly pastoral.

Traditional pastoral becomes peripheral to literary culture in
England as the Stuart monarchy died out. The prologue to Gay's
The Shepherds Week includes a mock-lumpen lament for Queen
Anne as part of the attempt of its complex pastoral to overwhelm
and enclose the simple by imitating it.

> Our clerk came posting o'er the Green
> With doleful Tidings of the Queen;
> That Queen, he said, to whom we owe
> Sweet *Peace that maketh Riches flow;*
> That Queen who eas'd our Tax of late,
> Was dead, alas! and lay in State.

But the mourning rustics fulfill their role with a mistaken as well
as an unseemly promptness.

> While thus we stood as in a Stound,
> And wet with Tears, like Dew, the Ground,.
> Full soon by Bonefire and by Bell
> We learnt our liege was passing well . . .[5]

Like Pope in *The Rape of the Lock*, Gay can maintain the traditional
royalist role of pastoral only through burlesque. But the shift in
taste that informs the pastoral controversy is dependent on a larger
social change; simple pastoral is a Whig taste, complex a Tory,

even in its most parodistic forms. The end of the Stuart line, and thus of its dream of absolutism, is the beginning of an attempt at constitutional stability to which the political games of traditional pastoral are no longer relevant. The pastoral society is no longer the model of a social ideal. It is no longer possible to present social class ironically. Simple pastoral insists unambiguously on the social distinctions from which the complex derives its artifice. It is a change to parallel the change I outlined in the last chapter, the imposition on the comic society of the ordering of law. Stability of the kind that interests the early Augustans implies a fixed view of class relationships, a view that both simplifies and restricts the world of pastoral, as it had that of Restoration comedy. In this context *The Beggar's Opera* (1728) is the beginning of a musical tradition, but the end of a literary one. It may have started the vogue of the ballad opera, but it closes, as a brilliant climax, the theatrical career of ironic pastoral.

More than a decade before the play appeared, Pope was considering 'pastorals' in a similar vein. In a famous letter, dated 30 August 1716, he conveys to Swift

> . . . a hint that a set of Quaker pastorals might succeed, if our friend Gay could fancy it . . . I believe farther, the pastoral ridicule is not exhausted, and that a porter, footman, or chairman's pastoral might do well. Or what think you of a Newgate pastoral among the whores and thieves there'.[6]

The term 'Newgate pastoral' has attached itself to *The Beggar's Opera* largely as a result of Empson's influential essay[7] but a question remains as to whether it could be called a pastoral in an eighteenth century sense; whether anyone could have thought of the final outcome of Swift's suggestion in the terms in which it was originally made. It is unlikely, I think, that 'Newgate pastoral' meant 'Newgate pastoral play' to either Pope or Swift. At this point in the history of pastoral 'a pastoral' was an eclogue, and it was largely Pope who made it so.[8] But whatever form Pope had in mind, his idea was strengthened by an intervention of coincidence. In 1717, a few months after Swift's letter, Thomas Purney published *A Full Enquiry into the True Nature of Pastoral*. One year later, at the age of 24, he was appointed chaplain of Newgate. Purney resigned in 1727, at about the same time that Gay offered *The Beggar's Opera* to Rich. His prison career was a controversial one, and satirical pamphlets made the obvious connection to his other career, as pastoralist. In ministering to his Newgate flock, Purney, perhaps unconsciously, fictionalized their experience. It was his responsibility to record the confessions and dying speeches of the inmates, some of whom complained that the chaplain misrepresented them, in pressing for confession of more crimes than they had actually committed, and rewriting their words as he recorded them.[9] The life that surrounded him could not easily be coerced into the simple moral truths of sentimental pastoral. It was surely Purney's career that kept the idea of prison-pastoral alive between the letter and the play. But to establish how and why this idea of pastoral *became* a play, one must look back over the traditions of the Restoration stage.

Newgate scenes are a minor convention of Restoration comedy. Steele insists with a moral seriousness on an issue broached by Farquhar in ironical hints – that a reformation of morality means law, and law means prisons. Aphra Behn's adaptation of Marston's *The Dutch Courtesan*, as *The Revenge, or a Match in Newgate* (1680) suggests in its treatment of the condemned highwayman and his wife, something of that odd mixture of burlesque and pathos that prison scenes bring out in eighteenth century writers. Earlier still, Thomas Duffet explored the idea of a translation of pastoral ideas into prison settings in his parodies of contemporary opera, *The Mock Tempest* (1675) and *Psyche Debauch'd* (1678).

The positive results are, in both pieces, the invention of a prison-pastoral to predate the *Beggar's Opera* – as does the occasional line, as when Prince Nick exclaims at his trial (Vi) that 'Justice may be better satisfied with Marriage than hanging – for 'tis now the greater punishment'.[10] The mock-bucolic tone acquires a pastoral feeling of its own –

Don't Birds grow upon Trees like Pears, what would she desire?
Don't Pyes grow in a little Brick-house, close by the fire?[11]

Duffet reduces everything to a rural, childhood, vision more truly pastoral than Shadwell's. *The Mock Tempest* reinstates Antonio's vision of the 'kingdom of Whores and Knaves' as Gonzalo's Golden Age. The inhabitants of a brothel are trapped in Prospero's Bridewell. Dryden makes a better target than Shadwell – 'If our fathers don't get us Husbands quickly . . .' Duffet's Dorinda cheerfully asserts, '. . . we'll make him lye with us himself, shall we sister?'[12] – a fair hit at Dryden's suggestiveness, even if it is only an opening out of Miranda's alarming 'I wou'd he were not old . . . .'.[13] The gap between burlesque and its object is seldom so narrow; it is simply a case of the dominant dramatic form claiming back its own.

In the Preface to *Albion and Albanius* Dryden defined the social class of the characters in opera, and pointed to the kind of dramatic tradition that the form can be aligned with.

> . . . at *Turin* . . . was performed the *Pastor Fido*, written by the famous *Guarini*, which is Pastoral *Opera* made to solemnize the Marriage of a Duke of *Savoy* . . . [and, in addition to supernatural beings] . . . shepherds might reasonably be admitted, as of all callings, the most innocent, the most happy, and who by reason of the spare time they had, in their almost idle Employment, had most leisure to make Verses, and to be in Love; without somewhat of which Passion, no *Opera* can possible subsist.[14]

Seventeenth and early eighteenth century opera cannot strictly follow the conventions of either comedy or tragedy; its tone is too 'high' for the first, its action too diffuse, too varied in feeling for the second. Pastoral tragicomedy is the only other dramatic genre that neo-classical theory allowed. Handelian opera seria, like Restoration comedy, is dramatically a kind of ironic artifice; it is a complex Ariostian pastoral, building largely on earlier Venetian libretti that expand classical stories into courtly intrigue. Handel both sharpens and humanizes his texts, and exploits their ironies in ways that seem to me to be precisely similar both to Restoration comedy and to Gay. It is Handel who achieves a definitive series of portrayals of the woman as plotter; the enchantress figures, the Armidas, Alcinas and Cleopatras, whose soprano coloratura spins the most dazzling webs of seductive intrigue, and with whom, as Winton Dean has finely pointed out, Handel seems to identify,[15] as the source of an enclosing, though tragically insubstantial artifice. Simple pastoral's answer to this is an opera like Addison's mindboggling *Rosamund* (1707), whose dramatic climax is a prophetic vision of Blenheim. Handel, as dramatist, seems to have much more in common with Gay than either has with such determinedly 'English' determinedly 'simple' taste. All Gay's plays are jokes on that basic uncertainty than seems to me to inform Farquhar's London comedies: what *kind* of people should plays be about? *The Beggar's Opera* is infinitely more successful than the others, in that the impulse to write an opera had focussed this uncertainty into a style. Gay's dialogue never differentiates character in even the broadest terms. It has the rattling impersonality of recitative. The songs of *The Beggar's Opera* provide its peaks of intensity. The only one to Handel's music, Matt of the Mint's, to the march in *Rinaldo* (1711), finds a laconic splendour in its conceits to match exactly the Handelian panache.

> Let us take the Road
>> Hark! I hear the sound of Coaches!
>> The hour of Attack approaches,
> To your Arms, brave Boys, and load.
>> See the Ball I hold!
>> Let the Chymists toil like Asses,
>> Our Fire their Fire surpasses,
>>> And turns all our Lead to Gold.[16]

In the 'Introduction', the Beggar (before pointing out his own use of the rival lady theme), claims 'I have introduc'd the Similes that are in all your celebrated *Operas*, the *Swallow*, the *Moth*, the *Bee*, the *Ship*, the *Flower* &c.'[17] Opera seria, like pastoral, places its characters in a kind of leisured vacuum, from which they can express themselves in elaborate flights of fancy. The verbal style of Restoration comedy tends to this after the nineties; Vanbrugh's dialogue, for example, seems extrovert and impersonal in its reliance on elaborated metaphor. Such an 'Assay of Wit' or 'Flirt of the Imagination'[18] as he called it, is an aspect of complex pastoral that Purney attacks. The kind of statement made by Gay's characters marks them as both operatic and pastoral, just as the 'rival ladies' theme makes the action both operatic *and* heroic. Gay, again, makes an analysis of common characteristics.

The songs in *The Beggar's Opera* condense and organise the even handedness of correspondence between image and referent that lies at the basis of Gay's individual poetic. Like the arias of opera seria they offer insights into a vivid imaginative world that the surface of recitative or dialogue would urbanely exclude. Mrs Peachum's famous song in I.viii ('And when she's drest with Care and Cost, all-tempting, fine and gay,/As Men should serve a

Cowcumber, she flings herself away')[19] make the traditional identification of girl and fruit in a context of urban waste. The contemporary joke on cucumbers was thay they were only fit to be
washed, dressed and thrown away. Mrs Peachum picks up the
point that Polly has made in the previous song: like most of them it
involves a small and perhaps comically trivial object that emerges
from the ferocity of the conceit much the worse for wear.

> Virgins are like the fair Flower in its Lustre,
> Which in the Garden enamels the Ground;
> Near it the Bees in Play flutter and cluster,
> And gaudy Butterflies frolick around.
> But, when once pluck'd, 'tis no longer alluring;
> To Covent-Garden 'tis sent, (as yet sweet,)
> There fades, and shrinks, and dies, and is trod underfeet.[20]

The references to Covent Garden, flower-market and brothel-
district (though not as yet an opera house) places the metaphor as
an image in little of that process of urbanized pastoral with which
this book is largely concerned. Like many of the songs, its last line
puts emphasis on monosyllabic and brutal verbs. Nothing could be
further from 'the soft'. When the whores dance for MacHeath,
their song contradicts a more basic pastoral assumption.

> Dance and sing,
> Time's on the Wing,
> Life never knows the return of Spring.[21]

Gay exploits a conventional image to deprive it of its usual comfort
– to point out that human life, unlike the seasons, is *not* a cycle; life
never knows the return of spring. As process, these 'flirts of the
imagination' may belong to pastoral; but the meanings they insist
on close up the pastoral irony.

There is one subject for which MacHeath never finds an apt
image; 'He that tastes Woman, Woman, Woman', MacHeath sings
after the whores have betrayed him, 'He that tastes Woman, Ruin
meets'.[22] The nearest he finds is that of music itself, though again
Gay falls back on repetition to express this;

> Like the Notes of a Fiddle she sweetly, sweetly
> Raises the Spirits, and charms our Ears.[23]

When faced by Polly *and* Lucy, MacHeath's grasp on language collapses altogether –

> How happy could I be with either,
>> Were t'other dear charmer away!
> But while you thus teaze me together,
>> To neither a word will I say;[24]

– he repeats the tune on nonsense words. 'Woman' is a fact for which MacHeath can find no adequate verbal formula. And so, finally, is death.

Pastoral always includes death in its statement, but only to propitiate and eventually cheat it. The 'cheat' of *The Beggar's Opera* is too crude, too ragged, to diffuse a disturbing sense of the gallows' imminence. *The Beggar's Opera* has more of a sense of mortality in it than any Restoration tragedy. There is a simple tragic pattern at the base of its ironies, a pattern that seems about to complete itself when the beggar relents and the opera ends happily. In the sequel, *Polly* (1728), MacHeath pays his dues. The American to which Gay transports him deprives MacHeath of an escape into London's comfortably ironic sense of itself. The play ends with his death at the hands of Indians as grave and ruthless as Sarastro's priests. Gay has exiled town-pastoral onto the bleak shores of the moralized exotic; the last of the libertines meets his end in an unforgiving Arcadia.

Appendix: a Chronological Checklist of Plays

	Plays	Other events
1580	Tasso: *Amyntas*	
1590	Guarini: *Il Pastor Fido*	
1632	Shirley: *Hyde Park* Shirley: *The Ball*	Market developed on Covent Garden Piazza by the Earl of Bedford
1633		St. Paul's, Covent Garden built by Inigo Jones
1635	Brome: *The Sparagus Garden*	
1638	Brome: *Antipodes*	
1640		Long Parliament – fall of Strafford and Laud.
1641	Brome: *The Jovial Crew* Cowley: *The Guardian* (see also *Cutter of Coleman St.*, 1661)	
1642		King tries to arrest five members of Parliament; First Civil War. Theatres closed by Parliament.
1646		End of 1st Civil War – Charles I surrenders to Scots.
1647	Fanshawe: *The Faithful Shepherd*	
1648		Second civil war.
1649		Execution of Charles I
1652		London's first coffee-house opened, in

		St Michael's Alley Cornhill. Hyde Park sold into private hands.
1656	D'Avenant: *The Siege of Rhodes*	
1658		Death of Cromwell.
1660	Tatham: *The Rump*	Restoration of Charles II. The King's and the Duke of York's companies are formed. Le Notre engaged to improve St James's Park.
1661	Cowley: *Cutter of Coleman St* Fountaine: *The Rewards of Vertue*	
1662	Howard, Robert: *The Committee*	Act of Uniformity. Charter granted to the Royal Society
1663	Dryden: *The Wild Gallant* Etherege: *The Comical Revenge* Howard, James: *The English Monsieur* Tuke: *The Adventures of Five Hours*	
1664	Dryden: *The Indian Queen* Flecknoe: *Love's Kingdom*	
1665	Dryden: *The Indian Emperour*	The great plague.
1665/7		War with Dutch
1666		The Fire of London.
1667	Dryden: *Secret Love*	Milton's *Paradise Lost* published.
1667	Dryden: *The Tempest*	
1668	'Faithful Shepheard' Cavendish, Margaret, Duchess of Newscastle: *The Convent of Pleasure* Cavendish, Margaret, Duchess of Newscastle:	The King's Company and the Duke agree to split the repertory between them. Dryden appointed Poet Laureate.

Phantasm's Masque
Etherege: *She Would if She Could*
Flecknoe: *Demoiselles a la Mode*
Sedley: *The Mulberry Garden*
Shadwell: *The Sullen Lovers*
Shadwell: *The Royal Shepherdesse*

1669 Dryden: *Tyrannic Love*

1670 Shadwell: The Humourists   New Royal Exchange Building completed.

1671 Villiers, Duke of Buckingham: *The Rehearsal*
Wycherley: *Love in the Wood*

Covent Garden Market granted Royal Charter. The Duke's Company open the Dorset Garden Theatre.

1672 Dryden: *Marriage a la Mode*
Shadwell: *Epsom Wells*
Wycherley: *The Gentleman Dancing Master*

1673 Behn: *The Dutch Lover*
Settle: *The Empress of Morocco*

1674 Cavendish, William, Duke of Newcastle: *The Triumphant Widow*
Dryden: *The State of Innocence*
Perrin: *Ariadne*

Death of Milton. The King's Company open the New Drury Lane Theatre.

1675 Crowne: *Calisto*
Duffet: *The Mock Tempest*

Wren's St Paul's begun.

1675 Shadwell: *Psyche*
Shadwell: *The Libertine*
Wycherley: *The Country Wife*

1676 Behn: *Abdelazar*
Crowne: *The Country Wit*
Etherege: *The Man of Mode*
Shadwell: *The Virtuoso*

Wycherley: *The Plain Dealer*

1677   Behn: *The Rover*
       Crowne: *The Destruction of Jerusalem (I + II)*
       Dryden: *All for Love*
       Lee: *The Rival Queens*

1678   Behn: *Sir Patient Fancy*   The 'Popish Plot'.
       Duffet: *Psyche Debauch'd*   Bunyan's *Pilgrim's*
       Otway: *Friendship in*   *Progress* published.
       Fashion
       Shadwell: *A True Widow*

1679   Behn: *The Young King*   Introduction of the
                                          Exclusion Bill.

1680   Behn: *The Revenge*   Death of Rochester.
       Lee: *The Princess of Cleve*
       Otway: *The Orphan*
       Otway: *The Soldier's Fortune*

1681   Behn: *The Roundheads*   Charles II dissolves
       Ravenscroft: *London*   Parliament.
       Cuckolds   Shaftesbury proposes
       Shadwell: *The Lancashire*   Duke of Monmouth as
       Witches   heir.

1682   Behn: *The City Heiress*   Thomas Creech published
       Blow: *Venus and Adonis*   his translation of
       Otway: *Venice Preserved*   Lucretius's *De Rerum*
                                         Naturae.
                                         The King's company and
                                         the Duke of York's
                                         Company merge to form
                                         the United Company.

1683   Crowne: *City Politicks*
       Otway: *The Atheist*

1684   Southerne: *The*
       Disappointment
       Wilmot, Earl of Rochester:
       Valentinian

1685   Crowne: *Sir Courtly Nice*   Etherege leaves England
       Dryden: *Albion and*   on diplomatic mission to
       Albanius   Ratisbon. Death of
       Dryden: *Albion and*   Charles II: James II
       Albanius   succeeds. Duke of

		Monmouth's Rebellion. Death of Otway.
1687	Sedley: *Bellamira*	Newton publishes the *Principia*.
1688	Shadwell: *Squire of Alsatia*	Expulsion of James II. William of Orange arrives in London.
1688/9	Mountfort: *Greenwich Park*	
1689	Behn: *The Widow Ranter* Dryden: *Amphitryon* Purcell: *Dido and Aeneas* Shadwell: *Bury Fair* Southerne: *Sir Antony Love*	William and Mary's accession. Aphra Behn dies. Shadwell is Poet Laureate. Kensington Palace improved by Wren for William and Mary.
1690	Crowne: *The English Friar*	Battle of the Boyne (final defeat of James II). Locke, *Essay Concerning Human Understanding*.
1691	Dryden: *King Arthur* Southerne: *The Wive's Excuse*	Etherege dies(?)
1692		Lee dies. Shadwell dies. Tate becomes Poet Laureate.
1693	Congreve: *The Old Batchelour* Southerne: *The Maid's Last Prayer*	
1694	Congreve: *The Double Dealer* Crowne: *The Married Beau* Ravenscroft: *The Canterbury Guests* Southerne: *The Fatal Marriage* Terence (trans Echard): *Plays*	Bank of England established by Royal Charter.
1695	Congreve: *Love for Love* Southerne: *Oronooko*	Thomas Betterton and other leading actors leave Drury Lane to form their own company at

Lincoln's Inn Fields.

1696 Cibber: *Love's Last Shift*
Vanbrugh: *The Relapse*
1697 Congreve: *The Mourning Bride*
Vanbrugh: *The Provok'd Wife*
1698 Crowne: *Caligula*
Farquhar: *Love and a Bottle*

Jeremy Collier publishes *A Short View of the Immorality and Profaneness of the English Stage.*

1699 Farquhar: *The Constant Couple*
1700 Congreve: *The Way of the World*
Vanbrugh: *The Pilgrim*

Death of Dryden.

1701 Farquhar: *Sir Henry Wildair*

War of the Spanish succession begins.

1702 Centlivre: *The Beau's Duel*

William's death.
Succession of Queen Anne.

1703 Steele: *The Lying Lover*
1704 Cibber: *The Careless Husband*

Marlborough victorious at Blenheim.

1705 Centlivre: *The Gamester*
Steele: *The Tender Husband*
Vanbrugh: *The Confederacy*

Vanbrugh and Congreve's Haymarket Theatre opened.
Vanbrugh begins Blenheim Palace.

1706 Farquhar: *The Recruiting Officer*
1707 Addison: *Rosamund*
Farquhar: *The Beaux Stratagem*

Union of Scotland and England.
Death of Farquhar.

1709 Centlivre, Susanna: *The Busy Body*
1710 Congreve: *Semele*
1711 Handel: *Rinaldo*
1713

War of the Spanish succession ends: treaty of Utrecht.

1714		Death of Queen Anne: George I succeeds. Whigs in power. Steele becomes licensee of Drury Lane. John Rich becomes manager of Lincoln's Inn Fields.
1715		Jacobite Rebellion. Death of Wycherley.
1718	Centlivre: *A Bold Stroke for a Wife*	
1719	Southerne: *The Spartan Dame*	
1721		Walpole becomes first Minister.
1722	Steele: *The Conscious Lovers*	
1727		Death of George I. George II succeeds. Gay's *Polly* refused registration.
1728	Gay: *The Beggar's Opera* Gay: *Polly*	
1729		Death of Congreve. Death of Steele.
1730		Cibber becomes Poet Laureate.
1732		Death of Gay. Covent Garden Theatre opened.
1737		Walpole's Licensing Act.

Notes

PREFACE

1. Hume argues against the usefulness of the term and argues for a more complex tanonomy of subgenres, derived mainly from 'effect'.

INTRODUCTION

1. *William Wycherley* in Bernard Harris and John Russell Brown (eds), *Stratford on Avon Studies 6* (London, 1965) p. 71.
2. William Van Lennep (ed.) *The London Stage 1660–1800* (Carbondale Illinois, 1965), *Part 1 1660–1700*, p. xxxvi.
3. Thora Burnley Jones and Bernard de Bear Nicol, *Neo-classical Dramatic Criticism 1560–1770* (Cambridge, 1976) pp. 13–17 and *passim*.
4. Though it is surely not written then, as Pepys presumes. *The London Stage, Part 1*, p. 44.
5. A. R. Waller (ed.), *The English Writings of Abraham Cowley* (Cambridge, 1905–6), *Essays, Plays and Sundry Verses*, p. 263.
6. Ibid., p. 262.
7. *The Triumphant Widow or the Medley of Humorists*, (London, 1677).
8. Quoted in Nicholas J. Perella, *The Critical Fortune of Battista Guarini's 'Il Pastor Fido'* (Firenze, 1973) p. 123. I am indebted to Tony Barley for telling me about Perella's book.
9. *Some Versions of Pastoral* (London, 1935) *passim*.
10. Michael Cordner (ed.), *The Plays of Sir George Etherege* (Cambridge, 1982), *The Man of Mode*, p. 322, v.ii.
11. This is from Poggiloli's description of the pastoral in his essay 'The Oaten Flute' (*Harvard Library Bulletin XI* (1957)) p. 152.
12. Jean Robertson (ed.), *The Countess of Pembroke's Arcadia (The Old Arcadia)* (Oxford, 1973) p. 56, ll.119–24.
13. Fredson Bowers (ed.), *The Beaumont and Fletcher Canon* (Cambridge, 1976) p. 497.
14. Thomas Purney, *A Full Enquiry into the True Nature of Pastoral* (Augustan Reprint Society, Michigan, 1948) p. 15; ll.26–7 see also *Conclusion*, pp. 243–6.
15. David Piper, *The English Face* (London, 1957) ch. v, p. 130.
16. R. B. McKerrow (ed.), *The Works of Thomas Nashe* (London, 1904) II pp. 328–4, 317.

17. C. F. Tucker Brooke (ed.), *The Works of Christopher Marlowe* (Oxford, 1910), p. 289, Act IV, ll.1800–16.
18. *The London Stage*, Part I, p. 169.
19. *The Myth of the Golden Age in the Renaissance* (London, 1970) ch. II, p. 37.
20. Pogglioli, pp. 149–50.
21. John Shearman, *Mannerism* (London, 1967) p. 92.
22. Perella instances Casanova, no less, using *Pastor Fido* as a seduction ploy; Perella, p. 100.
23. In *The Illusion of Power* (Berkeley, 1975) pp. 51–2.
24. Walter F. Staton Jnr. and William E. Simeone, *A Critical Edition of Sir Richard Fanshawe's 1647 Translation of Giovanni Battista Guarini's IL PASTOR FIDO* (Oxford, 1964) pp. 4–5.
25. James Turner, *The Politics of Landscape* (Oxford, 1979) p. 27.
26. Quoted in Antonia Fraser, *King Charles II* (London, 1979) p. 154.
27. Ghosh (ed.), *The Works of Thomas Otway* vol. II (Oxford, 1932) p. 472, ll.26–30.
28. David M. Vieth (ed.), *The Complete Poems of John Wilmot, Earl of Rochester* (New Haven, 1968) p. 41, ll.21–2.
29. G. Thorn Drury (ed.), *The Poems of Edmund Waller*, vol. II (London, 1893) p. 40, ll.23–4.
30. Ibid., p. 42, ll.61–2.
31. Ibid., p. 44, ll.109–14.
32. Richard Flecknoe, *Love's Kingdom: a Pastoral Trage Comedy; with a Short Treatise of the English Stage, etc. by the same Author* (London, 1664).
34. Montagne Summers, (ed.), *The Works of Thomas Shadwell* vol. I, (London, 1927) p. 125 II.
35. *The London Stage, Part 1*, p. 157.
36. Ibid., p. 137.
37. Ibid., pp. 130–1, ll.151–2.
38. *Il Pastor Fido*, p. 115 IV.vii 1.3844.
39. *The Faerie Queene*, Bk.I.
40. See the scenarii given in volume II of K. M. Lea's *Italian Popular Comedy* (Oxford, 1934).
41. Perella, p. 115.
42. Francois Truffaut, *Hitchcock* (London, 1978) pp. 157–60.
43. Perella, p. 27.
44. See Chapter 4 pp. 109–12 in this book.
45. See Chapter 2 pp. 56–8 in this book.
46. See William Gaunt, *Court Painting in England* (London, 1980) pp. 144–5.
47. Allan S. Jackson offers the best exposition of Restoration scene design in his article *Restoration Scenery 1656–1680* in *Restoration and Eighteenth Century Theatre Research*, vol. III, no. 2 (Chicago, 1964).
48. 'Monsieur P. P.' (Pierre Perrin), *Ariadne or the Marriage of Bacchus an Opera* (London $167\frac{3}{4}$ [sic.]).

1: FROM 'DECORUM' TO NATURE

1. See, for example, John Harold Wilson, *The Court Wits of the Restoration* (Princeton, 1948).
2. See Introduction, pp. 5–7 in this book.
3. Four New Plays, viz: *The Suprisal, The Committee, Comedies, The Indian Queen, The Vestal Virgin, Tragedies. As They were Acted by His Majesties Servants at the Theatre Royal. Written by the Honourable Sir Robert Howard* (London, 1665) p. 73, I.i.
4. Ibid., p. 106, III.
5. Ibid., p. 81, I. v i. pp. 123–4
6. Ibid., IV i. p. 110
7. Ibid., III. p. 106
8. Vivian de Sola Pinto (ed.), *The Poetical and Dramatic Works of Sir Charles Sedley*, vol. I (London, 1928) p. 185, v.v, ll.193.
9. Michael Cordner, (ed.), *The Plays of Sir George Etherege*, (Cambridge, 1982) p. 54, III.vi, ll.12.
10. Ibid., p. 83, IV.ii, ll.27–9.
11. Ibid., p. 5
12. Ibid., p. 85, V.ii, ll.76–9.
13. John Harrington Smith and Douglas McMillan (eds), *The Works of John Dryden* (Berkeley, 1962), vol. VIII *Prologue to the Wild Gallant Reviv'd*, p. 6, ll.15–22.
14. *The Works of Thomas Shadwell*, vol. I 'To the Reader', p. 100.
15. Dryden, *Works*, vol. VIII, p. 11, I.i, ll.106–7.
16. Ibid., p. 33, IV, ll.1151–9.
17. James Howard, *The English Monsieur*, (London, 1674) p. 4, I.
18. Ibid., p. 6, I.
19. Ibid., p. 40, IV.
20. Ibid., p. 57, V.
21. Ibid., p. 57, V.
22. Johan Huizinga, *Homo Ludens* (London, 1970; 1st edn, 1949) pp. 28–9.
23. Sedley, *Works*, vol. I p. 36.
24. *The Complete Poems*, p. 123, ll.61.
25. Sedley, *Works*, vol. I, p. 120 I.iii, ll.71.
26. Ibid., p. 120, I.iii, ll.72–3.
27. Ibid., p. 122, I.iii, ll.123–6.
28. Ibid., p. 120, I.iii, l.47.
29. Ibid., p. 129, II.i, ll.121–3.
30. Ibid., p. 131, II.i, ll.198–9.
31. Ibid., p. 131, II.i, ll.200–2.
32. Ibid., p. 130, II.i, ll.171–4.
33. Howard's *Four New Plays*, 'To The Reader' a4(r).
34. Ibid., a4(r).
35. Ibid., a4(r).
36. Ibid., a4(r).
37. Ibid., a4(v).
38. *The Plays of Sir George Etherege*, p. 111, I.i, ll.110–15.

39. Ibid., p. 129, II.i.
40. Ibid., p. 125, I.ii, ll.157–9.
41. Ibid., p. 124, I.ii, ll.130–1.
42. Ibid., p. 126, I.ii, ll.182–3.
43. Ibid., p. 147, II.ii, ll.224–7.
44. Ibid., p. 138, II.ii, ll.110–12.
45. Ibid., p. 140, II.ii, ll.171–4.
46. See Ch. 2, 'William Wycherley' pp. 53–4 in the book
47. Allan S. Jackson offers the best exposition of Restoration Scene design in his article *Restoration Scenery 1656–1680* in *Restoration and Eighteenth Century Theatre Research*, vol. III, no. 2 (Chicago, 1964).
48. Etherege *Plays*, p. 207, V.i, ll.638–9.
49. Ibid., p. 180, IV.ii, ll.54–6.
50. Ibid., p. 198, V.i, ll.300–5.
51. Ibid., p. 144, III.i, ll.2–3.
52. Ibid., p. 272, III.iii, ll.30–1.
53. *Complete Poems*, p. 103, ll.27–30.
54. *Dryden, Works*, vol. XI, p. 239, I.i, ll.352–6.
55. Ibid., p. 272, III.ii, pp. 470–2.
56. Ibid., p. 307, V.i, ll.314–19.
57. Ibid., p. 291, IV.iii, ll.145–52.
58. *Endeavors of Art: A Study of Form in Elizabethan Drama* (Madison, 1954) pp. 53–84.
59. See John Rupert Martin's *Baroque* for a further account (London, 1977) pp. 39–73. Martin however ascribes the move to realism as a reaction to the excesses of mannerism. This seems too limited in scope (and too purely aesthetic) to account for so widespread a phenomenon.
60. Harriet Hawkins, in *Likenesses of Truth* (Oxford, 1972), deals wittily with the religio-moral idiom of Restoration comedy criticism; see her chs 4 and 5, pp. 79–113.
61. Etherege *Plays*, p. 330, V.ii, l.435.
62. Ibid., p. 249, II.ii, ll.114–45.
63. Ibid., p. 249, II.ii, ll.146–8.
64. Ibid., p. 312, V, ll.158–62.
65. Ibid., p. 251, II.ii, ll.221–3.
66. Ibid., p. 251, II.ii, ll.212–16.
67. Ibid., p. 256, III, ll.74–6.
68. Ibid., p. 272, III.iii, ll.30–1.
69. Ibid., p. 272, III.iii, ll.32–4.
70. *Complete Poems*, pp. 40–6, ll.33–82.
71. Etherege *Plays*, p. 269, III.ii, ll.250–9.
72. Ibid., p. 221, I.i, l.154; p. 309, V.i, l.151.
73. Ibid., p. 328, V.ii, ll.372–5.
74. Frederick Bracher (ed.), *Letters of Sir George Etherege*, (Berkeley, 1974) p. 170.
75. *The London Stage*, part 1, p. 159.
76. Heinrich Wolfflin, *Renaissance and Baroque*, trans. Kathrin Simon (London, 1964) p. 88.
77. *The Origin of German Tragic Drama* trans, John Osborne (London, 1977)

p. 66. Benjamin, Writing in 1924, is partly quoting Hansenstein's *Vcm Geist des Barock* (Munich, 1921)

2   WILLIAM WYCHERLEY

1. Gerald Weales (ed.), *The Complete Plays of William Wycherley*, (New York, 1967) *Love in a Wood*, p. 30. II.i.
2. Ibid., p. 91, IV.i.
3. Ibid., p. 103, V.
4. Ibid., p. 27, I.
5. Ibid., p. 112, V.
6. Ibid., p. 111, V,l.12.
7. Ibid., p. 112, V.
8. Ibid., p. 78, IV.
9. Ibid., p. 65, III.
10. Ibid., *The Gentleman-Dancing-Master*, p. 138, I.
11. Rochester, *The Complete Poems*, p. 28, l.40, See Chapter 3 pp. 86–90 in this book.
12. Wycherley, *Complete Plays*, p. 184, III.
13. Ibid., *The Plain-Dealer*, pp. 419–21, II.
14. 'William Wycherley' in *Stratford on Avon Studies*, 6, pp. 71–91.
15. Wycherley, *Complete Plays; The Country-Wife*, p. 279, II.
16. Ibid., p. 313, IV.
17. Ibid., p. 293–4, III.
18. Ibid., p. 264, I.
19. Ibid., p. 263, I.
20. Ibid., p. 259, I.
21. Ibid., p. 336, IV.
22. Ibid., p. 350, V.
23. In *The Alchemist*; see C. H. Herford and Percy Simpson (eds) *Ben Jonson* (Oxford, 1937) vol. V, pp. 319–30, II.ii, ll.65–8.
24. Wycherley, *Complete Plays*, p. 275, II.
25. Ibid., p. 317, IV.
26. Ibid., *The Plain-Dealer*, pp. 420–21, II.i.
27. Ibid., p. 408, I.
28. Ibid., p. 484, IV.
29. Ibid., p. 425, II.
30. Ibid., p. 439, III.i.
31. Ibid., p. 386.
32. Ibid., p. 471–2, IV.
33. Ibid., p. 439, III.i.
34. Ibid., p. 454, III.i.
35. Ibid., p. 385.
36. See Chapter 5, pp. 114–27 in this book.
37. Ibid., p. 431, II.
38. Ibid., p. 483, IV.
39. Ibid., p. 479, IV.

40. Ibid., p. 430, II.
41. Ibid., p. 513, V.
42. Ibid., p. 515, V.

3 'THE WITS' GARDEN'

1. *Complete Poems*, pp. 104–12.
2. Eleanore Boswell, *The Restoration Court Stage* (1660–1702) (Cambridge, Mass., 1932) Part III, p. 179.
3. James Maidmont and W. H. Cogan (eds), *The Dramatic Works of John Crowne* (Edinburgh, 1873) vol. I; 'To the Reader', p. 237.
4. Ibid., vol. I p. 262.
5. Ibid., 'To the Reader', p. 239.
6. Ibid., Prologue, p. 243.
7. Ibid., vol. V, p. 318.
8. Ibid., Prologue, p. 246.
9. Ibid., vol. II, p. 264.
10. Ibid., vol. III, p. 275.
11. Ibid., vol. V, p. 309.
12. Ibid., vol. V, p. 310.
13. See Chapter 3, in this book pp. 77–8.
14. *Calisto*, vol. IV, pp. 301–2.
15. Crowne, *Works*, vol. V, p. 391.
16. Ibid., vol. V, p. 317.
17. *The Works of John Dryden*, vol. XV, p. 3, ll.11–17.
18. Ibid., p. 3, ll.18–20.
19. *The Dramatic Works of Sir William D'Avenant* (Edinburgh, 1873) vol. III, p. 28.
20. 'Monsieur P. P.' (Pierre Perrin), *Ariadne or the Marriage of Bacchus on Opera* (London $167\frac{3}{4}$ (sic)) 'The Prologue'.
21. Ibid., 'To the King's most excellent majesty'.
22. *The Works of John Dryden*, vol. XV, pp. 34–5, II.ii.
23. Thomas Duffet; *The Mock-Tempest or the Enchanted Castle* (London, 1675) p. 18, II.ii.
24. Berenice and Porphyrius, part of a rash of conversion occasioned by the arrival of the heroine, Catherine of Alexandria in the suite of the emperor Maximin, try to work out if they can meet up after martyrdom:

> Berenice: 'Tis want of knowledge, not of love, I fear,
> Lest we mistake when bodies are not there;
> O as a mark that I could wear a Scroul,
> With this Inscription, *Berenices Soul*.

(*The Works of John Dryren*), vol. X, p. 184, v.i, ll.490–3.
25. Ibid., vol. VIII, p. 209, III.ii, ll.96–7.

26. Montague Summers (ed.), Dryden, *The Dramatic Works* (London, 1932) vol. V, p. 287.
27. Ibid., vol. V, p. 284.
28. Ibid., vol. V, p. 284.
29. Ibid., p. 276, IV.i.
30. James Kinsley (ed.), *The Poems and Fables of John Dryden*, (Oxford, 1962) p. 830, ll.86–9.
31. Dryden, *Dramatic Works*, p. 488.
32. Anthony Lewis (ed.), John Blow, *Venus and Adonis* (Monaco, 1949), 'The Prologue', p. 17.
33. Ibid., vol. I, p. 44.
34. *Psyche Debauch'd: a Comedy* (London, 1675) II.i, p. 23.
35. *The Works of Thomas Shadwell*, vol. II pp. 299–300, Act II.
36. *Titus Lucretius Carus. His Six Books of Epicurean Philosophy Done into English VERSE with NOTES. The Third Edition* (London, 1683) (C2)^r–(C4)^r; (D3)^r–(D3)^v.
37. Rochester, *The Complete Poems*, p. 35; Shadwell, *Works*, vol. III p. 105, I.
38. Rochester, *The Complete Poems*, p. 122–3, ll.41–9.
39. Shadwell, *Works*, vol. III p. 26, I.
40. Ibid., p. 48, II.
41. Ibid., pp. 74–5, IV.
42. Ibid., p. 89.
43. This point of view is perhaps most eloquently put by Anne [Barton] Righter's essay 'Heroic Tragedy' in *Stratford upon Avon Studies, Restoration Theatre*, pp. 135–57.
44. *The Works of John Dryden*, vol. VIII p. 187, I.i, ll.82–3.
45. Ibid., p. 202, III.i, ll.34–7.
46. Ibid., p. 213, IV.i, ll.65–6.
47. Peter Elfred Lewis (ed.), John Gay, *The Beggars Opera*, (Edinburgh, 1973) p. 87, II.xiii, ll.28–32.
48. *Works of John Dryden*, vol. IX p. 89, IV.iv, ll.79–82. The role was written for Nell Gwynn, in itself a sign of Dryden's attempt to lighten and humanize the attitudes of the earlier play.
49. Elkanah Settle, *The Empress of Morocco: a Tragedy* (London, 1673) p. 49, IV.iii.
50. Ibid., p. 56, IV.iii.
51. Rochester, *The Complete Poems*, p. 50, ll.33–4.
52. *The Indian Queen*, p. 206, III.ii, ll.157–8, 165–6.
53. Thomas B. Stroup and Arthur L. Coke (eds), *The Works of Nathaniel Lee* (New Brunswick, NJ 1955) vol.II p. 153, ll.12–13.
54. Ibid., p. 203, IV, ll.261–3.
55. Ibid., p. 161, I.ii, ll.63–9; see also p. 162, I.ii, ll.85–108 and Rochester, *Poems etc. on Several Occasions with Valentinian: a Tragedy* (London 1691) p. 379, act 1.
56. Rochester *Poems etc. . . with Valentinian*, pp. 400–6, III.ii.
57. *The Works of Nathaniel Lee*, vol. II, pp. 179–180, II.iii, ll.84–99.
58. Ibid., pp. 175, II.i, ll.107–8.
59. Ibid., p. 182, II.ii, ll.206–10.
60. Rochester, *The Complete Poems*, p. 85, 1.5.

61. *The Works of Nathaniel Lee*, vol. II, pp. 188, III.i, ll.125–33.
62. Ibid., p. 178, II.iii, l.126.
63. Ibid., p. 186, III.i, ll.64–7.
64. Ibid., p. 202, IV.i, ll.218–19.
65. Ibid., p. 223, v.iii, ll.169–76.
66. Ibid., p. 225, ll.254–6.
67. Ibid., p. 134, ll.31–2.

4 SHADWELL AND CROWNE

1. Works, *Dryden*, vol. II p. 59, l.16.
2. George Birkbeck Hill (ed.), *Lives of the English Poets*, (Oxford, 1905) vol. II p. 212.
3. See Introduction, p. 9 in this book.
4. *The Complete Poems*, p. 124, II, ll.73–6.
5. Ibid., p. 123, l.145.
6. See Introduction, pp. 14–16 and Ch. 1, p. 28 in this book.
7. In MacFlecknoe, *Works*, II p. 58, ll.163–4.
8. *Works of Thomas Shadwell*, vol. III, p. 101.
9. Ibid., vol. II, p. 181, V.
10. Ibid., p. 182, V.
11. Ibid., p. 109, I.i.
12. See Chapter 1, p. 40 in this book.
13. *Works of Thomas Shadwell*, vol. III, p. 104.
14. Ibid., p. 124, II.
15. Ibid., p. 127, II.
16. Ibid., p. 140, III.
17. Ibid., pp. 129–30, II.
18. Ibid., 'To Sir Charles Sedley', p. 283.
19. Ibid., 'Drammatis Personae' (sic), p. 287.
20. Ibid., p. 300, I.
21. Ibid., p. 330, I.
22. Ibid., p. 361, V.
23. Ibid., pp. 341–3, IV.
24. Ibid., Prologue, p. 285.
25. Ibid., Epilogue, p. 363.
26. Ibid., vol. III, 'To Sir Charles Sedley', p. 283.
27. See *Letters*, pp. 96, 129, 186.
28. Sedley, *Poetical and Dramatic Works*, vol. II, p. 97, Epilogue, ll.7–18.
29. *Terence's Comedies Made English* (London, 1694) The Preface (i).
30. Shadwell, *Works*, vol. III, 'To Sir Charles Sedley', p. 284, ll.303–5.
31. Ibid., vol. I, p. 278, V.
32. Sedley, *Works*, p. 19, I.ii, ll.98–101.
33. Ibid., pp. 25–6, II.i, ll.46–107.
34. See Oliver Millar, *Sir Peter Lely* (London, 1978) p. 63. Millar's illustration shows her as shepherdess. The Minerva portrait is illustrated in *The Poetrical and Dramatic Works of Sir Charles Sedley*, vol. II, facing p. 1.

35. Sedley, *Works*, p. 28, II.i, ll.145–50.
36. Ibid., p. 63, IV.iii, ll.55–78.
37. Ibid., p. 79, IV.v, ll.19–20.
38. Shadwell, *Works*, vol. IV, Prologue, p. 296.
39. Ibid., I, p. 305. It may indeed be possible to read Oldwit as portrait of Newcastle.
40. See Charlotte Bradford Hughes, *John Crowne's Sir Courtly Nice: a Critical Edition* (The Hagee 1966) pp. 13–22, for a lucid biographical account of Crowne's career.
41. See Chapter 3, pp. 68–72 in this book.
42. *The Complete Poems*, p. 121, ll.10–11.
43. Crowne, *Dramatic Works*, vol. III, p. 71, III.
44. Ibid., p. 57, III.
45. Ibid., p. 44, II.
46. Ibid., 'To the Right Honourable Charles, Earl of Middlesex', p. 17.
47. Ibid., vol. II, p. 116, I.ii.
48. Ibid., p. 117, I.ii.
49. Ibid., p. 182, IV.
50. Ibid., p. 160, III.
51. Ibid., p. 310, IV.
52. Ibid., p. 312, IV.
53. Ibid., p. 294, III.
54. Ibid., pp. 263–4, III.i.
55. Ibid., p. 261, I.
56. Ibid., vol. IV, 'The Preface to the Reader', p. 22.
57. Ibid., Dramatis Personae, p. 28.
58. Ibid., p. 116, V.
59. Ibid., 'To the Right Honourable William, Earl of Devonshire', pp. 14–15.
60. See Chapter 7, pp. 149–55 of this book.

5 THOMAS OTWAY

1. *The Orphan*, 'with Remarks by Mrs Inchbald' (London, 1823) p. 3.
2. J. C. Ghosh (ed.), *The Works of Thomas Otway* (Oxford, 1932) *The Orphan*, vol. I, p. 430, V, ll.795–6.
3. Ibid., *Friendship in Fashion*, p. 349, I, ll.436–8.
4. Ibid., p. 364, II ll.434–5, Etherege *Works*, vol. I, pp. 21–2, II.i 152–70.
5. Otway, *Works*, pp. 389–408, IV.
6. Ibid., p. 339, I, ll.73–4.
7. Ibid., p. 382, III, ll.468–70.
8. Ibid., p. 359, II, ll.254–8.
9. Ibid., pp. 359–60, II, ll.260–79.
10. Ibid., p. 399, IV, l.348.
11. Ibid., p. 371, III, ll.39–91.
12. Ibid., p. 419, V, l.366.
13. Ibid., IV, p. 398, l.304, and p. 402, l.462.
14. Ibid., p. 410, V, ll.41–4.

15. Ibid., p. 429, V, ll.693–5.
16. Ibid., p. 430, V, ll.728–31.
17. Ibid., p. 400, IV, l.396.
18. Ibid., p. 423, V, ll.487–91.
19. In John Dovers *The Mall or The Modish Lovers* (1674), a play which echoes Otway's closely, if in a lighter and more relaxed vein.
20. Ibid., p. 430, V, ll.732–6.
21. Ibid., p. 408, IV, ll.651–9.
22. Ibid., p. 409, V, ll.7–14.
23. Ibid., p. 430, V, ll.744–7.
24. Ibid., vol. II *The Soldier's Fortune*, p. 398, V ll.1039–40.
25. Ibid., p. 112, II, ll.1–7.
26. Ibid., p. 103, I, l.239.
27. Ibid., p. 127, II, ll.510–17.
28. Ibid., p. 109, I, ll.438–40.
29. Ibid., p. 111, I, ll.529–30.
30. Ibid., p. 108, I, ll.414–17.
31. Ibid., p. 138, III, l.221.
32. Ibid., p. 168, IV, l.584.
33. Ibid., p. 164, IV, ll.451–5.
34. Ibid., pp. 181–2, V, ll.342–6.
35. Ibid., p. 182, V, ll.368–70.
36. Ibid., p. 189, V, ll.576–7.
37. Ibid., p. 167, IV, l.538.
38. Ibid., p. 119, II, ll.261–3.
39. Ibid., p. 175, V, ll.121–6.
40. Ibid., vol. II, *The Atheist*, p. 328, III, ll.12–16.
41. Ibid., p. 390, V, ll.775–9.
42. Ibid., vol. II, pp. 445–6, ll.101–16.
43. Ibid., p. 317, II, ll.149–50.
44. Ibid., p. 374, V, ll.255–7.
45. Ibid., p. 363, IV, l.550.
46. Ibid., p. 398, V, ll.1037–8.
47. See George Birbeck Hill (ed.), Samuel Johnson, *Lives of the English Poets*, (Oxford, 1905), vol. I, p. 247, and below.

6 APHRA BEHN

1. Margaret Cavendish, Duchess of Newcastle, *Poems and Phancies* (London, 1664) p. 17.
2. Margaret Cavendish, Duchess of Newcastle, *Plays Never before Printed* (London, 1668), *The Convent of Pleasure*, p. 7, I.ii.
3. Ibid., pp. 22–6, III.i–iv.
4. Ibid., p. 30, III.x.
5. Ibid., Epilogue, p. 53.
6. *The Duchess of Newcastle* in *Collected Essays* (London 1966) vol. III, pp. 51–8.

7. Margaret Cavendish, Duchess of Newcastle, *Poems and Phancies* (London, 1664) p. 190.
8. Ibid., pp. 155–68.
9. This is especially apparent in the *Poems upon Several Occasions, Works*, vol. VI pp. 113–290.
10. See Chapter 2, pp. 56–57 and Chapter 3, pp. 86–90 in this book.
11. See Chapter 10, pp. 239–40 in this book.
12. Montague Summers (ed.), *The Works of Aphra Behn*, (London, 1905) vol. VI, pp. 163–4.
13. *Works*, vol. II, pp. 114–8, I.i.
14. In *The Rover, Sir Patient Fancy* and *The Emperour of the Moon*.
15. Susanna Centlivre, *The Dramatic Works* (London, 1872) vol. I, *The Gamester*, p. 134 I.i.
16. Ibid., p. 171, IV.
17. See Chapter 10, pp. 230–3 in this book.
18. Maureen Duffy's recent biography does much to rescue the facts of Behn's life from its apparent fictionalization. *The Passionate Shepherdess; Aphra Behn 1640–89* (London, 1977).
19. Behn, *Works*, vol. V, p. 169.
20. Behn, *Works*, vol. V, p. 131.
21. Ibid., p. 130.
22. E. R. Dodds, *The Greeks and the Irrational* (Berkeley, 1951) p. 106.
23. Behn, *Works*, vol. V, p. 184.
24. Ibid., vol. I, p. 20, I.ii.
25. Ibid., pp. 69–70, IV.ii.
26. Ibid., vol. I, p. 103, V.i.
27. Ibid., vol. I, p. 223.
28. Ibid., vol. IV, p. 116.
29. Ibid., vol. IV, p. 22, I.i.
30. Ibid., p. 26, II.
31. Ibid., pp. 29, II.
32. Ibid., vol. IV, p. 95, V.i.
33. Compare *Sir Patient Fancy* (*Works*, vol. IV) p. 86, IV.iv with A. H. Bullen (ed.), *A Mad World, My Masters, The Works of Thomas Middleton*, (London, 1885) vol. III, p. 355, V.ii. See also Behn's *The Lover's Watch* (1686), a sequence of poems and prose pieces organized around the hours of the day. It is an adaptation of *La Montre* (1666) by Balthazar de Bonnecorse. See *The Works of Aphra Behn*, vol. VI, pp. 3–111.
34. *The Dutch Lover*, 'An Epistle to the Reader', *Works*, vol. I, p. 222.
35. Behn, *Works*, vol. I, p. 353, I.ii.
36. Ibid., p. 398, IV.iii.
37. Ibid., p. 401, IV.iv.
38. Ibid., vol. I, p. 399, IV.iv.
39. Ibid., p. 405, V.i.
40. Ibid., vol. II, p. 229, II.ii. It is, of course, equally possible to read it as an allusion to the Middleton, on Wilding's part.
41. Ibid., vol. II, p. 228, II.ii.
42. Ibid., p. 258, III.i.
43. Ibid., p. 231, II.ii.

44. Ibid., vol. II, p. 236, II.iii.
45. Ibid., pp. 215–6, I.i.
46. Ibid., vol. II, p. 268, IV.ii.
47. Ibid., p. 296, V.v.
48. Ibid., p. 298, V.v.
49. Duffy, p. 218.
50. Behn, *Works*, vol. VI, p. 117.

7 MARRIAGE AND THE COMEDY OF THE 1690s

1. See, for example, Gilbert Burnet's *An Essay on the Memory of the Late Queen* (London, 1695) *passim*.
2. Swedenberg (ed.), *The Works of John Dryden* (Berkeley and Los Angeles, 1976) vol. XV, pp. 224, ll.2–22.
3. Burnet, pp. 37–8.
4. *The Works of John Dryden*, vol. XV, pp. 317, ll.23–5.
5. Ibid., pp. 224–5.
6. See Chapter 3, pp. 68–72 in this book.
7. *The Works of John Dryden*, vol. XV, p. 257, II.ii, ll.48–9.
8. Ibid., p. 235, I.i, ll.129–30.
9. Ibid., p. 258, II.ii, ll.81–2.
10. Ibid., p. 311, V.i, ll.269–70.
11. Ibid., p. 315, V.i, l.392.
12. Ibid., p. 240, I.ii, ll.10–11.
13. Ibid., p. 256, II.ii, ll.25–6.
14. Ibid., p. 315, V.i, l.410.
15. Ibid., p. 302, V.i, ll.540–4 and ll.566–7.
16. Ibid., p. 281, III.i, l.553.
17. Ibid., p. 225, ll.22–3.
18. Crowne, *Dramatic Works*, vol. IV, 'To the Right Honourable The Lord Marquess of Normanby, Earl of Mulgrave', p. 234.
19. Ibid., I, p. 245.
20. Ibid., I, p. 243.
21. See Chapter 3, pp. 74–7 in this book.
22. Crowne, *Dramatic Works*, vol. IV, p. 243, I.
23. Ibid., p. 277, II.
24. Ibid., Dramatis Personae, p. 242.
25. Ibid., p. 257, I.
26. Ibid., p. 278, II.
27. Ibid., p. 261, II.
28. Ibid., p. 288, III.
29. Ibid., p. 295, III.
30. Ibid., p. 299, III.
31. Ibid., pp. 314–5, IV.
32. Ibid., pp. 315–6, IV.
33. Ibid., p. 321, V.
34. Ibid., p. 317, IV.

35. Ibid., p. 324, v.
36. Ibid., p. 332, v.
37. Ibid., p. 287, III.
38. Ibid., 'An Epistle to the Reader' pp. 238–9.

8   SOUTHERNE, CIBBER AND VANBRUGH

1. See *On the Artificial Comedy of the Last Century* in *Elia* (1823), E. V. Lucas *The Works of Charles and Mary Lamb* (London, 1903) vol. II, pp. 141–7.
2. Arthur L. Hayward (ed.), Tom Brown, *Amusements Serious and Comical and other Works*, ed. Arthur L. Hayward (London, 1927), p. 31, 'Amusements IV'; The Playhouse.
3. See Dryden's Prologue *To My Dear Friend Mr. Congreve, On His COMEDY, call'd The Double Dealer* in Herbert Davis (ed.), *The Complete Plays of William Congreve* (Chicago, 1967) p. 35.
4. Norman Ault and John Pitt (eds), *Poems of Alexander Pope*, (London, 1964), vol. VI, p. 399.
5. Thomas Southerne, *The Fatal Marriage* (London, 1694)] p. A2 (v).
6. Thomas Southerne, *The Disappointment or The Mother in Fashion* (London, 1684) p. 27, III.i.
7. Ibid., p. 22, III.i.
8. Ibid., p. 60, v.
9. Thomas Southerne, *The Spartan Dame* (London, 1719) Preface A3 (r).
10. Thornton Wynnwood (ed.), Thomas Southerne, *The Wives Excuse or Cuckolds Make Themselves* (Pennsylvania, 1972) pp. 88–9, III.ii, ll.1543–6 and 1556–60.
11. Ibid., p. 108, IV.ii ll.2213–17.
12. Ibid., pp. 67–8, II.ii, ll.800–5.
13. Ibid., p. 124, V.iii, ll.2759–64.
14. Ibid., p. 100, IV.i, ll.1968–9.
15. Ibid., p. 69, II.ii, ll.845–9. ˙
16. Southerne's Lady Trickit is reminiscent of Wycherley's Olivia in her first reference to his suitor – 'of all things he's my aversion' (p. 8, I.i) – and, of course, in her secret affair with Garnish. Indeed the change from Vernish (in Wycherley) to Garnish is so slight as to seem designed to point up the connection between the plays.
17. Thomas Southerne, *The Maids Last Prayer: Or, ANY, rather than Fail* (London, 1693) pp. 18–19, II.ii. Compare the situation of the speaker in *Timon*, Rochester, *Complete Poems*, pp. 65–72.
18. It is she for example, who presides at the raffle at Mrs. Siam's, ibid., p. 31; III.i pp. 33–4.
19. Ibid., p. 8, I.i. See also p. 11, II.i, where the speaker is Wishwell.
20. The best account of these events is to be found in Judith Milhous's *Thomas Betterton and the Management of Lincoln in Fields* (Southern, Illinois, 1979).
21. Charles Gildon, *A COMPARISON Between the TWO STAGES with an EXAMEN OF THE GENEROUS CONQUEROR; AND some Critical*

Remarks on the Funeral or Grief Alamode, The False Friend, Tamerlane and other (London, 1702) p.I.

22. See Patrick Conner's *Oriental Architecture in the West* (London, 1979) pp. 26–44.
23. *The Wives Excuse*, p. 98, IV.i, ll.1834–6.
24. Colley Cibber, *Three Sentimental Comedies*, ed. Maureen Sullivan (New Haven, 1973) *Love's Last Shift*, p. 46, III.iii, ll.105–8.
25. Cibber's famous *Apology* is in part a description and justification of this process. His account of Mrs. Verbruggens Melantha seems to me to be the best account of this style of Restoration acting. See B. H. Stone (ed.), *An Apology for the life of Mr. Colley Cibber, Comedian, with an historical account of the stage during his own time* (Ann Arbor, 1968) pp. 95–7.
26. Ibid., p. 40, III.i, ll.162–6.
27. Ibid., p. 16, I.i, ll.250–1.
28. Ibid., pp. 22–3, I.i, ll.503–13.
29. Ibid., pp. 24–35, II.i.
30. Ibid., p. 60, IV.iii, ll.194–6.
31. Ibid., p. 20, I.i, ll.417–18.
32. Ibid., p. 68, V.ii, l.12.
33. Ibid., p. 72, V.ii, l.143.
34. Ibid., pp. 52–3, IV.i, ll.92–113.
35. Bonamy Dobree and Geoffrey Webb (eds), *The Complete Works of Sir John Vanbrugh* (London, 1928) vol. I, p. 49, III.i.
36. Ibid., vol. I, p. 158, IV.iii.
37. Ibid., pp. 26–9, I.iii.
38. Ibid., p. 19, I.i.
39. See *The State of Innocence*, Act V, *The Dramatic Works*, vol. III. p. 426.
40. *The Relapse*, p. 20, I.i.
41. Torquato Tasso, *Amyntas*, trans. Leigh Hunt in Eric Bentley (ed.), *The Genius of the Italian Theatre* (New York: 1964) pp. 167–8, II.ii.
42. Ibid., p. 20, I.i.
43. Ibid., p. 42, II.i.
44. Ibid., p. 54, III.ii.
45. Ibid., p. 55, III.ii.
46. Ibid., pp. 89–90, V.iv.
47. Ibid., p. 97, V.v.
48. Ibid., p. 93, V.iv.
49. Jeremy Collier, *A Short View of the Immorality and Profaneness of the English Stage, 1698* (Scolar Press Reprint, 1971) p. 213.
50. *The Relapse*, p. 60, III.iv.
51. See note 3, Chapter 8, p. 000.
52. Ibid., p. 116, I.i.
53. Ibid., p. 117, I.i. See Hill, *The World Turned Upside Down* (London, 1972) 'When Vanbrugh's Lady Brute countered the New Testament command to return for evil by saying "that may be a mistake in the translation", who knows how much she owed to Clement Wither and Samuel Fisher?', p. 215.
54. *The Provok'd Wife*, p. 120, I.i.

55. Ibid., pp. 125–6, II.
56. Ibid., p. 127, II.
57. Ibid., p. 145, III.
58. Ibid., pp. 161–5, IV.iv.
59. Ibid., p. 168, V.ii.
60. Ibid., p. 180, V.v.
61. Ibid., p. 181, V.v.
62. *Works*, vol. I, p. 208.
63. Ibid., vol. III, p. 19, I.ii.

9 CONGREVE

1. *Incognita: or, Love and Duty Reconciled 1692* (Scolar Press reprint, Menston, 1971) pp. 11–12.
2. Ibid., pp. 67–8.
3. Ibid., p. 107.
4. Ibid., pp. 88–9.
5. Ibid., pp. 89–90.
6. Ibid., 'The Preface', A 6 (v).
7. Ibid., pp. 1, 4.
8. Ibid., p. 70.
9. Ibid., p. 111.
10. Herbert Davis (ed.), *The Complete Plays of William Congreve* (Chicago, 1967) p. 35.
11. In *Sir Patient Fancy*, p. 139. See Chapter 4 in this book. Behn is, of course, enlarging on a hint in Etherege's *She Would If She Could*. (See Chapter 1, p. 40 in this book.)
12. Congreve, *The Old Batchelour*, in *Complete Plays*, pp. 37–8, in this book I.i, ll.22–32.
13. Ibid., p. 42, ll.210–15.
14. Ibid., p. 41, ll.146–7.
15. Ibid., p. 55, II.ii, ll.33–5.
16. Ibid., p. 40, I.i, l.118.
17. Ibid., p. 54, II.ii, ll.8–10.
18. Ibid., p. 80, IV.i, l.172.
19. Ibid., p. 58, II.ii, ll.114–17.
20. Ibid., p. 112; (see also pp. 66–7).
21. See Montague Summers (ed.), *The Complete Works of William Congreve* (London, 1923) vol. III, *Samele*, p. 101, II.iii.

    Handel, whose version has displaced that of John Eccles, for whom *Semele* was originally written, does not set these lines. Instead he expands the pastoral vision at the end of the scene; that pathetically insubstantial fantasy world which alone can hold the illusion of humanly achieved perfection. The libretto is itself a kind of mask; Handel puts a face behind it.
22. Congreve, *The Old Batchelour*, p. 58, II.ii, ll.153–4.
23. Ibid., p. 59, II.ii, l.175.

24. Ibid., p. 60, II.ii, ll.197–8.
25. See Chapter 8, p. 168 in this book.
26. Ibid., p. 88, IV.iv, ll.188–9.
27. Ibid., p. 58, II.ii, ll.140–3.
28. Ibid., p. 37, I.i, l.14.
29. See Summer's Introduction to *The Complete Works of William Congreve*, vol. I. p. 18.
30. Congreve, *The Old Batchelour*, 'The Epistle Dedicatory', pp. 29–30.
31. Ibid., 'To Mr Congreve', p. 31..
32. Congreve, *The Double Dealer*, in *Complete Plays* p. 123.
33. Ibid., p. 129, I.i, ll.68–78.
34. In her introduction to the Scolar Press reprint; *The Double Dealer* 1964 (London, 1973) p. 4.
35. Congreve, *The Double Dealer*, Dedication, p. 120; Dramatis Personae, p. 126.
36. Ibid., p. 138, I.i, ll.421–2.
37. Ibid., p. 155, III.i, ll.176–86.
38. Ibid., p. 150, II.i, ll.440–2.
39. Ibid., p. 150, II.i, ll.465–8.
40. Ibid., p. 150, II.i, ll.460–4.
41. Ibid., p. 167, III.ii, ll.624–32.
42. Ibid., p. 177, IV.i, ll.377–80.
43. Ibid., p. 168, IV.i, ll.20–6.
44. Ibid., p. 148, II.i, ll.389–90.
45. Ibid., p. 184, IV.ii, ll.19–23.
46. The most blatant reminiscences are of Richard III and Lady Anne (pp. 197–8, V.i) of Iago, and Edmund. A full account of the play's glancing but persistent verbal reference to Shakespeare would be outside the scope of this chapter; though it is perhaps another aspect of that self-conscious theatrical 'monumentality' evoked by Dryden's prologue. For an account of Betterton's Hamlet, of his style and status as an actor of Shakespeare, see B. R. S. Fone (ed.), *An Apology for the Life of Colley Cibber* (Ann Arbor, 1968) pp. 60–1.
47. Congreve, *The Double Dealer*, p. 187, V.i, ll.2–3.
48. Congreve, *Love for Love*, in *Complete Plays* Prologue, p. 213.
49. Ibid., Prologue, p. 213.
50. Ibid., p. 219, I.i, ll.120–1.
51. Ibid., p. 220, I.i, ll.151–2.
52. Ibid., p. 226, I.i, ll.388–90.
53. Ibid., p. 217, I.i, l.60.
54. Ibid., p. 219, I.i, ll.108–9.
55. Ibid., p. 216, I.i, l.5.
56. Ibid., p. 233, I.i, ll.624–33.
57. Ibid., Dedication, p. 210.
58. Ibid., pp. 255–6, I.i, ll.363–7.
59. Ibid., p. 240, II.i, ll.199–201.
60. Ibid., p. 243, II.i, l.129.
61. Ibid., p. 244, II.i, ll.339–42.
62. Ibid., p. 224, I.i, ll.313–16.

63. Ibid., p. 221, I.i, ll.211–2.
64. Ibid., p. 215.
65. Ibid., p. 251, II.i, ll.610–14.
66. Ibid., p. 259, III.i, ll.227–30.
67. Ibid., p. 254, III.i, ll.40–1.
68. Ibid., p. 260, III.i, ll.245–8.
69. Ibid., p. 277, IV.i, ll.66–8.
70. Ibid., p. 290, IV.i, ll.247–8.
71. Ibid., p. 292, IV.i, ll.231–9.
72. Ibid., p. 294, IV.i, ll.707–8.
73. Ibid., p. 295, IV.i, ll.749–50.
74. Ibid., p. 296, IV.i, ll.775–6.
75. Ibid., p. 296, IV.i, ll.786–90.
76. Ibid., p. 297, IV.i, ll.815–16.
77. Congreve, *The Way of the World*, in *Complete Plays*, p. 442, III.i, l.654.
78. Peter Holland discusses some of the implications of this in *The Ornament of Action* (Cambridge, 1979); see pp. 204–43.
79. Congreve, *The Way of the World*, p. 395, I.i, ll.7–10.
80. Ibid., p. 413, II.i, ll.121–2.
81. Ibid., p. 415, II.i, l.214.; p. 442, III.i, l.631.
82. Ibid., p. 404, I.i, ll.337–8.
83. Ibid., p. 409, I.i, ll.534–5.
84. Ibid., p. 408, I.i, l.501.
85. Ibid., p. 417, II.i, ll.265–6.
86. *The Old Batchelor*, Dedication, p. 29.
87. Congreve, *The Way of the World*, p. 420, II.i, ll.385–8.
88. Ibid., p. 420, II.i, ll.393–400.
89. Ibid., pp. 447–8, IV.i.
90. Collier, *A Short View*, p. 142.
91. Ibid., p. 175.
92. Congreve, *The Way of the World*, p. 418, II.i, ll.317–20.
93. Ibid., p. 429, III.i, ll.167–8.
94. Ibid., p. 448, IV.i, ll.121–6.
95. Ibid., p. 416, II.i, l.246.
96. Ibid., p. 465, V.i, ll.134–5.
97. Ibid., p. 429, III.i, l.148.
98. Ibid., p. 462, V.i, ll.15–17.
99. Ibid., Dedication, p. 391.

10 FARQUHAR, CENTLIVRE AND STEELE

1. A. C. Ewald (ed.), *The Dramatic Works of George Farquhar*, ed. A. C. Ewald (London, 1892); *The Constant Couple; or, A Trip to the Jubilee*, 'Another Prologue', vol. I. pp. 127–8.
2. Ibid., Preface to the Reader', p. 119.
3. Ibid., vol. I; *Love and a Bottle*, p. 15, I.i.
4. Ibid., p. 15, I.i.

5. Ibid., pp. 77–8, IV.ii. See also Charles Stonehill (ed.), *A Discourse upon Comedy; The Complete Works of George Farquhar* (London, 1930) vol. II, p. 339.
6. *Dramatic Works*, vol. I, *The Constant Couple*, pp. 130–1, I.i.
7. Ibid., p. 134, Ii.
8. Ibid., p. 134, Ii.
9. Ibid., vol. I, pp. 141–2, I.ii.
10. Ibid., pp. 157–8, II.iv.
11. Ibid., p. 167, II.v.
12. Ibid., p. 168, II.v.
13. Ibid., I, pp. 185–7, III.v.
14. Ibid., I, p. 210, vi.
15. Ibid., p. 216, Vii.
16. *A Comparison Between the Two Stages*, p. 55.
17. Dramatic Works, *Sir Harry Wildair*, p. 319, V.vi.
18. The Southerne plays are *Sir Antony Love* (1689) and *Oroonoko* (1695); the Behn, *The Widow Ranter* (1689); the Ravenscroft *The Canterbury Guests* (1694); the Shadwell and Mountfort *Bury Fair* (1689) and *Greenwich Park* (1688/9).
19. *Dramatic Works*, vol. II, *The Recruiting Officer*, p. 130, I.i.
20. Ibid., p. 135, I.ii.
21. Ibid., p. 135, I.ii.
22. Ibid., II, p. 127, I.i.
23. Ibid., p. 132, I.i.
24. Ibid., p. 181, IV.i.
25. Ibid., vol. II, p. 140, II.i.
26. Ibid., p. 144, II.ii.
27. Ibid., I, *Sir Harry Wildair*, p. 248, I.i.
28. Ibid., I, *Love and a Bottle*, p. 113–4, V.iii.
29. Ibid., II, *The Recruiting Officer*, p. 160, II.i.
30. Ibid., p. 168, III.ii.
31. Ibid., p. 170, III.ii.
32. Ibid., p. 143, II.ii.
33. Ibid., II, *The Beaux Stratagem*, p. 247, I.i.
34. Ibid., p. 248, I.i.
35. Ibid., p. 248, I.i.
36. Ibid., p. 278, III.ii.
37. Ibid., II, p. 244, I.i.
38. Ibid., p. 278, III.ii.
39. Ibid., p. 342, V.v.
40. Ibid., p. 278, III.ii.
41. See Chapter 7, p. 149 and Chapter 9, p. 186 in this book.
42. *Dramatic Works*, vol. II, *The Beaux Stratagem*, p. 251, I.i.
43. Ibid., II; p. 278, III.ii.
44. Ibid., pp. 259–60, II.i.
45. Ibid., II, p. 300, III.iii.
46. Ibid., p. 318, IV.i.
47. Ibid., III; pp. 302–3, IV.i.
48. Ibid., p. 302, IV.i.

49. Ibid., p. 309, iv.i.
50. Ibid., p. 331, v.iii.
51. Ibid., ii; p. 328, v.i.
52. Ibid., ii; p. 330, v.ii.
53. Ibid., p. 347, v.v.
54. Ibid., ii; *The Recruiting Officer*, p. 117; Congreve, *Complete Plays; The Way of the World*, iii; 1551, p. 439.
55. Ibid., ii; *The Beaux Stratagem* 'Prologue', p. 241.
56. Ibid., ii; 'Prologue' p. 241.
57. Ibid., p. 241.
58. See John Loftis, *Steele at Drury Lane* (Berkeley, 1952) pp. 13–25.
59. See Chapter 8, pp. 160–1 and 169–75 of this book.
60. Susanna Centlivre, *The Dramatic Works* (London, 1872) vol. i, *The Beau's Duel*, p. 95, iii.i.
61. Shirley Strum Kenny (ed.), *The Plays of Richard Steele* (Oxford, 1971), *The Lying Lover*, 'Preface', p. 115, ll.8–9.
62. Ibid., p. 115, ll.12–16.
63. Ibid., p. 122, i.i, ll.112–3.
64. Ibid., p. 158, iii.ii, ll.189–90.
65. Ibid., p. 152, iii.i, l.83.
66. Ibid., p. 133, ii.i, ll.22–5.
67. Ibid., p. 127, ii.i, ll.292–4.
68. Ibid., pp. 187–8, v.iii, 327–36.
69. Steele, *Plays, The Tender Husband*, p. 229, i.ii, ll.120–1.
70. Ibid., *The Lying Lover*, p. 162, iv.ii, ll.7–8.
71. Ibid., *The Tender Husband*, p. 000, ii.ii, ll.247–9.
72. Ibid., p. 251, iii.ii, l.99.
73. Ibid., *The Conscious Lovers*, p. 342, iii, ll.124–6.
74. Ibid., p. 358, iv.ii, ll.18–29.

CONCLUSION: THE BEGGARS OPERA

1. For accounts of this see Richard E. Jones, 'Eclogue Types in English Poetry of the Eighteenth Century' (*JEGP*, 24, 1925) pp. 33–60, and Thomas G. Rosenmeyer, *The Green Cabinet; Theocritus and the European Pastoral Lyric* (Berkeley, 1969) pp. 3–33.
2. In his introduction to The Augustan Reprint Society's edition of Thomas Purney; *A Full Enquiry into the True Nature of Pastoral* (1717) (Ann Arbor, 1948) p. 1.
3. Ibid., pp. 60–2; ('How to attain to the Soft in Writing').
4. Quoted by Jones, pp. 43–4.
5. John Gay, *The Shepherd's Week* (1714) (A Scolar Press Facsimile, London, 1969) 'Prologue', [A6(r) – A6(v)].
6. Jones, pp. 41–2.
7. William Empson, *Some Versions of Pastoral* (London, 1935) pp. 195–253.
8. Jones, p. 38.

9. For an account of Purney's life and career see H. O. White (ed.) *The Works of Thomas Purney*, (Oxford, 1933) pp. xi–xxiv.

10. Thomas Duffet, *Psyche Debauch'd, A Comedy* (London, 1675) p. 18, II.ii.

11. Ibid., p. 4, I.i.

12. *The Mock Tempest*, p. 13 II.i.

13. *The Works of John Dryden*, vol. X, p. 24, I.ii, l.323.

14. Ibid., vol. XV p. 3, ll.11–17.

15. Winton Dean, *Handel and the Opera Seria* (London, 1970) p. 82.

16. Peter Elfred Lewis (ed.), *The Beggar's Opera* (Edinburgh, 1973) p. 72, II.ii, ll.44–5.

17. Ibid., p. 50, ll.15–17.

18. *A Full Enquiry into the True Nature of Pastoral*, p. 55.

19. Gay, *The Beggar's Opera*, p. 59, I.vii, ll.5–6.

20. Ibid., p. 58, I.vii, ll.9–16.

21. Ibid., p. 75, II.xxii, ll.39–41.

22. Ibid., p. 80, II.viii, ll.6–7.

23. Ibid., p. 73, II.iii, ll.10–11.

24. Ibid., p. 88, II.xiii, ll.39–43.

Bibliography

1 THE CRITICAL DEBATE

The literary study of Restoration comedy has been relatively restricted in its scope, but it is marked by fierce and apparently irresolvable controversy as to the nature and value of the form. I have concentrated in this section of the bibliography on important contributions to the debate.

Archer, W., *The Old Drama and the New* (London, 1923).
Bateson, F. W., 'Comedy of Manners', *Essays in Criticism* 1 (1951).
Bateson, F. W., '*Second Thoughts*: L. C. Knights and Restoration Comedy', *Essays in Criticism* 7 (1957).
Collier, Jeremy, *A Short View of the Immorality and Profaneness of the English Stage* (London, 1698).
Hawkins, H., *Likenesses of Truth* (Oxford, 1972).
Hazlitt, W., *English Comic Writers* (London, 1951).
Hume, R. D., *The Development of English Drama in the Late Seventeenth Century* (Oxford, 1976).
Hume, R. D., *The Rakish stage* (Southern Illinois, 1983).
Knights, L. C., *Explorations* (London, 1963).
Lamb, Charles, 'On the Artificial Comedy of the Last Century', in E. V. Lucas (ed.), *Elia, and the Last Essays of Elia* (London, 1902).
Rothstein, E., *Restoration Tragedy* (Madison, Milwaukee, 1967).
Staves, S., *Players' Scepters: Fictions of Authority in the Restoration* (Nebraska, 1979).
Stratford upon Avon Studies 6: Restoration Theatre (London, 1965) (Includes a number of excellent essays, including Ann Righter on Wycherley and on Heroic Tradgedy, Jocelyn Powell on Etherege, and Hugh Hunt on Restoration acting.
Underwood, D., *Etherege and the Seventeenth-Century Comedy of Manners* (Yale, Conn., 1957).
Wain, J., 'Restoration Comedy and Its Modern Critics', *Essays in Criticism* 4 (1956).

2 STAGING AND CONTEXT

The indispensable guide to the theatrical and social context of Restoration drama is Scouten and Van Lennep's encyclopaedic set of volumes, the

272

London Stage. The subject has attracted several likely studies, of which Powell's and Holland's are the most notable recent examples.

Boswell, E. *The Restoration Court Stage* (Cambridge, Mass., 1932).

Brown, Tom in Arthur L. Hayward (ed.), *Amusements Serious and Comical, and other Works* (London, 1927).

Cibber, Colley in B. R. Stone (ed.), *An Apology for the Life of Mr Colley Cibber, Comedian, with an Historical View of the Stage During His Own Time,* (Ann Arbor, 1968).

The History of the English Stage from the Restoration to the Present Time, compiled from the papers of Thomas Betterton by E. Curll (London, 1741).

Gildon, Charles, *A Comparison between the Two Stages* (London, 1702).

Gildon, Charles, *The Life of Thomas Betterton* (London, 1710).

Holland, P., *The Ornament of Action: Text and Performance in Restoration comedy* (Cambridge, 1979).

Jackson, A. S., 'Restoration Scenery 1656–1680', *Restoration and Eighteenth Century Theatre Research,* vol. III no. 2 (Chicago, 1964).

Jose, Nicholas, *Ideas of the Restoration in English Literature, 1660–1671* (London, 1984).

Luckett, R., 'Exotick but Rational Entertainments; the English Dramatick Operas', in Marie Axtonand Raynard Williams (eds), *English Drama: Forms and Development, Essays in Honour of M. C. Bradbrook* (Cambridge, 1977).

McAfee, H., *Pepys on the Restoration stage* (New Haven, Conn., 1916).

Milhous, J., *Thomas Betterton and the Management of Lincoln's Inn Fields 1695–1708* (Southern Illinois, 1979).

Authentick Memoirs of the Life of Mrs Ann Oldfield (London, 1730).

Powell, Jocelyn, *Restoration Theatre Production* (London, 1984).

Sorelius, G., *The giant Race Before the Flood: Pre-Restoration Drama on the Stage and in the Criticism of the Restoration* (Uppsala, 1966).

Waith, E. M., *Ideas of Greatness; Heroic Drama in England* (London, 1976).

Wilson, J. H., *The Court-Wits of the Restoration* (Princeton, 1948).

Zimbardo, R., *Wycherley's Drama: a Link in the Development of English Satire* (New Haven, Conn., 1965).

Index

Dramatic texts are listed both under their titles and under the author's name.
Other texts are listed only under the author.